A Complete Identity

A Complete Identity

*The Youthful Hero in the Work of
G. A Henty and George MacDonald*

RACHEL E. JOHNSON

☙PICKWICK *Publications* • Eugene, Oregon

A COMPLETE IDENTITY
The Youthful Hero in the Work of G. A Henty and George MacDonald

Copyright © 2014 Rachel E. Johnson. All rights reserved. Except for brief quotations in critical publications or reviews, no part of this book may be reproduced in any manner without prior written permission from the publisher. Write: Permissions, Wipf and Stock Publishers, 199 W. 8th Ave., Suite 3, Eugene, OR 97401.

Pickwick Publications
An Imprint of Wipf and Stock Publishers
199 W. 8th Av.e, Suite 3
Eugene, OR 97401

www.wipfandstock.com

ISBN 13: 978-1-62564-238-7

Cataloging-in-Publication data:

Johnson, Rachel E.

A complete identity : the youthful hero in the work of G. A Henty and George MacDonald / Rachel E. Johnson, with a foreword by Jean Webb.

xvi + 240 p. ; 23 cm. Includes bibliographical references and index.

ISBN 13: 978-1-62564-238-7

1. MacDonald, George, 1824–1905—Criticism and interpretation. 2. Henty, G. A. (George Alfred), 1832–1902. 3. English fiction—19th century—History and criticism. 4. Children's stories, English—History and criticism. I. Webb, Jean, 1949–. II. Title.

PR4969 J544 2014

Manufactured in the U.S.A.

*To my father, Basil Brown,
a mine of Henty information,
and the late Freda Levson 1911–2004,
MacDonald family descendant,
and greatly missed friend*

"We are men looking at puzzling reflections in a mirror. The time will come when we shall see reality whole and face to face."

1 Cor 13:12 (J. B. Phillips translation)

Contents

List of Illustrations   *viii*

Foreword by Jean Webb   *ix*

Preface   *xi*

Acknowledgements   *xiii*

Introduction   *xv*

1. My Hero: Method and Text   1
2. Historical Context   11
3. Genre, Mode, and Ideology   52
4. Child and Hero: The Construct of the Child 1850–1900   91
5. The Construct of the Hero 1850–1900   125
6. The Ideology of the Hero and the Representation of the "Other"   170
7. My Hero: The Complete Identity   205

Bibliography   *211*

Index   *225*

Illustrations

Figure 1:   George MacDonald's bookplate   137

Figure 2:   "I wish I had been a boy instead of a girl"   157

Figure 3:   Charlie encounters Ben Soloman in the wood   183

Foreword

It is a refreshing delight when one finds a text which brings new thinking to authors and texts which have been highly researched and become set into seemingly unbreakable moulds. Rachel Johnson's *A Complete Identity: The Youthful Hero in the Work of G. A Henty and George MacDonald* is a deeply and thoroughly researched book which brings new readings and understandings of the work of G. A. Henty and George MacDonald, plus new ways of thinking about the construction of heroism in the nineteenth century. This book emanates from a lifetime's engagement as a reader with these two authors which resulted in her successful PhD thesis upon which this book is based. The work is set against and illuminates the nineteenth-century context in terms of historical event, philosophy, ideology, and prevalent attitudes. Having been the Director of Studies for Rachel's doctoral work I was constantly impressed by her depth and range of knowledge which is now incorporated into this text and which will bring new ways of understanding and reading to the work of Henty and MacDonald. She has disrupted and exploded the "given" knowledge and stereotyping accorded to these two influential authors and demonstrates that instead of being on opposing poles of a continuum, that there are, in fact, considerable cross-over points and places where one might have otherwise not positioned each writer.

The notion of the hero is one which has been central to writing for children since fairy tales were first told and literary texts for children were produced. As Lord Byron wrote at the beginning of *Don Juan*:

> "I want a hero: an uncommon want
> When every year and month sends forth a new one,
> Till, after cloying the gazettes with cant,
> The age discovers he is not the true one."
> —Byron, *Don Juan*

The desire for an heroic focus is strong: the need to have the embodiment of that which is valued philosophically and morally and then brought to life through characterization, action, and plot. Heroic attributes can often be attached to characters without substantial proof, especially in the contemporary age of celebrity. Johnson's *A Complete Identity* rectifies the populist and academically constructed images of Henty and MacDonald and re-positions their work to articulate the complexities which lie beneath the populist reputations of Henty as the "Boy's Historian," intent upon creating the imperialist boy hero, and MacDonald as a writer of fairy tales. In conclusion, Rachel Johnson's work strips away clichéd thinking and draws the reader closer to discovering the "true" hero in the nineteenth century, albeit satisfyingly subject to multiplicity in a postmodern age.

Jean Webb
Professor of International Children's Literature,
University of Worcester, UK

Preface

WHERE DID THE IDEA for an investigation of the hero figure in Henty and MacDonald come from? Initially, there were those who were puzzled when I mentioned the two authors in the same breath. And there were those who were not, who immediately grasped the significance of investigating these two authors within their historical context and with a focus on the hero figure. The work of George MacDonald has been for me a source of interest, inspiration and study for over three decades. The pictorial covers of G. A. Henty's work were a background to my childhood although I did not read more than two or three of his stories until the idea of examining their work together coalesced with my interest in the history of children's literature and the nineteenth century milieu. The result is the following work.

Acknowledgements

I WOULD LIKE TO record my thanks to my father, Rev. A. B. E. Brown, whose longstanding interest in G. A. Henty has met my interest in George MacDonald in this book. His knowledge of Henty and his enthusiasm for the work has been unwavering.

My enduring thanks go to Professor Maria Nikolajeva and Professor Jean Webb. Maria encouraged me to send in the book proposal after the manner of Bishop Odo "comforting" Duke William's troops, and Jean spent many unstinting hours discussing aspects with me, helped by her everlasting supply of hot chocolate. Their warm support never fails. Without the privilege of their friendship and their confidence in my work, this book would never have appeared.

My thanks also to members of the Henty Society; particularly Ann King and Dennis Butts who were always prepared to share their knowledge with me.

Library colleagues from the University of Worcester, UK, deserve thanks for their support, especially Su and Catherine, the best Interlibrary Request Team I have ever met, and John and Andy, who never complained about the amount of book-carrying from the store to the Library. Special thanks go to Catherine who agreed to read through the text with her expert and intelligent eye for detail.

Finally, on the basis that "the last shall be first," thanks to Terry, my husband whose support surely qualifies him as the compassionate fairy tale hero.

Introduction

There is a threefold rationale behind this investigation. Firstly, to reassess the current critical view which perceives the work of G. A. Henty and George MacDonald as oppositional, secondly to revaluate the ideology in their work as it relates to the construction of the identity of the hero figure, and thirdly to indicate the continuing influence this figure has on contemporary children's literature. This third point can only be indicative since a thorough examination of influence would require a book of its own.

An investigation into the construct of the hero in the work of G. A. Henty (1832–1902) and George MacDonald (1824–1905), raises questions about the accepted critical position which views the work of these writers as oppositional. Henty and MacDonald wrote for both children and adults. The focus of this book is the construct of the hero in their writing for children within the context of the social, political, and religious conditions of the second half of the nineteenth century (1850–1900). Such an enterprise invites reflection of the current application of the hero figure construct to subsequent children's literature through to the twenty-first century. Although a thorough application would be the subject of another work, the relevance for contemporary children's literature cannot be ignored since the characteristics found in this figure are recognizable and constantly recur in contemporary fiction for children. A related area of study, and pertinent to contemporary education, would be to examine the implications of the reprinting programmes of the works of Henty and MacDonald. The rationale of contemporary American publishers is that their reprinting programmes are worthwhile because the values found in the work of these writers should be communicated to the present generation of children in the firm belief that those values are needed in the contemporary world.

The organization of this book aims to progress from the general to the particular beginning with an explanation of my method of approach to the hero figure in the work of these two authors. Chapters 2 to 4 set the historical scene, gradually narrowing the focus onto the hero figure found in the analysis of specific texts in chapters 5 and 6. A discussion as to why this hero figure was so psychologically important in Western culture's perception of itself leads into the final chapter.

1

My Hero

Method and Text

A KEY TO THE construct of the hero figure in the nineteenth century lies in the realms of both the real and the imagined. The image as an ideal represents a combination of both these aspects of the figure. I begin my investigation of the construct of the image of the hero with an analysis of story and character in terms of the ideological implications of genre.

Method

G. A. Henty and George MacDonald are cited as writing not only in different but in opposing genres, that is, historical/realism as opposed to fantasy/fairy tale. The extent of this perceived difference can be gauged from Hugh Walpole's comment in 1926, on writing for children, "... children divide into the two eternal divisions of mankind, ... Romantics and Realists, Prosists ... and Poets, Business Men and Dreamers, Travellers and Stay-at-Homes, Exiles and Prosperous Citizens. ... I fancy that all the children of my day who gloried in Henty were Realists and Hans Andersen was for the others."[1] Walpole makes clear that his reference to Andersen is representative of fairy tale writers or retellers. The continued critique in terms of opposition is evident in John Stephens' statement that the distinction between realism and fantasy

---

1. Walpole, *Reading*, 17–18.

is "the single most important generic distinction in children's fiction."[2] These quotations demonstrate the enduring nature of the perceived gulf between writing critiqued as realism and writing critiqued as fantasy or fairy tale. My intention is to interrogate this oppositional categorization with reference to the work of Henty and MacDonald and to demonstrate the mixing of genre apparent in the narrative structures of their writing. I examine this narrative structure from the position of generic conventions previously determined by critics so that I may investigate the structure as a vehicle to convey ideology and values. Critical opinion from F. J. Harvey Darton (1932)[3] through Guy Arnold (1980), Humphrey Carpenter and Mari Pritchard (1984)[4] to William Potter (2000)[5], categorizes Henty's writing as historical adventure story within the broader genre of realism. Critics contributing to works on the history of children's literature such as those cited above have drawn on previous histories thereby perpetuating the stereotypical criticism of Henty's work, using the same texts as examples. The exception to this predominant critique is Dennis Butts (1992), who notes the aspects of romance in Henty's stories.

The most critiqued stories in MacDonald's writing for children are those categorized as fantasy and fairy tale, for example *At the Back of the North Wind*, *The Golden Key*, *The Wise Woman*, *The Princess and the Goblin*, and *The Princess and Curdie*. Specialist studies such as *The Bright Face of Danger: An Exploration of the Adventure Story* by Margery Fisher, and *Fairy Tales and the Art of Subversion* by Jack Zipes, have furthered the categorical generic distinctions between Henty and MacDonald.

It therefore appears that the genres represented by Henty and MacDonald are so different that readers are expected by the critic to approach them with differing expectations based upon their knowledge of the conventions of the two broad categorizations of realism and fantasy. The assumption that Henty is a realistic children's writer because of his historical approach and his description of specific battles, causes the reader to focus on this aspect of the text rather than on the narrative structure to be found in the progress of the hero through this realistic landscape. MacDonald's writing for children, critiqued as fantasy and

2. Stephens, *Language and Ideology*, 7.
3. Darton, *Children's Books in England*, 302–3.
4. Carpenter and Pritchard, *The Oxford Companion*, 244–47.
5. Potter, *The Boy's Guide*, 19.

fairy tale, challenges conventional categorization. For example, in the instances where fantasy and realism intertwine, such as *At the Back of the North Wind* (1871), critiqued predominantly as fantasy, and *A Rough Shaking* (1891), in which the critical emphasis is on realism. Walpole noted the preference for realism in the active, out-going child, a stereotypical perception of the male reader and aligning with the assumed audience of Henty. The "dreamers ... and stay-at-homes"[6] who read fairy tales are aligned with the stereotypical perception of the female reader. Appealing to a more passive audience who live in the world of the imagination, the fairy tale is seen to appear less threatening to the status quo. Yet the way in which the author structures the narrative in order to present reality to the reader carries ideological implications. The apparent lack of political threat from the fairy tale resulted in its use as a vehicle for societal critique, a precedent set in seventeenth-century France with the development of the literary fairy tale. The way the text interweaves with the dominant or subordinate discourse and draws on familiar narrative patterns to enhance the process of what Louis Althusser has described as interpellation,[7] that is, the drawing-in of the reader to the ideological position of the text, is therefore significant.

Whilst "every use of language carries freight, a freight of what I am calling 'values' and others might call 'ideology,'"[8] the writing of Henty and MacDonald was intended to carry value-laden "freight." They wrote with the intention of not only engaging the attention of young readers, none of whom were divided in their preference for enjoyable stories, but with the stated objective of educating the reader. Henty began the majority of his stories with a short preface in which he stated his intention "to mix instruction with amusement,"[9] specifying which part of the story was historical "fact" and which part fiction. He also encouraged emulation of the hero with a view to success in life, success in this instance majoring on character development and work ethic. The influence of this intent on contemporary decisions to reprint the work of Henty and MacDonald is primary. In the preface to *The Boy's Guide to the Historical Adventures of G. A. Henty*, Schmitt notes, "the rich legacy

---

6. Walpole, *Reading*, 17.
7. Althusser, *On Ideology*, 308.
8. Booth, *Are Narrative Choices*, 65.
9. Henty, *Young Buglers*, Preface.

which Mr Henty left to the boys of the world."[10] The author of this book spells out this "rich legacy" in terms of how the Henty hero behaves and the need for such role models in the context of contemporary children's literature. Johannesen Printing and Publishing, who reprint the work of George MacDonald, also emphasize the ethical benefits of reading MacDonald. His books are advertised as, "Century-old literature that transcends time, culture and history . . . stimulating higher, nobler & purer thinking."[11] George MacDonald's son Greville wrote of his father that his "message was all in his books,"[12] but MacDonald's "message" is neither so clearly defined nor always so explicit as is Henty's. MacDonald's essay on the fantastic imagination and his recorded response to a direct question as to the meaning of his work; "You may make of it what you like. If you see anything in it, take it and I am glad you have it; but I wrote it for the tale,"[13] suggests a less didactic intent but his emphasis on the spiritual development of his protagonists signifies his moral intent.

In the European variation of ethical criticism found in the work of Emmanuel Levinas, the emphasis is on responses to alterity. This emphasis is particularly significant in the case of Henty, whose portrayal of the British imperialistic response to, and interpretation of, responsibility towards colonized peoples continues to be influential beyond the time in which he wrote. Recognizing the importance of context to the production of the texts and to the construct of the hero figure within them, I endeavor to, "isolate and categorize the various social factors which meet and interact . . . and finally to explain those interactions."[14] The ideological interests running through the text may have been so interpellated into the society out of which the text was written, that they were not recognized or questioned. In the case of Henty, this acceptance is demonstrable. MacDonald's writing falls into the literature described by Louis Montrose as both promoting and containing subversion.[15] MacDonald promotes subversion in that his stories critique his society whilst at the same time being contained by that society. This view is part of the larger debate as to whether societal norms can be subverted at

10. Schmitt, *Preface to the Boy's Guide*, 12.
11. Johannesen, *Johannesen Printing and Publishing*, website.
12. MacDonald, *George MacDonald*, 2.
13. MacDonald, *Fantastic Imagination*, 318.
14. McGann, *The Text, the Poem*, 295.
15. Montrose, *New Historicisms*, 402.

all, given the constraints of historical circumstance under which any individual writer lives. I argue that both Henty and MacDonald have "a potential for power of subversion"[16] that does transcend their immediate historical context.

Clarence Walhout argues that the extent to which an author recognizes and addresses issues he sees as problematic within his own society determines his value beyond his own age.[17] This view needs explanation and definition. Questions such as: value to whom? in what context? and from which or whose perspective? The influence of both authors is currently reaching beyond their own time period into the twenty-first century. Some cultural values which were recognized and critiqued by MacDonald were equally part of the fabric of Henty's cultural context but are not questioned in his work. Other issues are critiqued by Henty and not by MacDonald. It could therefore be argued that the "value," to use Walhout's term, or influence of Henty's and MacDonald's work beyond their own time is due to the same issues not being recognized in the present (twenty-first century) promotional context, whilst there is a recognition of other, stated, "values" contained in their work, which are deemed worthy of promotion. Examples of these values include courage, truthfulness, and generosity. MacDonald also addresses socially radical issues in the domestic context and often, "turned the world upside down and inside out to demonstrate that society as it existed was based on false and artificial values."[18] Society "as it existed" and exists does not, for example, always recognise truthfulness and generosity as praiseworthy in a world where financial profit was and is often the paramount criteria of success. George Levine points out that literature written within the historical Victorian period (1837–1901) could critique society whilst still participating in it and that resistance to the dominant discourse can be absorbed into society in ways that appear supportive rather than subversive.[19] The construct of the hero, as it appears in Henty and MacDonald, can be mapped to the discourses of these writers' cultural context which in turn integrates their contribution into its own construction.

16. Brannigan, *New Historicism*, 6.
17. Walhout, and Ryken, ed. *Contemporary Literary Theory*, 76.
18. Zipes, *When Dreams*, 125.
19. Levine, *Victorian Studies*, 133–34.

Despite the colonial implications of the nineteenth-century English authorial position, with which MacDonald, although a Scot, was conversant, I have made the decision not to investigate the writing of Henty and MacDonald from a postcolonial theoretical viewpoint since it could be argued that because both authors were writing during a time of rapid imperial expansion, they were active participants in the construction of the empire and colonies rather than postcolonial critical commentators. I have applied the theories of postcolonial critics to my argument where it is appropriate and particularly in chapter 6 in which the ideology of the hero is examined in relation to "the other."

Text

The work of Henty and MacDonald is extensive. Henty published approximately[20] eighty boys' stories as well as five novels for adults, collections of short stories and documentary reports on historical events. MacDonald published three volumes of sermons and two of poetry as well as fantasy, fairy tales, and twenty-nine novels. I have chosen texts that typify the narrative techniques and ideological positioning of both authors. The texts chosen for discussion from the work of Henty and MacDonald represent the hero figure in different cultures, circumstances, and time periods (both actual and mythical) which emphasise aspects of his or her character. Taken together, these characteristics build the composite, identifiable persona, the ideal character of the hero figure.

G. A. Henty (1832–1902)

I have chosen to analyze seven texts published between 1871 and 1906 (posthumous publication) from G. A. Henty's approximately eighty stories. These texts are chosen as representative of his work. They include events ranging historically between AD 70 and 1899. The hero figures also demonstrate Henty's inclusion of the black hero, the female hero and the flawed hero which has been overlooked by critics to date in their focus on the male, Caucasian boy.

Out on the Pampas (1871), Henty's first published text for children, is a pioneer story based on the adventures of one family rather than on a particular historical event. This text differs from the majority of

---

20. The complexities of Henty bibliography has been expertly documented in, Newbolt, *G. A. Henty*.

Henty's work in that it does not include a major historical battle and does not refer to known historical figures. The foremost characters are four children, two boys and two girls, Charley, Hubert, Maud, and Ethel. Although the eldest boy is represented as the primary agent of action, the other three make their contribution as individuals, displaying heroic characteristics when confronted by life-threatening situations, setting a precedent for active female characters which Henty followed in subsequent writing. In 1891 Henty returned to the pioneer story with the New Zealand based *Maori and Settler*. The historical focus in *Maori and Settler* is on the Hwa uprising (1870) and, unusually in the Henty story, the boy hero, Wilfred, remains in the land of his adventure. Although these two texts do not receive such close analysis as others, I refer to them to demonstrate points discussed.

By Sheer Pluck (1884) exemplifies significant consistent characteristics of the Henty hero and is an instance of Henty's use of his own experience since the story draws on his work as newspaper correspondent for *The Evening Standard*, covering the first Ashanti war and the march to Coomassie in 1873.

The setting for *The Young Buglers* (1880) is the Peninsular War of 1810 and includes the classic Henty motifs of the hero's loss of parents and of fortune, and his subsequent journey to regain the latter. In this text, Henty's two young male protagonists, Tom and Peter Scudamore, display characteristics that establish the core construct of his hero figure. *The Young Buglers* includes a major black character who could arguably be presented as the real hero of the story, initiating discussion on Henty's representation of race.

For the Temple (1888) covers events leading up to the siege of Jerusalem by the Romans (AD 70). The exploits of the Jewish hero John raise questions about strategies of resistance employed by an oppressed people. Henty's depiction of a guerrilla fighter as the hero interrogates the nature of individual heroism.

I have chosen to analyze the story *Captain Bayley's Heir* (1889) in my discussion of genre because this text demonstrates the combination of genre in Henty's work. The protagonist of this story, Frank Norris, is fatherless, and, wrongly accused of theft, flees the country to find his fortune. Frank's narrative includes a sub-plot in which, through Frank's compassionate behavior before he leaves England, Captain Bayley's true heir is found.

The plot of *Rujub the Juggler* (1892), set in India during the Sepoy uprising (1856), hinges on the gift of second sight. The hero *of Rujub the Juggler*, Ralph Bathurst, differs from the critiqued stereotype in that he is paralyzed by fear at the sound of any loud noise including gunfire. This fear affects the way Henty portrays his hero and initiates discussion within the narrative on the nature of courage.

In *The Tiger of Mysore* (1896) Henty traces the eighteenth-century war with Tippoo Saib and includes discussion on mixed race marriage and again features second sight as integral to the story. This text demonstrates the pivotal importance of the English boy's Indian friend Surajah.

The action of *A Soldier's Daughter*, published posthumously in 1906, takes place on the unsettled border of northern India in 1860. The female protagonist, Nita, is an exceptionally strong example of Henty's inclusion of a girl in the role of hero. His female hero is discussed from the point of view of gender related to the characteristics of the male hero. I refer to many texts not included as primary in this section, where illustrative examples are needed to substantiate points within the context of the argument. Such texts include *Condemned as a Nihilist* (1893), *For Name and Fame* (1886), *A Jacobite Exile* (1894), *Sturdy and Strong* (1888), *True to the Old Flag* (1885), and *The Young Franc-Tireurs* (1875).

George MacDonald (1824–1905)

From the eight publications by George MacDonald that are regarded as written for a child audience I have chosen six texts. They range in publication date from 1867 to 1891 and include fairy tales, fantasy, parable, and realism. These twenty-five years saw MacDonald's highest literary output and include his editorship of the periodicals *Good Words for the Young* and *Good Things for the Young of All Ages* (1869–73).

In the first text, *At the Back of the North Wind* (1871), MacDonald blends fantasy and realism into a full length story that includes descriptions of social conditions in Victorian London. His main protagonist is a male, feminized, idealized Romantic child.

The focus of the discussion on *Ranald Bannerman's Boyhood* (1871), my second text, is the construct of the male hero which is mapped to the investigation into the nineteenth-century construct of the hero.

MacDonald's longer fairy tales, *The Princess and the Goblin* (1872), *The Wise Woman* (1874), and *The Princess and Curdie* (1883) demonstrate reality, "viewed through the fine gauze of MacDonald's imagination."[21] These texts encourage the reader to look at the world MacDonald creates in such a way as to understand their own world differently. Whereas much of Henty's work can be viewed as expansive adventures in the geographical context of English imperialism, MacDonald's work focuses on situations in Britain or Europe, either in actuality or in an imaginative reconstruction. MacDonald's writing for children chronicles the educative process on a spiritual level. The narrator's voice frequently comments on aspects of character that contribute towards the construction of an ideal. In *The Princess and the Goblin* and *The Princess and Curdie*, this heroic construct is equally applicable to both the male and female heroes, a less usual application at a time when the male hero was the focus of an idealized heroic construct, and one which demonstrates MacDonald's high view of the feminine elements of character. His strong female child characters often appear in positions of leadership and equality with the male hero.

In *A Rough Shaking* (1891), superficially a realistic text, the blurring of the real and the marvellous focuses on the main male character who displays the same feminine idealized male child characteristics as does Diamond in *At the Back of the North Wind*, whilst also displaying the masculine physical courage which comes to the fore in Henty's work. With its improbable fairy tale ending, *A Rough Shaking* raises questions about the boundaries between realism, fantasy, and fairy tale and bridges the gap referred to by Walpole in 1926 as, "the eternal division," and John Stephens writing in 1992 termed the "polarization" of these genres. I draw other texts by MacDonald into the discussion as they are needed in order to exemplify particular points.

I have already noted that one particularity of the writing of these authors lies in the construction of an essential hero, whose attributes, if combined, exemplify both the physical and the spiritual ideal of their time in one identity. Both Henty and MacDonald incorporate values from the same sources, filtered in ways that both reflect and construct their present, and influence their future societal context. These values are personified in the hero figure in their work. By analyzing the chosen texts, read in relation to historical context and focusing on genre, it is possible to see this set of values and their ideology reflected through the lens of the hero figure.

21. Blanch, *My Personal Debt*.

Both writers are located in time and place using biographical material drawn from existing sources. In order to establish Henty and MacDonald within the milieu of the period 1850–1900, I begin with an overview of three specific areas. The first area is the political landscape in England, both domestic and foreign. The intellectual, social, and religious challenges facing English society are included. In the second area, since the focus of the investigation is Henty and MacDonald's writing for children, I examine the progression towards the Victorian construct of the child, since it is inextricably linked to the third area, which is the dominant English nineteenth-century construct of the hero. The term Victorian is used literally to mean the years during which Queen Victoria reigned (1837–1901). The second half of this period (1850–1900) coincides with the years during which the majority of the texts analyzed were written and published. I have used the personal pronoun "he" to refer to the hero figure in most instances since it indicates the continuing prevalence of associated masculinity.

2

Historical Context

> "a large part of any book is written not by its author
> but by the world its author lives in."[1]

BECAUSE IT IS NOT possible to entirely disengage any author from the world he or she lives in, I need to include an overview of the historical context in which Henty and MacDonald wrote and published their work. Such an overview provides a base from which to investigate the values apparent in their texts.

Although the major contemporary influences on their work were not entirely the same, those concepts which emerged from the historical context, and influenced the work of both authors to a greater or lesser extent, include the concept of muscular Christianity; the English public school ethos developed by Thomas Arnold, (headmaster of Rugby School); the gospel of self-improvement and the expansion of English commercial interests leading to further colonization beyond Europe. The work of G. A. Henty demonstrates that these influences contributed to the construct of "the Henty hero" in his stories. George MacDonald's major influences were his Christian beliefs; German Romanticism; the atmosphere of religious doubt; the rise in scientific enquiry and the development of Christian Socialist thinking. Henty's Christian beliefs and extensive reading in natural history are less overt in his writing. These differing lines of influence superficially indicate a divide in their

---

1. Hollindale, *Ideology*, 15.

work, but together they set a foundational context from which I examine the construct of the child and the construct of the hero in their writing. MacDonald's Scottish origin also strongly influenced his writing and shaped his views as an outsider in England. From this position he was able to critique English politics and society as an observer. The Scottish influences on his work originate in the local context of his formative years[2] and lie at the micro rather than macro level of Scottish social and political history. During the period in which he published (1855–99), MacDonald's position as an outsider translates into his work in the observation of people in the English context where he lived most of his adult life.

A. N. Wilson describes the second half of the nineteenth century in England as, "an alarming triumph song," when Great Britain grew wealthier, more powerful and less sensitive to the needs of the weak in society."[3] This sense of growing power was balanced by a sense of insecurity induced by the unprecedented pace of change in all aspects of life experienced by people living in the Victorian era.

The two major influences, identified by John Houghton as driving transition during this time were the growth of industrial bourgeois society, and doubt about the nature of man, society and the universe.[4] The changes in society from the beginning of Victoria's reign (1837) until the end of it (1901) were encapsulated in Thomas Carlyle's essay *Past and Present* written in 1843, as a movement from an essentially medieval, feudal society to a modern society characterized by chaos and disintegration. Carlyle contrasted the way of life in a twelfth-century English Abbey with that of contemporary, that is, mid-nineteenth-century, industrial England. He drew a contrast between the "past" order and recognized hierarchical nature of society and the "present" confusion and disorientation he observed around him.[5] The consequent sense of instability within society was a factor in the perceived need for an ideal hero figure to stand as a consistent and stable icon in the midst of uncertainty and change.

---

2. See Raeper; *George MacDonald*, 24–40; Triggs, *George MacDonald*, 7–14; Triggs, *The Stars and the Stillness*, 1–16.

3. Wilson, *The Victorians*, 120.

4. Houghton, *The Victorian Frame of Mind*, 22.

5. Carlyle, *Past and Present*, 408–17.

The Growth of Industrial Society

The inescapable population growth in an industrial society and developments in technology fuelled the breakdown of agrarian society and the consequent population movement into cities. A perception of continual movement and hurry was documented in the memoirs of Frederic Harrison[6] and compounded anxieties caused by changes in the structure of society, as industry, and consequently cities, expanded to accommodate both factory workers, and others displaced by unemployment.

At the same time, the utilitarian philosophy of Jeremy Bentham (1748–1832) and laissez-faire economics that had seeped into the Victorian worldview, altered priorities. Commercialism and materialism became more dominant motivational factors, particularly amongst industrial managers. Movement within society slowly became more fluid. As the feudal structures disintegrated, so the possibility of changing a person's position in the hierarchy of society appeared within the reach of many more people. Manuals such as Samuel Smile's *Self-Help* (1859) encouraged upward movement towards a middle class position in society through education and hard work. Although Smile's exhortation to improve oneself may have resulted in movement up the social ladder in some instances, it did not attempt to remove the ladder. However hardworking and capable a person proved themselves to be, acceptance into a higher social class was never guaranteed. A position on the next rung of the social ladder was maintained through long working hours as aspirations and goals took the form of material goods which indicated one's status to others. Social mobility was not confined to the working, lower middle classes, and middle classes. An example of Henty's rare exploration of successful Smilesian self-help can be found in his novel *Facing Death*, a story of the Staffordshire coal mines in which the orphan son of a miner eventually becomes pit manager through hard work and application to study. In MacDonald's short tale *Cross Purposes* equality between social classes is only seen as possible in Fairyland, despite the superior capabilities of the lower class male protagonist. The characteristics of the main character in both of these stories are consistent with the need for a morally superior hero figure who could negotiate the volatility of social upheaval even when he could not overcome existing barriers.

---

6. Harrison, *Autobiographic Memoirs*, 19.

Doubt and the Need for the Hero Figure

At the same time as the outward, demographic movement gathered pace, the internal worlds of people's minds were turning from spiritual to material concerns. From a consciousness of their place in society within a secure structure, they were assailed by religious controversy and the growth of a scientific, empirical philosophy of life. This change is the second major shift cited by Houghton, that of, "doubt about the nature of man, society and the universe." These two changes, the growth of bourgeois society and doubt, were factors which undermined certainties that had previously been accepted and unquestioned by the majority of people. A major impetus to theological doubt arose from the publication in 1859 of Charles Darwin's *Origin of Species* which brought into question "the nature of man" and his place in the natural world.

John Stuart Mill noted in his diary the pervasive doubt and uncertainty which educated people experienced. He observed that the multifaceted argument, "only breeds increase of uncertainty," so that, "they [the educated classes] feel no assurance of the truth of anything."[7] As early as 1831, Carlyle observed that although old certainties were passing, there was nothing to replace them.[8] In the worlds of commerce, industrialism and nature the survival of the fittest was demonstrated on a daily basis, creating a society, "less sensitive to the needs of the weak."[9] As the theory of selection in the natural world was applied to competition experienced in the industrial world, a growing awareness of the concept of natural selection and inter-relatedness began to encourage the growth of socially aware political ideas and movements. This development did not penetrate the consciousness of the majority of people until much later and was primarily reflected by writers critiquing the contemporary scene. George MacDonald was one of these writers. In Henty's work, the behavior of any protagonist indicates his recognition of the importance of the relationship between the strong and the weak since one of the Henty hero's central tenets was protection of the weaker individual. This tenet is demonstrated by, for example, Frank Hargate,[10]

---

7. Elliot, ed., *The Letters of John Stuart Mill*, 359, Appendix A. *Mill's Diary*, January 13, 1854.

8. Carlyle, *Characteristics*, 67–108.

9. Wilson, *The Victorians*, 120.

10. Henty, *By Sheer Pluck*, 32.

Dick Holland[11] and any number of other Henty heroes. The importance of this tenet at a societal level is not overtly argued.

Houghton asserts that despite the doubt, change and uncertainty, belief in the existence of truth was not abandoned during the Victorian period. In tune with evolutionary theory, the "age of transition" was regarded by thinkers such as John Stuart Mill as a process through which the human mind would move towards a time when it, "satisfied itself of truth."[12] Pamela Jordan, in her study of three novels of faith and doubt, cites the growth of interest in the newly articulated philosophies of population theory, phrenology, and psychology as contributory to, not only religious doubt, but also doubt as to whether certainty could be reached at all. As the divide between theology and science grew, so did the divide between the belief in absolute truth and relativism. During the period 1850–1900 there was more concern about the divide between theology and science amongst religious leaders than that between absolute truth and relativism. The divide between theology and science was compounded by the unwillingness of religious leaders to examine new scientific ideas which initially appeared to be so threatening to previous certainties. MacDonald, trained as a scientist,[13] incorporated scientific ideas into his stories, an aspect of his work discussed at length by F. Hal Broome.[14] MacDonald's application of Darwinian theory is discussed later in this book in relation to particular texts. Henty's interest in natural history and his comprehensive reading on the subject is not discussed by critics but frequently appears in his stories, for example in the interests and career of Frank Hargate in *By Sheer Pluck* (1884).

England 1850–80: The Young Hero

Compared to the political upheaval in many parts of Europe, the situation in England in 1850 appeared to be peaceful. This was partly because the unrest on "English" soil was no longer happening in England. The Chartist Movement, begun in the 1830s as a movement to extend suffrage and improve the lives of the working class poor had been crushed not only by the show of force used by the government in 1848,

11. Henty, *Tiger of Mysore*, 17.
12. Elliot, ed. *The Letters of John Stuart Mill*, 359, Appendix A. *Mill's Diary*, January 13, 1854
13. Raeper, *George MacDonald*, 54
14. Broome, *The Scientific Basis*, 87–108.

but by lack of support and an emphasis on self-interest rather than the common good that hardened over the following decades. The imperial enterprise was growing so rapidly that political dissidents and criminals could be exported to the colonies alongside goods produced by the equally rapid growth of industrial processes in Britain. Transportation of undesirables served both to relieve pressure on the prison population in England and to strengthen the colonial labour force. By 1850, additions to the empire since the beginning of Victoria's reign (1837) included Hong Kong (1843), Gambia (1843), and Orange River in South Africa (1848). The perceived Russian threat to British interests in India led to the first Afghan wars (1842) and the annexation of the Punjab (1848) following the Sikh wars.[15] Wilson points out that although England's main interest at the time was in trade, the need to create peace so that trade may flourish led to the suppression of disturbances that might threaten trade, followed by annexation in order to secure the peace needed for the continuation of trade.

Starting as it did with the Great Exhibition in 1851, a display of British manufacturing superiority and global influence, the decade 1850–60 fulfilled Carlyle's earlier (1829) description of the time as "the mechanical age"[16] and, as Carlyle had foreseen, men "grown mechanical in head and heart,"[17] showed less flexibility of thought and less compassion than they had in less mechanized times. By the late 1840s and 1850s, Benthamite philosophy had influenced political attitudes to such an extent that there was reluctance within government to act in any way that might interfere with the free market by the provision of any form of state aid. This attitude included the lack of response to the Irish famine of 1845. The government may have been reluctant to provide aid for the Irish but many individuals were actively involved in doing so. Greville MacDonald (George's son) notes that his mother Louisa's younger sister Phoebe "collected a great deal of money for the cause,"[18] the cause being the Irish famine.

Samuel Smiles' (1812–1904) philosophy of self-help may have encouraged, "aspiration over occupation,"[19] amongst the lower-middle

15. James, *The Rise and Fall*, 374, 223.
16. Carlyle, *Signs of the Times*, 34.
17. Tennyson, ed. *A Carlyle Reader*, 37.
18. MacDonald, *George MacDonald*, 101.
19. Rodrick, *The Importance of Being an Earnest Improver*, 39.

and upper-working classes, but amongst the urban poor, the poverty was so deep that only an individual of exceptional energy could grasp any rung of the social ladder sufficiently firmly to begin the climb by self-help. Prior to 1850, Charles Dickens, and later in the century, General Booth founder of the Salvation Army, began the educative process of exposing urban poverty. Booth continued the work by Henry Mayhew whose document *London Labour and the London Poor* (1861–62) was the first systematic attempt to record the reality of the lives of the urban poor. Despite the pervasive influence of utilitarianism and the extensive ignorance about levels of urban poverty, there were voices, both within the government and within the Anglican Church, which questioned Benthamite philosophy.

Throughout his investigation of the Victorians, Wilson repeatedly draws attention to the, "British capacity for adaptation of its system, based on ... acute self-criticism."[20] This ability of the British governmental system to critique itself from the inside provides an example of Stephen Greenblatt's premise that, "a gesture of dissent may be an element in a larger legitimation process."[21] That the political structure could contain, absorb and act upon such subversion was a factor in enabling England to avoid the revolutionary upheaval experienced elsewhere in Europe. These critical voices were not coming from the margins of society, but from respected figures such as Shaftesbury (Anthony Ashley Cooper, seventh Earl of Shaftesbury, earlier Lord Ashley), Charles Kingsley (1819–75) and Rev. F. D. Maurice (1805–72). Maurice and Kingsley promoted the Christian Socialist Movement, which, although it only lasted six years as an organization (1848–54), left a lasting influence and became a magnet for critics of the dominant discourse, including George MacDonald, who had already aligned himself with the theological position of Maurice in his rejection of Calvinist ideas of eternal damnation. Within the religious community, George Eliot's translations of David Friedreich Strauss' *Das Leben Jesu* (The Life of Jesus, 1844) and Ludwig Andreas Feuerbach's *Das Wesen des Christenthums* (The Essence of Christianity, 1854), questioning Christ's divinity, led churchmen such as Samuel Wilberforce, Bishop of Oxford, to address the doubts assailing believers by advocating an anti-intellectual position in order to preserve what he perceived as traditional orthodoxy. The defensive reaction by

20. Wilson, *The Victorians*, 149.
21. Greenblatt, *Resonance and Wonder*, 308.

the religious establishment to the perceived threat of heresy meant that thinkers such as Maurice, Alexander Scott,[22] and George MacDonald were unable to continue within the mainstream churches, Maurice and Scott as Anglicans and MacDonald as a Congregationalist. Maurice was ejected from his Professorial Chair at Kings College London following the publication of his *Theological Essays* in 1853 and MacDonald was forced to leave his pastorate in Arundel in 1853.

Youth: our Hope for the Future

In such a period of great change, an emphasis on the younger generation emerged as a hope for the future. In 1862, Benjamin Disraeli, then Prime Minister, wrote a letter to Mrs. Brydges Williams, quoted in George Earle Buckle's biography, in which he described the age in which he lived as, "one of infinite romance . . . like a fairy tale."[23] Disraeli was speaking about the personal opportunities he believed to be available in a prosperous, socially fluid, and economically successful nation. The growing prominence and influence of the middle class falls in with Simon Dentith's assertion of class as one of the major fault lines of nineteenth-century society, dovetailing as it does with his designation of gender as another fault line and both reinforced by Thomas Arnold's reform of the public school. Arnold's vision of a school system which would turn out boys whose character, impregnated by the ethos of an Arnoldian education, would influence not only their immediate community but also the life of the whole nation and carry further to become the foundation for the continuation and development of the empire. Dentith's "fault lines" of nationalism, imperialism, and ethnicity and race[24] can also be tracked through the Arnoldian public school ethos demonstrating from its microcosmic world major warps running through the wider fabric of nineteenth century society. The concept of the Arnoldian boy features in the creation of Henty's construction of boy as hero, discussed in a later chapter.

During the 1860s educational developments in England included debates about the desirability of science education. It was already

---

22. A. J. Scott had his licence as a minister revoked when he declared himself "unable to subscribe any longer to the Westminster Confession." Triggs, *The Stars and the Stillness*, 32.

23. Buckle, *The Life of Benjamin Disraeli*, 331.

24. Dentith, *Society and Cultural Forms*, 4.

well established in Germany and in the Scottish universities. George MacDonald had studied natural philosophy (chemistry) at Aberdeen and his biographer William Raeper states that he would have continued his study of chemistry in Germany had funds permitted.[25] Objections to a greater emphasis on science in education, by Lords Derby, Stanhope and Carnarvon included the argument that science education would eat into time needed for games. The implications of losing such time was, in their view, global, and would ultimately impact upon the continuing influence of imperialism, given that the inculcation of team spirit, courage and endurance learnt on the games field was believed to be carried over into every area of life including the battlefield. Sir Henry Newbolt encapsulated this train of thought in his poem *Vitai Lampada*,

> The river of death has brimmed his banks
> And England's far, and Honour a name,
> But the voice of a schoolboy rallies the ranks:
> "Play up! Play up! And play the game!"
> . . .
> This they all with joyful mind
> Bear through life like a torch in flame,
> And falling fling to the host behind—
> "Play up! Play up! And play the game!"[26]

In this game, as the master in *Tom Brown's Schooldays* says, "he (the boy) doesn't play that he may win, but that his side may."[27] Although the character of the Arnoldian boy is a factor in the construction of the Henty hero, the Arnoldian boy does not display the individualism and initiative necessary for Henty's ideal boy. The proliferation of the new public (fee paying) schools invented "a social instrument"[28] whose influence was broadened further after the 1870 Education Act to provide schools for those who could not pay as much as those aspiring to be gentlemen, but the epithet "social instrument" applied equally to what would now be termed state (non-fee paying) schools, since the continuing migration to the cities created a need, so it was perceived by the ruling classes, for "instruments" of social control.

25. Raeper, *George MacDonald*, 54.
26. Newbolt, *Poems*, 78–79.
27. Hughes, *Tom Brown's Schooldays*, 355.
28. Wilson, *The Victorians*, 286.

F. D. Maurice was prominent in the promotion of women's education, although the embryonic women's movement in the political sense was given impetus during the 1860s and 1870s by the outrage triggered by the Contagious Diseases Acts of 1864 and their amendments throughout the 1860s. Repealed in 1886, the CD Acts served to throw the legal discrepancies between the treatment of men and women into such sharp relief that the gender fault line opened in a demand for change. Maurice's pupils included two women, Frances Mary Buss and Dorothea Beale who were to change the face of women's education both by reforming existing schools and by founding new schools for girls where academic achievement was taken seriously. They were also active in the campaign to allow girls to sit public examinations, a concession eventually given in the late 1860s. Women were then able to gain places at Oxford and Cambridge, but only London University allowed them to sit examinations and receive degrees until post 1918. MacDonald was invited by Maurice to give lectures to women's classes at Birkbeck College, London, in 1859. As an advocate for women's education who held a high opinion of the intellectual capabilities of women, MacDonald supported Maurice's innovations and encouraged female participation in organized education, although he was initially reluctant to support their inevitable desire to participate in public life and the male-dominated professions, such as doctors and lawyers, once educated.

Maurice's particular brand of Christian expression, advocated through the Christian Socialist Movement and shared by Charles Kingsley and Thomas Hughes, came to be known as "muscular Christianity" because of the emphasis on spirituality and athleticism. In his book *Muscular Christianity* (1994), Donald Hall draws a parallel between the association of physical strength and religious endeavor with the ability to influence and control one's own internal and external world. Henty describes his protagonists as physically strong, and MacDonald's protagonists, both male and female, display courage, endurance and spiritual awareness. In characters such as Curdie in *The Princess and the Goblin* and *The Princess and Curdie*, Curdie's physical strength as a miner boy is apparent in his activity but not commented on as a separate attribute. Although the need to counteract the insecurity and perceived chaos caused by doubt, loss of belief and rapid social and technological change focused initially on personal control, the masculine characteristics cited by Hall, such as a striving to achieve excellence in any undertaking, sought a wider control which Hall relates to, "projects for control of the unknown, the threatening."[29] The muscular Christian ethic reinforced the construct of masculinity as projecting social and economic power. The moral and spiritual emphasis of the muscular Christian ethic dovetailed with the growing justification for empire as bringing civilization to wild, untamed places, which culminated in the evangelical mission to reach into every aspect of character and culture. The baseline emphasis which muscular Christianity developed was the heavenly and earthly rewards of "pluck" and hard work. Hall notes that Kingsley regarded "pluck" as "the primal stuff of virtue" and states that "this expression pervades nineteenth century thought and imagery."[30] A dictionary definition of "pluck" is given as, "showing determination to fight or struggle; bold, courageous, spirited."[31] These attributes bring together the mid-nineteenth-century drive for self-help; the muscular Christian character of physical strength, self-reliance, resourcefulness, self-control and spiritual development and the public school ethos following Thomas Arnold's reforms. Although from the 1870s the self-help movement became increasingly individualistic and moved away from the earlier formation of self-help co-operatives,[32] the muscular Christian characteristics culminate in the construction of the superior character of the British boy who is born to a life of leadership and adventure in the furthest corners of the ever-widening empire. This is the individual central to Henty's historical adventure stories, epitomized by the character of Frank Hargate in *By Sheer Pluck* (1884). In keeping with Kingsley's and Maurice's emphasis, the Henty boy's physical fitness and strength was due more to his skill and practice of boxing than to participation in team games. MacDonald forged his own interpretation of the muscular Christian by his emphasis on "spiritual" muscularity, although his male heroes Curdie and Clare Skymer also display the physical strength essential to the Henty hero.

29. Hall, *Muscular Christianity*, 8.
30. Ibid., 30.
31. New Shorter Oxford English Dictionary
32. Rodrick, *The Importance of Being an Earnest Improver*, 47.

The Self-Made Hero

During the two decades 1860–80, there were a number of significant political and social landmarks both at home and abroad. At home the 1867 Reform Bill and the 1870 Education Act were two notable instances whilst abroad these years marked the rapid expansion of colonial annexation, mainly in the east.

The successful passing of the Reform Bill meant the enfranchisement of over nine hundred thousand voters. Despite the fear of some Liberals that socialism would increase, it enabled working class Tories to vote and consequently decreased sympathy towards socialism. As an example of "controlled subversion" of the status quo, the extent of the Reform Bill gives an instance of the ability of Victorian England to adapt to circumstance. Carlyle, in his pamphlet *Shooting Niagara* (1867) depicted the reform as the beginning of the end of civilization. Carlyle, regarded as the prophet of his age, was, as Rainer Emig points out, the spokesman for "an age of contradiction."[33] He was against revolution as experienced in France, but equally against aristocratic government where he perceived the aristocracy to be parasitic. Emig argues that Carlyle's eccentric logic, that is, "on the margins of the acceptable and conventional but not outside it,"[34] enabled not only Carlyle himself but the society into which he wrote to "contain remarkable tolerance, often indeed against its own explicit intentions."[35] This level of tolerance enabled influential figures, such as John Ruskin,[36] as well as Carlyle, to present strong views on issues, although these views often appear to contradict other views in their writing when considered from a twenty-first-century perspective. This apparent lack of consistency within the work of the same person can be found in both Henty, whose view of race was not as stereotypical as critics imply and in MacDonald, whose support for women's education was not complemented by a support for women's suffrage and full participation on public life. Carlyle's seemingly reactionary stance was also contradicted by his view of the outsider presented in *On Heroes and Hero Worship* where he attempts to prise open Victorian closedness to the "other."

---

33. Emig, *Eccentricity Begins at Home*, 386.
34. Ibid., 380.
35. Ibid., 383.
36. See Rosenberg, *The Genius of John Ruskin*.

Historical Context 23

The second significant landmark noted, the 1870 Education Act, provided for some kind of school attendance to the age of thirteen, although provision was strictly on grounds of class or income and not completely free unless extreme poverty was proven. Figures show that literacy levels rose from 80.6 percent to 93.6 percent in the twenty years following the Act,[37] possibly indicating that formalizing education made a comparatively small impact upon basic literacy, although no definition of basic literacy is given in this comparison. Gerald Jordan, investigating the effect of popular literacy on imperial sentiment, notes that during the same period (1870–90), "the basis was laid for an imperial sentiment which, by the last decade of the century, was to transcend social differences and bind English people of all classes to the cause of imperial expansion."[38]

The period 1870 to 1900 was the time of Henty's most prolific production. Jordan's investigation shows Henty's popularity in a survey of major public library borrowing when he records Henty as, "after Rider Haggard, the most called-for author"[39] Although Henty wrote his stories for boys, this survey covered all borrowing and so indicates the pervasive influence of what Jordan in the same passage describes as "the sun-drenched, blood-stained prose of empire," throughout the borrowing public. Wilson goes further when he writes of Henty, "who ... probably had more influence than any other, in shaping the way that the British thought about the other people in the world,"[40] with the implied assumption of unquestioned superiority.

It was with "the other people in the world," that the British army had most to do from 1860 to 1880, if the term is applied to non-Europeans. After the Crimean War, the British army fought nine wars ranging geographically from New Zealand through India, Africa, South Africa, and back through Burma to China during the decades 1860–80. Some of these wars took place simultaneously and all were ostensibly defending English interests in trade and commerce. As the presence of the growing empire pervaded the mental landscape, Dentith, for example, implies that attitudes to other races and black races in particular, were hardening by the end of the 1860s as imperialistic expansion became

37. Altick, *The English Common Reader*, 171.
38. Jordan, *Popular Literature*, 149.
39. Ibid., 150.
40. Wilson, *The Victorians*, 259.

more overt. This date is quite early for such a change of attitude, which became more obvious in popular literature after the turn of the century. Henty frequently subverts his own stereotype. In *The Young Buglers* for example, Sam the black drummer, depicted as a figure of fun in the wider context of the regiment, is the character whose resourcefulness, courage and imaginative action rescues the boy heroes on several occasions.

James Walvin adds to Dentith's note on stereotypical constructions of other races by pointing out that the growing influence of scientific racism amongst the British led to, "a firm belief in British superiority."[41] Stemming from the rise of science in the Enlightenment period and perpetuated through Hume, Kant, and Hegel, this belief extended beyond the person to laws, institutions, and the concept that only the British could carry civilization and government to those who by English definition were "uncivilized," that is non-Western. The conclusion therefore was that because the English were the best suited to carry civilization to "the other people in the world," they were under an obligation to do so. It is worth mentioning that French thinking ran along the same lines. Darwin's *Origin of Species* (1859) was used to bolster the existing scientific position. Edward Said points out that the consequences of viewing non-western, and especially black people, as "savages" inevitably meant they were also seen as incapable of independence or self-organization and therefore in need of English rule. Said quotes Ruskin's view of England as, "for all the world a source of light, a centre of peace."[42] As the colonized were seen as without culture and without history, effectively in spiritual and intellectual darkness, the mission of carrying England's "light and peace" was seen to legitimise imperial expansion. Henty's stories were frequently situated in exotic locations, investing the place with a history linked to an event which happened in it, a history predominantly voiced through the English boy hero and one which emphasized British interests. In the European context the "mission civilisatrice"[43] of France developed post 1870 since the political climate in France earlier in the nineteenth century was strongly anti-imperialist. Suzanne Howe observes that the change came about not only as an economic necessity but in order to assert national pride and honour. German colonial expansion was motivated initially by the need for trade in the 1870s.

41. Walvin, *Victorian Values*, 116.
42. Said, *Culture and Imperialism*, 94.
43. Howe, *Novels of Empire*, 27.

The German sense of mission developed after 1900 and tended toward health and education provision.[44]

Although the beliefs about a civilizing mission outlined above predominated in England, there were dissenting voices, ranging from James Beattie and Johann Gottfried Herder writing in the late eighteenth century, through to a rise in anti-imperialist sentiment in the late nineteenth century.[45] Bernard Porter records that anti-imperialism in the 1860s and 1870s led to a feeling of resentment against, "unco-operative peoples whose recalcitrance had forced people to take them over."[46] This attitude savors more of guilt for colonialism by the use of force than respect for the colonized as entitled to their independence. It is reminiscent of one of Hegel's arguments for black inferiority which was the lack of respect for life demonstrated by "negroes (who) allow themselves to be shot down in thousands in their wars with Europeans."[47] Despite minimal dissent, Porter emphasizes that during the 1870s statesmen generally assumed that public opinion was on the side of the imperialists following the greatest period of industrial and commercial growth at home.

Impact on the Work of Henty and MacDonald

In this final section of the overview of the general historical context I will concentrate on three concepts that influenced and informed both domestic and foreign policy and which occur in the discussion of specific texts in a later chapter.

The first concept stemmed from the dominant views on race which led to a parallel between the urban poor in the domestic context and the colonized people in the context of empire. The connection between these two groups included the representation of both women and the colonized as children who needed to be educated and governed. The second concept is found in a correlation between the exploration of exotic geographical spaces and the exploration of the uncharted psychological spaces of the subconscious. Such an association brought the exotic space into the domestic arena, influencing views of the self both on a personal and a collective level. The third concept lies in the relationship between

---

44. Ibid., 13, 14, 18, 115.
45. Eze, ed. *Race and Enlightenment*, 34, 65, 153.
46. Porter, *The Lion's Share*, 50, 64.
47. Eze, ed. *Race and Enlightenment*, 136.

the renewed exploration of spiritualties, including alternatives to orthodox Christianity, and a wider awareness of and concern for social problems. These interests grew partly as a reaction to the unprecedented emphasis on wealth creation and the growth of national power.

The last two decades of the nineteenth century saw Britain falling behind Europe economically. As a result more energy was diverted towards imperial expansion, resulting in significant territorial gains whilst "securing British interests."[48] The apologetic that the "conquests were forced upon us," printed in the *Manchester Guardian* 7 April 1884 was an attempt to counter the change in attitude to the empire that became more apparent towards the end of the century following Disraeli's aggressive foreign policy. In the years leading up to 1880 Britain was involved in a number of small wars and had gained control of the Suez Canal[49] which was the main trade route to India. Said asserts that the doctrine of empire came to be accepted even by women's and working class movements,[50] an indication of its all-pervasive nature. Despite the acceptance of English superiority, reinforced by a racial interpretation of Darwinian theory, anti-imperialistic voices became stronger and alternative views to imperialism were articulated and disseminated through a proliferation of papers and periodicals. Correspondents were reporting not only on the numerous wars in the colonies, but some, for example William Thomas Stead and William Howard Russell, were presenting aspects of both domestic society and foreign involvement which were far from triumphalistic or plauditory. A link between home and foreign policy emerged on the issue of race. Walvin writes, "Pride in empire and overseas settlement was tempered by worry about the degeneration of the British race at home."[51] This worry stemmed from the consequences of the decline in agriculture between 1860 and 1880 which resulted in an influx of rural poor who then added to the existing numbers of urban poor. Scientific racism and the eugenics movement predicted a cumulative degeneration of the British race, in which "the ill-nourished poor bequeathed their physical and mental deficiencies to their large numbers of offspring."[52] Carlyle's *Shooting Niagara* (1867) was an

48. Porter, *The Lion's Share*, 88.
49. James, *The Rise and Fall*, 196–97.
50. Said, *Culture and Imperialism*, 62.
51. Walvin, *Victorian Values*, 118.
52. Ibid., 118.

early warning of what developed into a sense of impending disaster. MacDonald's fairy tale *The Princess and the Goblin* (1872) reflected the potential for degeneration in both the domestic and the colonial context. The sequel, *The Princess and Curdie* (1883), addressed the self-destructive potential in a society that is preoccupied with a self-interested pursuit of wealth. At the same time the imperialist machine became more ruthless in its methods of preserving British commercial interest abroad. In his bio-critical study of Henty's work Guy Arnold comments that Henty's later adventure stories become more mechanistic, which, he believed, reflected the hardening attitude toward colonial rule during these two decades.[53] Work on popular magazines for boys by Geoffrey Fox notes that an unquestioning, hardening of attitude toward colonial rule and the foreigner escalated *post* 1900.[54] The fact that Henty was producing stories to tight deadlines may account for some of the mechanistic nature of the stories if not the increased level of violence found in the example given by Arnold, *With the Allies to Pekin* (1904) which was a posthumous publication hurriedly written, since the events described took place in 1900 and Henty died in 1902. Henty continued to include opinions in the dialogue of his characters which presented political situations from both an English and a non-European point of view. *With the Allies to Pekin* includes a discourse on the unacceptable nature of the European use of disproportionate force to requisition Chinese ports. The hero's father observes, "the last murder of two German missionaries gave Germany an excuse for seizing the port of Kiaochow. ... [N]aturally it seems a preposterous price to pay for the murder of two foreigners. ... Suppose two Chinese had been killed in Germany, what do you think the Germans would say if China were to demand as compensation Bremerhaven?"[55]

The growth of empire fiction alongside the growth of empire draws attention to the fictional quality of some of the characters involved in both exploration and administration. I use the word fictional in the sense that the experiences of some of these people parallels invented, imaginative narratives found in contemporary novels. Kathryn Tidrick

53. Arnold, *Held Fast for England*, 73.

54. This discussion was developed in a seminar led by Geoffrey Fox in relation to Boys' Magazines and Comics. Conference, Children's Literature Comes of Age, Faculty of Education, Cambridge, 2004.

55. Henty, *With the Allies to Pekin*, 40.

spells this out in her study *Empire and the British Character* (1992), giving Frederick Courtenay Selous as an example of a, "prototype for (Rider Haggard's) Allan Quatermain."[56] Michael Brander's suggestion that Samuel White Baker was the inspiration for the Henty hero is too sweeping to stand without qualification, but Brander's account of Baker's colonial adventures with seemingly miraculous escapes, "native" sidekicks, rapid language acquisition, and ever-present resourcefulness in the face of danger does resemble a Henty story, with the inclusion of an equally resourceful wife. With such characters' exploits in the newspapers and their fictional counterparts proliferating in literature, the empire was so integral to British national life that, as Porter states, statesmen "generally assumed public opinion was on the side of the imperialists"[57] and Africa, or any other exotic location, was part of their psychological landscape. Whilst Henty wrote of adventures into unknown geographical territories, MacDonald's work reflected the unknown in terms of psychological territory.[58] These two areas of exploration intersected in the person of Henry Morton Stanley, the originally British, adoptive American journalist, whose psychological "struggle" is noted by Thomas Pakenham[59] and interpreted by Wilson who comments that Stanley "saw Africa, as many explorers and missionaries did, as the metaphor for the uncharted territory of their own personal 'struggle.'"[60] This comment typifies the relationship between geographical and psychological exploration. Henty and Stanley met in 1868 when Henty was sent to report on the Magdala campaign[61] and during the Ashanti campaign of 1873–74; both were correspondents following Sir Garnet Wolseley's force. Henty later put his experiences into his story *By Sheer Pluck* (1884).

The need for young men educated in English public schools, molded to carry forward British interests, whether in "the two scrambles for Africa"[62] or in the containment of uprisings in India, was a factor in the change in attitude to education, at least in the public schools. The "less

56. Tidrick, *Empire*, 57.
57. Porter, *The Lion's share*, 64.
58. See essays in McGillis, *For the Childlike*, and Raeper, *The Gold Thread*.
59. Pakenham, *The Scramble for Africa*, 25.
60. Wilson, *The Victorians*, 488.
61. King, *G. A. Henty in West Africa*, 3.
62. James, *The Rise and Fall*, 288.

Latin and more chemistry" argument sought to promote the less well-off who could succeed in public examinations. Their practicality was seen as an asset if they were placed in a remote colonial administrative post. The "less cricket and more rifle shooting" argument[63] exhibited some confusion as to the product required for the extension of the empire. Whilst "the product" was expected to "play the game" in the sense of acting upon the limited set of collective dominant ideas inculcated into the boy at public school, he was also expected to be a resourceful individual, able to act alone and able to survive in isolation for months or years as Sir Hugh Charles Clifford, Administrator in Malaya (1866–1941) did in fact. In this situation Clifford had his interest in hunting big game to console him. The Henty hero became a combination of these requirements and it is a point of interest that Samuel White Baker, mentioned above, attended school for only a few months, suggesting that what was needed in the last decades of the century was independence and resourcefulness in the Administrative posts whilst the team-player followed the ever-present colonial wars, distinguishing himself by his courage, physical stamina and leadership qualities in a collective arena.

If, as Wilson states, the nineteenth century was "an era of faith ... as much as one of doubt,"[64] then the question is, "faith in what?" Not only was there belief in the continuation of empire, the materialistic creed of wealth creation, trade, and economic domination, but also a rise in new religious movements such as Mormonism, Christian Science and Theosophy. Within the orthodox stream of belief there was a rise in the influence of Roman Catholicism alongside the growth of "broad church" theology and fundamentalist evangelicalism. According to Claude Welch, writing in 2002, the major controversies within the Christian community, both protestant and Roman Catholic, reflected the "continuing struggle of the church within the larger society," and culminated in social gospels at the end of the century.[65] All these movements were reflected in the fiction of the period. Anthony Trollope's critique of materialism in *The Way We Live Now* (1874) and MacDonald's writing for both children and adults point towards an alternative to what MacDonald believed was the self-destructive tendency of greed, whether for wealth or power. Interest in alternative spiritualities also

63. Porter, *The Lion's share*, 130.
64. Wilson, *The Victorians*, 549.
65. Welch, *Confidence and Questions*, 139.

found a place in MacDonald's adult novels. Hypnotic control and séances feature, for example, in *David Elginbrod* (1863) and *Robert Falconer* (1868). The inclusion of social reform in imperialist expansion, based on the evangelical cult of personal example, found fictional outlets not only in the fiction of Henty but also in MacDonald's novels, such as *The Vicar's Daughter* (1872) and *Robert Falconer*. The social work of William Booth, which led to the foundation of the Salvation Army in 1878, was part of the trend towards widening social awareness and calls for action to address, for example, poverty, homelessness, and unemployment. Politically these problems were addressed by the thinking of Thomas Hill Green (1836–82), a pioneer of social egalitarianist thought in England.[66] After the demise of the Christian Socialist Movement in 1854, the growing influence of Marx's writing resulted in Henry Myers Hyndman (1842–1921) founding the Social Democratic Federation in 1881, later to become the British Socialist Party. Hyndman was an old Etonian who became a journalist. Although committed to furthering social justice, he displayed instances of the Victorian ability to hold contradictory views without apparently needing to reconcile them. For example, although an anti-imperialist, he praised the merits of British imperialism in the Pall Mall Gazette for which he wrote. Whilst reporting on the Italian war in 1866 he met Henty who was also reporting on the Italian campaign. In his autobiography Hyndman recalls an incident in which he and Henty were involved. This incident is recorded in some detail in Hyndman's biography, and describes Henty as "ordinarily the most good-natured, buoyant-spirited, and long-suffering man that ever lived."[67] Hyndman also records Henty's reaction to the Dreyfus second trial which Henty attended in Paris in January 1895 and which is discussed in Hyndman's biography of Clemenceau. Whilst acknowledging that "Henty was a thorough-going Tory," and therefore expected to take the view that Dreyfus was a traitor, Hyndman continues "but he had no doubt that Dreyfus was a terribly ill-used man." Hyndman also notes that Henty "understood what was going on"[68] in this complicated political episode. The full accounts of these incidents indicate a relationship that stretched beyond the workmanlike towards friendship and record Henty's understanding of the political complexities of the period.

66. Wilson, *The Victorians*, 519.
67. Hyndman, *The Record*, 42.
68. Hyndman, *Clemenceau*, 167, 168.

By the time of the South African wars (1893-94, 1896-97, 1899-1902) dissenting voices on the subject of imperial expansion, and particularly on tactics used to preserve existing British interests in South Africa, were becoming louder. These events are well documented, for example by James. Henty's South African novels *The Young Colonists* (1885) and *With Buller in Natal* (1901) were explicit in his derogation of the Boers, although one of his characters, an English officer, comments "'they are a splendid set of men . . . they are magnificent riders and good shots.'" [69] Henty was equally explicit about the apathy, indecision, and arrogance of the British government in the face of unrest. His character comments, "a handful of miserable curs at home . . . were ready to betray the honour of England, in order that they might make matters smooth for themselves at home."[70] Henty was never afraid to criticize English policy if he believed it was at fault as will be seen in a closer look at Henty's life.

G. A. Henty from 1832-50:
Influences that Shaped His Thinking

Henty's biographer, George Manville Fenn (1911) subtitled his biography *The Story of an Active Life*, an intimation that his work lays more emphasis on what Henty did than on the man himself. Private letters from Henty, held by the libraries of the University of Indiana (Bloomington), Yale, Hove (UK), and Wandsworth (London, UK) and by private collectors reveal little more,[71] dealing almost exclusively with practical matters. Manville Fenn approaches his subject as Henty approached one of his fictional heroes, by tracing Henty's adventures after the initial two chapters on his early life. The result is that Manville Fenn's biography is eulogistic and episodic. Arnold's *Held Fast for England* (1980) does not claim to be a biography, but "an attempt to assess his (Henty's) importance and influence as a boys' writer."[72] With no definitive biography to date, Arnold's work is the most recently published source of biographical information.

69. Henty, *The Young Colonists*, 238.
70. Henty, *With Buller in Natal*, 368-69.
71. Photocopies of correspondence made available courtesy Ann King, Henty Society.
72. Arnold, *Held Fast for England*, preface.

Although Henty could be described as an "insider" in Victorian society, his early life was atypical and did not presage his later career in any way. I use the term "insider" in the sense that he was born in the southern part of England, to middle class parents, was a product of the English public school system and pursued a career as a war correspondent attached to a newspaper which supported the Tory party and by which he was trusted to reflect the moral and ideological values of established English society. From his position as "insider" he was able to report critically on, for example, government policy, when he believed criticism was needed. Henty's analyzes of policy both at home and abroad verify his political understanding of the often conflicting interests of the period. His construction of heroism endeavored to draw the ideal and the achievable into the context of contemporary historical events.

George Alfred Henty was born in Trumpington, Cambridgeshire on December 8th 1832, although the family were living in Godmanchester at the time. He was baptized in Godmanchester in 1836 with his younger brother Frederick.[73] Manville Fenn quotes Henty as recalling, "I spent my boyhood, to the best of my recollection, in bed." Manville Fenn records that when Henty was confined to bed due to illness he read avidly, "romance, adventure, everything,"[74] although he also points out that Henty's grandfather was interested in science and fostered Henty's interest in natural history, including it in his reading matter. This information is corroborated by an interview with Henty conducted by George Knight and published in the periodical for boys, *The Captain* in 1899. Scientific interest in natural history was widespread and growing in the early to mid-nineteenth century. Charles Kingsley's writing reflects his own expertise in this area of study in, for example, his observations of the natural world in *The Water-Babies: A Fairy Tale for a Land Baby* (1863). Henty's interest in natural history was communicated through his boy heroes, notably Frank Hargate *(By Sheer Pluck),* whose talent resulted in his appointment as assistant naturalist on the expedition to Coomassie. The story is based on the events in West Africa in 1873 which Henty covered as correspondent to *The Standard* newspaper. There is no record of the individual books Henty read on natural history, but Eze

---

73. I am indebted to Ann King, Chair of The Henty Society for this information gathered from parish records.

74. Fenn, *George Alfred Henty*, 3.

observes that the authors of the texts available continually drew upon each other's work. The taxonomy they used included the human species placed on a hierarchical scale by racial characteristics and "rational and moral, evolutionary capacity" with the consistent allocation of the European (Caucasian) as the superior race. Eze continues, "the writings of Hume, Kant and Hegel played a strong role in articulating Europe's sense not only of its cultural but also racial superiority. In their writings . . . 'reason' and 'civilization' became synonymous with 'white' people and northern Europe, while unreason and savagery were conveniently located among the non-whites . . . outside Europe."[75] Responses to such assertions, for example James Beattie's to Hume, were not strong enough to mitigate the predominant view, "that every practice and sentiment is barbarous which is not according to the usages of modern Europe." Beattie countered what he termed this "fundamental mental maxim with many of our critics and philosophers" by turning the tables when he wrote that, "A plain historical account of some of our most fashionable duellists, gamblers, and adulterers (to name no more) would exhibit specimens of brute barbarity, and sottish infatuation such as might vie with any that ever appeared in Kamschatka, California, or the land of the Hottentots."[76] Humphrey Carpenter indicates that Henty's representation of race did not always reflect the dominant view of his time[77] and Dennis Butts notes that sympathetic treatment of races, such as the Irish poor in *Orange and Green* (1888), reflected some of the ideological divisions within Victorian society, and served to critique the dominant imperialistic policies.[78]

Henty's physically active adult life tends to take precedence over the record of his semi-invalid childhood, eclipsing the breadth of reading which he brought to his own later writing and political comment. When he was well enough, he attended a Dame School until the age of ten before being sent to a private boarding school in London where his education was punctuated by bouts of illness until he reached the age of fourteen. The turning point for Henty came when he was sent to Westminster School where his interests in poetry, books and natural history invited bullying. In order to survive in the world of the English

75. Eze, ed. *Race and Enlightenment*, 5.
76. Beattie, *An Essay on the Nature and Immutability of Truth*, 36.
77. Carpenter and Pritchard. *The Oxford Companion*, 246.
78. Butts, *True to Whose Flag?* 5.

public school, he took lessons in boxing and later in wrestling, both skills he strongly advocated in his later writing for boys. Westminster School features prominently in *Captain Bayley's Heir* (1889) and *In the Reign of Terror* (1888, subtitled *The Adventures of a Westminster Boy*). Manville Fenn builds upon the popular view of Henty, a view typified by James Barr's description of Henty as "a splendid specimen of an Englishman."[79] Barr's comment rests upon his English public school education and subsequent career, but his early life was atypical. His childhood spent reading romance, poetry, natural history, and "anything and everything" meant that by the time he reached Westminster School his interests were broader and his knowledge deeper than those of his less widely-read contemporaries. At this school, Henty internalized the Arnoldian model of the ideal English Schoolboy. Thomas Hughes' Tom Brown of *Tom Brown's Schooldays* (1857) was typical of the exemplary Arnoldian boy. The second half of the nineteenth century was, as Julia Duin points out, "an exciting time if you were, like Henty and the heroes of many of his novels, intelligent, talented, middle class and English, with a thirst for adventure and plenty of pluck."[80]

Again atypically, it was nearly fifteen years before Henty became established in his profession. His educational route deviated from the traditional clear passage through university and his career evolved out of his subsequent experiences which I will track through the decades 1850–1900.

G. A. Henty from 1850–80:
War Correspondent, Novelist, and Writer for Boys

In 1852, Henty entered Gonville and Caius (known as Caius) College Cambridge, to read classics. He continued to box and row but both Manville Fenn and Arnold record that at the end of the year he collapsed and took a year off to rest from study. He spent part of the year working in Wales where his father owned a coal mine and iron works. The knowledge of mining and engineering he acquired during this period enabled him to pass as an engineer in 1866 on an assignment as a correspondent for *The Standard* newspaper in Italy and gain access to one of the new ironclads, the fighting ships in the battle of Lissa engaged

---

79. Barr, *A Great Writer of Christmas Books*, 45.
80. Duin, *Victorian Children's Books*, 23.

in the war between Italy and Austria. Henty's experience in Wales also gave him the material for *Facing Death* (1882), a mining story in which the hero of humble origin rises to the position of pit manager through courage, perseverance, hard work and ingenuity, a classic Smilesian self-help combination of virtues. Henty's return to Cambridge was brief since England declared war on Russia in March 1854. The Crimean was an Imperial war, the only one fought against a European power during the nineteenth century, although, as James notes, there were some who regarded Russia as an Asiatic power.[81] Henty left Cambridge without taking a degree and took up a post with the Commissariat's Department of the army. His letters describing the conditions he found in the Crimea and the disorganisation he faced in the Purveyor's Department provided his entry into journalism. His father offered the letters to the London *Morning Advertiser*. The publication of these letters, and correspondence from other minor journalists endorsed William Russell's high profile reports for *The Times* describing the appalling conditions in the Crimea. As a result public opinion forced the government to improve organization of the venture in order to ensure that the soldiers received the supplies and medical support they needed, although it came too late for those who had already died from disease due to the conditions, including Henty's brother Frederick who died of cholera only two weeks after his arrival in the Crimea. Henty was invalided back to England in 1855. He incorporated this experience into his fiction in the novel *Jack Archer* (1883), which is set in the Crimea, and has two brothers as the major characters. Arnold notes the recurrence of the "brother pattern"[82] in other stories, notably *The Young Buglers* (1880). Henty's army career ended four years later (1859) but he did not become a full-time journalist until 1865. Apart from a posting to Italy in 1859 during the Italian war with Austria, Henty remained within the UK. He married Elizabeth Finucane in 1858 with whom he had four children between 1858 and 1865 when Elizabeth died.

Whilst in Italy, Henty's brief was to organize the hospitals for Britain's Italian Legion. He met Garibaldi for the first time and became familiar with the language and country he returned to seven years later on his first assignment as a war correspondent for *The Standard* newspaper. Henty's belief in the benefits of learning the language of the host

81. James, *The Rise and Fall*, 182.
82. Arnold, *Held Fast for England*, 7.

country is emphasized in his stories for boys. One of the many accomplishments of his heroes is their ability to pick up languages easily. This gift inevitably places them in a good position to be noticed and gain rapid promotion. Instances include Gregory Hilliard (real name Hartley) in *With Kitchener in the Soudan* (1903), and this language ability became integral to Henty's construct of the hero figure.

Henty's first published novel, *A Search for a Secret* (1867) was intended for an adult audience and as A. B. E. Brown, writing in 1997, notes, "in a precedent that was rarely followed thereafter, the narrator and central character is a woman." Brown also notes, "the discerning can perceive something of the ideas and personality of the author himself coming through."[83] This precedent for a strong, resourceful female character was taken up again in *A Soldier's Daughter* (1906), one of the last of Henty's stories to be posthumously published. The creation of a courageous female hero at the beginning and end of his writing career (there are others, less prominent, in between), indicates Henty's consistency in his perception of women as other than the dominant construct of the weak and childlike epitomized, for example, by the person of Rose La Touche (1848–75). It could be argued that Rose embodied the logical conclusion of such a construct by adding "invalid" to "weak" and "childlike." Female characters who appear in his books display unexpected physical and emotional strength given the stereotypical perception of Henty's attitude to women found in Arnold et al. Examples are Annie in *The Tiger of Mysore* (1896), Mary in *Cuthbert Hartingdon* (1889), and Alice in *Captain Bayley's Heir* (1889).

The years 1867–77 were Henty's most intense period of travel. He joined Lord Napier's expedition to Abyssinia in 1867–68 and published the resultant correspondence as a book, *The March to Magdala* (1868), primarily for an adult audience. Napier undertook the expedition in order to rescue hostages taken by the Emperor Theodore. Henty later incorporated his experience of both this expedition and his assignment to cover what James refers to as "a large-scale punitive war against the Asante of the Gold Coast"[84] into his boy's story *By Sheer Pluck* (1884). Henty's next assignment was to report on the Franco-Prussian war, initially from the German side in Berlin. His experience of the French side resulted not only in copy for the *Standard*, but also in *The Young*

83. Brown, *A Search for a Secret*, 5.
84. James, *The Rise and Fall*, 190.

Franc-Tireurs (1872), one of four stories with brothers as the heroes. This story was the second of his books for boys[85] and Henty had not yet begun to employ the formula he was later to follow more consistently, although the story does include disguise, in the use of which the Henty hero was a master. In 1875, Henty was selected to travel with the Prince of Wales and his retinue on a tour of India. Departing from Bombay in November 1875, the Prince and his retinue visited Baroda, Goa, Ceylon, Madras, Calcutta, Benares, Lucknow, and Nepal, returning to Bombay in March 1876. In May 1876, Queen Victoria was declared Empress of India. Manville Fenn, whose version of place names I have used above, records the pageantry in the language of an Eastern fairy tale, echoing Disraeli's sentiment that the age was "one of infinite romance . . . like a fairy tale." "[T]he Prince mounted the elephant in waiting, his host having provided a majestic beast, richly caparisoned and gorgeously painted. The howdah was of silver, beautifully decorated with cloth of gold. It was a resplendent spectacle."[86] Manville Fenn's chapter describing the tour continues in this manner. Research done by Ann King into newspaper reports of the tour has established the difficulty of conclusively identifying articles written by Henty. Newspaper articles were rarely signed since copy was telegraphed as quickly as possible to the newspaper's editor, who wrote up the information received for publication.[87]

G. A. Henty from 1880–1900: The Stories, Content, and Character

By the end of 1876, having covered the Carlist insurrection in Spain (1874) and the Turco-Serbian war in Serbia (1876), the physical stress of travel and the rough living conditions he experienced as a war correspondent contributed to a breakdown in Henty's health. Arnold notes "except for a visit to California in 1885 when he examined mining camps his travelling days were over."[88]

The stereotypical image of Henty, presented by Arnold, is partially borne out by Henty himself when he acknowledged, "To endeavour to inculcate patriotism in my books has been one of my main objects . . ."

---

85. The first was *Out on the Pampas* (1871).

86. Fenn, *George Alfred Henty*, 279.

87. Conversation between Ann King, Chair of the Henty Society, and RJ 9 Sept 2008.

88. Arnold, *Held Fast for England*, 10.

but he continues, "My object has always been to write good history."[89] Henty then elaborates on his techniques and reasons for adhering to them, including the need for his stories to feature an English boy hero. His rationale hinges on the appeal to his target audience and the need to sell his books. In the same article Henty notes that he regarded *The Young Carthaginian* (1887), *The Cat of Bubastes* (1889), and *The Destruction of Jerusalem (For the Temple)* (1888) as "the three stories that I rather expected would do especially well," although he does not elaborate on why he particularly thought so. Unfortunately they did not fulfil his expectations, a failure he attributes to their lack of an English hero. Henty's perceived need to cast an English boy as the protagonist gives an illustration of the circular nature of the growth of imperialism. Eric Stokes considers that "no other writer for the young exercised a tithe of his [Henty's] influence,"[90] yet Henty is recorded in the above quotation as having responded to market demand in his production of stories with a prominent English hero. As I have outlined in this chapter, many factors contributed to the imperialist mind-set, which fed on itself and so grew more influential. Although Henty's influence is clearly partially the result of his embedding in the contemporary political discourse in which he lived, nevertheless, on reading Henty's material, it becomes clear that he often subverts the critically perceived stereotypes. Stokes perceives that, "Having set them [stereotypes] up, Henty deliberately punctures the partition walls between them."[91] Stokes was referring to ethnic stereotypes in his review of Arnold's work, but the analogy could equally be applied to politics, religion, nationalism (as opposed to patriotism) and conservation. In *Condemned as a Nihilist* (1893), despite the hero's denunciation of revolutionary terrorism, there is a passage giving insight into the motivation to political violence which condemns a system that drives the socially concerned to such extremities. The hero's Russian employer observes, "I cannot but think the government has made a terrible mistake by its severity. . . . . These people . . . see that things are not as they should be. It is cruelty that has led them to use the only weapon at their disposal, assassination." In the same book, Henty puts an atypical gloss on hunting for sport, in terms of his own historical period, and a high value on the lives of animals. Godfrey, the hero,

---

89. Henty, *Writing Books for Boys*, 105.
90. Stokes, *From Mexico to Mysore*, 406.
91. Ibid.

speaks, "It is right to kill what we require for food, but to my mind there is nothing more wicked than taking life merely for amusement."[92] Henty's continuing interest in natural phenomena and his love of animals confirms Arnold's assertion that passages such as the above demonstrate Henty's own views. His emphasis on respecting and retaining the culture and identity of "the other" peoples tends to be overlooked as a result of his propagation of English superiority voiced through native speakers. An example of such a change in viewpoint is found in *With Kitchener in the Soudan* (1903). The wife of a Mahdi warrior, saved by the hero when she falls overboard from a ship, speaks, "To be always raiding, and plundering, and killing cannot be good. It used to seem to me natural and right, but now I have come to think differently."[93]

Following Carlyle, Henty advocates the "good in all creeds" philosophy whilst ensuring his heroes always thank God for deliverance from awkward situations. Unlike MacDonald, whose heroes' spiritual awareness is essential to their actions, Henty's heroes often appear superficially pious.[94] In spite of this apparent superficiality Henty, in an article entitled *True Heroism*, writes "To be a true hero you must be a true Christian; true heroism is inseparable from true Christianity."[95] In this statement Henty demonstrates the closeness of his ideal hero to that of George MacDonald, the trajectory of whose life and work I now address.

George MacDonald 1824–60: Intellectual Development

If Henty is described as the "insider" in English society, then MacDonald could be described as the "outsider," that is, as a Scot, he reflected upon English society from the outside. The effect upon his work of this reflection will be considered when I examine MacDonald's texts.

MacDonald was born in Huntly, Aberdeenshire, Scotland, on December 10th 1824. His great grandfather had been a piper who joined the Jacobite forces and fought at Culloden (1745). MacDonald's biographers Greville MacDonald (1924), William Raeper (1987), and Rolland Hein (1993) emphasize the importance of his Scottish roots both to his

92. Henty, *Condemned as a Nihilist*, 65–66, 226.
93. Henty, *With Kitchener*, 202.
94. See for example Henty, *Condemned as a Nihilist*, 231, 307.
95. Henty, *True Heroism*, 56.

work and to his character. His novels *Alec Forbes of Howglen* (1865) and *Ranald Bannerman's Boyhood* (1871) depict vivid pictures of the landscape and life of MacDonald's boyhood. His grandfather, Charles Edward, brought the family to Huntly from Portsoy, a fishing village in the north east of Scotland. He started the family business of bleaching and thread spinning, a business adapted by MacDonald's father, also George, to include the production of potato flour. MacDonald grew up on the small farm owned by the family where he developed a love of animals and horses in particular. His adult novel *Paul Faber* (1879) advocates his antivivisectionist views whilst *At the Back of the North Wind* (1871) and *A Rough Shaking* (1891) both feature horses as significant characters in the story. Although prone to illness, MacDonald attended one of the two schools in Huntly. Raeper notes that the school MacDonald attended was the new "adventure school" "mainly supported by the dissenting families of the town–especially by the Missionars"[96] as opposed to the Parish School. MacDonald drew a graphic depiction of the school in *Alec Forbes of Howglen* (1865), from his experiences at the adventure school, including the harsh schoolmaster who, fortunately for MacDonald, emigrated to Australia and was replaced by a master who recognised and fostered MacDonald's ability, enabling him to gain a bursary to King's College Aberdeen in 1840. As a boy, MacDonald, like Henty, read whatever he could find. Greville MacDonald cites John Bunyan's *Pilgrim's Progress* (1678), John Milton's *Paradise Lost* (1667) and Friedrich Gottlieb Klopstock's *Messiah* (1773) as high on his reading list but MacDonald's long poem *A Hidden Life* (1857), noted by Raphael Shaberman[97] as autobiographical, includes the lines,

> The boy knew little; but read old tales
> Of Scotland's warriors, till his blood ran swift
> As charging knights upon their death-career.[98]

Henty's boyhood reading echoes such tales of romance.

MacDonald's biographers, MacDonald and Raeper, record that he was often ill with pleurisy and unable to go to school. Raeper notes that "on one occasion he was kept in bed for four months and bled from

---

96. Raeper, *George MacDonald*, 29. The Missionar Kirk is described by Raeper as "a zealous alternative to the established church." Raeper, *George MacDonald*, 19.

97. Shaberman, *George MacDonald*, 10.

98. MacDonald, *The Poetical Works*, 135.

the arm."⁹⁹ Like Henty, MacDonald had ample reading time. Greville MacDonald also notes MacDonald's "keen observation of nature"¹⁰⁰ and interest in the way of life of shepherds and crofters who gathered in Huntly at *The Gordon Arms* and to whose talk MacDonald listened as a boy. MacDonald later fed this information, together with his observations and local stories and legends, into his fictional work.

His admittance to King's College Aberdeen in 1840, just before his sixteenth birthday, began a period of spiritual questioning for MacDonald. At an age when Henty was imbibing the ethos of an English public school, MacDonald was experiencing the life of a university student. The 1840s in Scotland witnessed such controversy within the Church of Scotland that it caused a split (1843). Politically, the campaign for the abolition of the Corn Laws was at its height. Richard Cobden (1804–65), one of the founders of the Anti-Corn Law League, visited Aberdeen in 1844. The gradual removal of protection leading up to the abolition of corn duty in 1846 affected small farmers, one of whom was George's father. Due to the family's financial difficulties, George was unable to attend King's College during the 1842–43 session. This enforced gap in his studies differs significantly from Henty's year out due to the breakdown in his health. Henty's family was wealthy enough for him to recover at home before taking up some employment in the family coal mine, whereas MacDonald was dependent on finding work both to survive and to continue his studies. Although Henty's heroes, such as Frank Hargate (*By Sheer Pluck*) and Dick Holland *(The Tiger of Mysore)* are often placed in a position of poverty on a temporary basis because of family circumstances usually entailing the loss of a father, they always reclaim a comfortable middle class social position on reaching adulthood. MacDonald reflects deeply upon, and writes about, poverty, in his novels and sermons, from personal experience, but the heroes of his children's stories rarely remain poor. Curdie becomes a king and Clare Skymer (*A Rough Shaking*) and Willie *(Gutta Percha Willie)* become well-off professionals in their chosen field. When Diamond *(At the Back of the North Wind)* dies, his family and the waif Nanny are left in an improved social position. Only Richard in the tale *Cross Purposes* remains poor.

99. Raeper, *George MacDonald*, 29.
100. MacDonald, *George MacDonald*, 57.

There is some dispute as to how MacDonald spent his year out of university in 1842–43. Greville MacDonald states that Rev. Robert Troup, married to MacDonald's first cousin and friend of MacDonald, recorded that George "spent some summer months in a certain castle or mansion in the far North . . . in cataloguing a neglected library."[101] Raeper notes this may have been Thurso Castle, owned by Sir George Sinclair, a German scholar. Other options are discussed by both Greville MacDonald and Hein. Notably the image of a library recurs in MacDonald's adult novels and is particularly significant in his second adult fantasy *Lilith* (1895). Deirdre Hayward's study *George MacDonald and Three German Thinkers* (2000) analyzes the major influences on MacDonald's thought and work, particularly the magnitude of the influence of German Romanticism which was, Greville MacDonald believes, fostered by the opportunity to encounter the breadth of material found in this library. Raeper notes that, "MacDonald, who read deeply in Carlyle and imbibed the same German influences, wrote under his shadow, espousing many of the same theories."[102] Carlyle's work was influenced by German idealist philosophy which, as G. B. Tennyson records, "affected Carlyle powerfully."[103] Tennyson also notes that Carlyle frequently analyzed Calvinist theological tenets in terms of the philosophy of Goethe, Fichte, Novalis, Kant, and Schelling. Although not directly recorded, it is likely that MacDonald read Carlyle's analysis at a time when he was questioning the Calvinism of his upbringing and forging his own theological position. Whilst he was studying at Aberdeen, MacDonald was influenced by what became known as the Morisonian heresy which broke in 1844. In the previous two years, MacDonald's encounters with social deprivation and involvement with Sunday School teaching had given him a lasting concern for the poor and exacerbated his unease with Calvin's doctrine of election. Morison preached that Christ died for all men and not just for the elect, taking his authority from 1 Corinthians 15:3–4. MacDonald's sympathy with Morison's interpretation of this Pauline, early church doctrine led to his removal from the Sunday school and paved the way for later influences upon his theological thought.

101. MacDonald, *George MacDonald*, 72.
102. Raeper, *George MacDonald*, 183.
103. Tennyson, ed., *A Carlyle Reader*, xxvii.

Rolland Hein's biography puts forward another view as to how MacDonald spent his gap year, which is that he "found a position as a teacher of arithmetic... from February to November 1843."[104] According to Greville MacDonald, both the work in the library and the teaching post took MacDonald through the year until he re-entered King's in November 1843 and graduated in March 1845. MacDonald spent the next five years working out what he believed about Christianity and finding out what to do with his life. Unable to continue his scientific studies because of financial constraints, he travelled to London where he became a private tutor. During this period, he was introduced to the Powell family through his cousin Helen McKay who had married Alexander Powell, and here he met Louisa, his future wife. Still struggling with matters of faith, MacDonald applied to, and was accepted into, Highbury Theological College to train as a Congregational minister. He spent the summer of 1848 at home in Huntly before returning to London to begin his theological training in the autumn of 1848. Contextually, the pace of change in England had gathered momentum during the five years 1845–50. By 1848 five thousand miles of railway had been built; and revolt in Europe had revived fears of revolution in England as the Chartist Movement gathered strength. MacDonald spent the summer of 1849 as a locum minister in Ireland, whose population had been decimated by famine and emigration. Caroline Moore, in a brief comment on lycanthropes in MacDonald cites *The Gray Wolf*, a short story published in 1871, as "a fictionalised reaction to the Irish poor."[105] Moore does not elaborate, but MacDonald's experience of Ireland so soon after the famine affected him deeply, and is recorded by Raeper.[106] MacDonald as "outsider" responded to the poverty of the Irish compassionately.[107] Since MacDonald already had an MA, he did not need to complete the usual four years of theological study and left Highbury after two years when he was offered the position of minister at Trinity Congregational Church Arundel. He commenced his duties in the autumn of 1850. MacDonald was already aligning himself with views outside of perceived orthodoxy. At Highbury he had problems with, as Louisa termed it in her letters, his

104. Hein, *George MacDonald*, 20.
105. Moore, *The Questions Dated*, 61.
106. Raeper, *George MacDonald*, 71.
107. In contrast, Kingsley's "insider" English response was one of revulsion. He viewed the Irish as an inferior race, thus aligning them with other colonial subjects. See Kingsley, *The Water Babies*, 96 and Chitty, *The Beast and the Monk*, 209.

"heresy."[108] In non-conformist circles correct doctrine was regarded as of paramount importance. MacDonald's Scottish upbringing, his non-conformist religious and social circle and his interest in German literature all removed him from the mainstream of English society during this period. Raeper records that Dissenters were still unable to enter Oxford, Cambridge or Durham universities. Church of Scotland controversies did not feature on the English religious scene, pre-occupied as it was with the "second spring" of English Catholicism[109] and the consequent rise in Roman Catholic political power.

MacDonald's pastorate in Arundel was dogged by difficulty. After only one month he became too ill to preach following a lung haemorrhage and was unable to return to Arundel until January 1851. Most of his convalescence was spent on the Isle of Wight where he wrote the narrative poem *Within and Without*. Raeper plots the development of this work, noting the Romantic influence on MacDonald. Soon after his return to Arundel in March 1851, George MacDonald married Louisa Powell and, so he thought, settled into life in Arundel. This stability was short-lived. By June of the following year some members of his congregation began to question his orthodoxy. Not only did he write poetry and read and translate German, but there was a rumor that "he had expressed a hope that the lower animals would be sharers in the better life to come."[110] The situation escalated when the suggestion that "the young pastor thought that the heathen would have some period of probation"[111] gained circulation. By the end of June 1852, the deacons cut his stipend, hoping that he would resign. Realizing that dissatisfaction with his preaching with references to these two points of doctrine was confined to only a few, albeit influential, members of the congregation, MacDonald continued in Arundel until May 1853 when he had no option but to resign. Louisa's attempt to start a small school to supplement the family income had not been successful. Leaving Arundel meant that MacDonald left behind the life he had anticipated, that of a pastor and preacher, and moved to Manchester where his brother Charles lived. Louisa joined him after the birth of their second child, Mary, in June 1853. MacDonald's move to Manchester was not only

---

108. See Raeper, *George MacDonald*, 69.
109. Wilson, *The Victorians*, 140.
110. MacDonald, *George MacDonald*, 178.
111. Raeper, *George MacDonald*, 90.

to be near his brother. Alexander Scott was based in Manchester and, although in difficulties himself because of charges of heresy, he was able to sympathize with MacDonald's position and to help him to find some tuition and lecturing, even the occasional preaching placement, in order to earn a living. The implications of such circumstances for MacDonald's thought and future work were profound. MacDonald was now in the position where he could develop his intellectual position in the company of like-minded thinkers such as Scott. Unable to pastor a church on a full time basis and unable to preach and teach frequently because of his health, MacDonald's main source of income was his writing. The publication of F. D. Maurice's *Theological Essays* in the same year (1853), and Maurice's consequent expulsion from his chair at Kings College London meant that MacDonald was sharing the experience of, as Raeper notes, "the men whom he admired most" [112] and whose views resonated most closely with his own. MacDonald's experience as an impoverished clergyman unable to comply with required beliefs finds a parallel in Mrs Gaskell's novel *North and South* (1855) which provides a fictionalized account of this not unusual position.[113]

Industrial Manchester in the 1850s did not provide a helpful climate for a man with lung disease and in 1856, soon after his first son, Greville, was born; MacDonald had his worst lung haemorrhage to date. The family moved away from Manchester, eventually settling briefly in Hastings after spending a winter in Algiers. The family moved from Hastings to London in 1859 when MacDonald accepted the professorship of English Literature at Bedford College. In his biography, Raeper documents MacDonald's support for the cause of women's education[114] although it was another thirty two years before Cambridge University opened its exams to women and only then in a limited way.

Two significant events in MacDonald's career during these four years were the publication of his narrative poem *Within and Without* (1855) and the publication of *Phantastes: a Faerie Romance for Men and Women* (1858). *Within and Without* was MacDonald's first published work and caught the attention of Lady Byron[115] who subsequently

112. Raeper, *George Macdonald*, 96.

113. This position is explored in depth in Pamela Jordan's study *Clergy in Crisis* (1997).

114. Raeper, *George MacDonald*, 162, 67, 259.

115. Anne Isabella Milbanke, married Byron in 1815 and parted from him in 1816.

provided considerable financial support for the MacDonald family at times of particular hardship. The significance of her patronage lay not only in her provision of freedom from financial worry, thereby enabling MacDonald to continue writing without having to seek lecturing engagements, but also in her introducing MacDonald to other wealthy and influential individuals through whom his work became more widely recognized. She entered MacDonald's fiction in the character of Lady Bernard in *The Vicar's Daughter* (1872). *Phantastes* was MacDonald's first adult fantasy, which, as Raeper notes "contains shades of Spenser and echoes of Bunyan."[116] *Phantastes* is one of MacDonald's most critiqued works. Contemporary reviews were mixed but subsequent recognition of the uniqueness of the work, which, when reviewed with his last published fantasy *Lilith* (1898), "stands at the junction in literature from which emerged the three different strains: fantasy writing, science fiction and the parable mode, used by writers such as Kafka and Borges who create other worlds that closely mirror our own."[117] Raeper's comment here signals the significance of MacDonald's work as seminal to the canon of fantasy literature. His immersion in German Romantic literature provided the inspiration for *Phantastes*. Discussion around its content and structure remains vibrant. By the end of the decade 1850–60, the foundation for MacDonald's reputation as a writer of poetry and fantasy had been laid. His vantage point as a Scot placed him in a position to observe English society, enabling him to critically assess what he perceived.

George MacDonald 1860–1900: The Magic Mirror

MacDonald communicated his ideas in his writing, in which he used the fairy tale form as a vehicle for his societal critique, presenting his views on race, women's education and social concern. As an outsider MacDonald was able to hold a mirror up to dominant views. For example, he was able to empathise with the colonized races, as his essay *An Invalid's Winter in Algeria* (1864) illustrated. He commented on the personal dignity of the Arab and questioned how authority in the colony was retained, since it was a dignity above that of any European, including the English. He wrote of the beauty of the black African, in

---

116. Raeper, *George MacDonald*, 144.
117. Ibid., 384–85.

Historical Context

contrast to the accepted perception that black Africans were uniformly ugly.[118] He wrote of an experience whilst walking back to the house after visiting friends one night, "It was a night of stars . . . and suddenly to my soul came a scent of earth, of damp spring earth, an odour well known from childhood. . . . Then I recognised the common mother–knew that England and Africa were of the same earth, and rejoiced that she bore me."[119] This understanding contrasts with the dominant view of Africa as entirely "other," the "wide enormous blank"[120] waiting to be explored. This sense of humanity as a community of likeness rather than "otherness" in terms of race also extended to groups viewed as "other" such as women and children.

It is indicative of the strength of the dominant view that such men as Maurice and MacDonald, themselves in the forefront of the promotion of women's education, were against medical education for women in the late 1860s. MacDonald, although open to the possible rightness of political rights for women, writes in his novel *The Seaboard Parish*, "I should not like to see any woman I cared much for either in Parliament or in an anatomical classroom."[121] This view changed when, through Lady Byron, MacDonald met Elizabeth Garrett Anderson, the first woman doctor, and other influential figures within the women's rights movement. The daughters of Mr and Mrs Leigh-Smith,[122] whom George and Louisa met in Algiers in 1856, had at that time seemed "fast, devil-may-care sort of girls" in their free-thinking, independent mode of life, but Anna, the daughter for whose health the family were in Algiers, seemed to Louisa "sweet and womanly,"[123] another indication of the hold the construction of the feminine as delicate, patient, "sweet" and tending towards invalidity had on the contemporary mind. This construct has been explored in depth in Ann Hogan and Andrew Bradstock's study *Women of Faith in Victorian Culture* (1998). Raeper explains "there was, however, a

---

118. See Eze, Race and Enlightenment.
119. MacDonald, *An Invalid's Winter*, 144–45.
120. Ashcroft, *Primitive and Wingless*, 187.
121. MacDonald, *The Seaboard Parish*, 291.
122. Mr Leigh-Smith was MP for Norwich. His daughter Barbara Leigh-Smith Bodichon (1827–91) was the benefactress of Girton College, Cambridge. Raeper, *George MacDonald*, 400.
123. MacDonald, *George MacDonald*, 270.

disparity between some of MacDonald's precepts and his practices"[124] in that only Irene (MacDonald's third daughter) continued into Higher Education, when she attended the Slade School of Art, art being an acceptable accomplishment for a young lady. The female protagonists in MacDonald's stories are frequently leaders, but demonstrate, "an ability to have it both ways."[125] Lissa Paul points out that such heroines conformed to the nineteenth century norms of the woman's place as secondary to the man's in the home, demonstrating the female ethic of care, described in Carol Gilligan's study, *In a Different Voice*.[126] At the same time they subvert this order by their active independence and leadership roles. Examples of such initiative can be found in MacDonald's *The Princess and the Goblin* and *Princess and Curdie* and in the shorter fairy tales such as *The Light Princess* and *Little Daylight*.

MacDonald's first novel, *Alec Forbes*, was published in 1865. This novel was the first of twenty-nine adult novels which were, as David Robb writes, "designed to keep the wolf from the door of himself and his large family."[127] The metaphor is a suitable one, wolves conjuring images of fairy tale. Robb indicates the correspondence between MacDonald's adult novels and the fairy tale in his study of MacDonald's fiction when he writes, "the transition from desperate travail to secure felicity is so complete that it has some of the quality of a fairy tale. Indeed . . . all MacDonald's 'realistic' novels (have) many fairy tale characteristics."[128] MacDonald's most intense period of writing covered the years 1860 to 1880. Not only was he producing novels to feed his family, but he also edited the periodical *Good Words for the Young* between 1869 and 1873. All his long fairy stories appear in this periodical, also *At the Back of the North Wind* (Nov. 1868–Oct. 1870) and *Ranald Bannerman's Boyhood* (Nov. 1869–Oct. 1870). In his prolific production of novels, MacDonald was not substantially different from any of his contemporaries. As Raeper points out, "when Victorian novelists sharpened their pens they did so with a purpose."[129] Raeper's focus in this statement is on "serious" novelists, those who aspired to educate as well as to entertain. For example,

---

124. Raeper, *George MacDonald*, 260.
125. Paul, *Reading Otherways*, 54.
126. Gilligan, *In a Different Voice*, 30–31, 62–63.
127. Robb, *Realism and Fantasy*, 275.
128. Robb, *George MacDonald*, 49.
129. Raeper, *George MacDonald*, 183.

Dickens and Mrs Gaskell revealed the conditions of city life for the poor, who were separated geographically from the better off and therefore invisible to many of them. Charles Kingsley brought religion and politics together in *Yeast* (1848) and *Alton Locke* (1850). MacDonald contributed *Thomas Wingfold, Curate* (1876) and *Robert Falconer* (1868) to the body of novels of faith and doubt, whilst *The Vicar's Daughter* (1872) *Guild Court* (1868) and *At the Back of the North Wind* (1871) are examples of his work addressing social conditions. A close friend of Octavia Hill, the housing reformer, MacDonald gained first-hand knowledge of the living conditions she was working to improve. Prevented by his health from preaching in a conventional pulpit, MacDonald believed, as he explained to his son Ronald, that he was, "no less impelled than compelled to use unceasingly the new platform whence he had found his voice could carry so far,"[130] that is, in his writing. His sense of mission is also noted by Greville, his eldest son and extended beyond the novels into his participation in the family's production of *Dramatic Illustrations from the Second Half of The Pilgrim's Progress by John Bunyan*, adapted for performance by Louisa and toured by the MacDonald family between 1877 and 1891.

MacDonald's "mythopaeic"[131] imagination, coupled with his sense of mission and financial need to write novels, produced work which had, in Robb's terminology, "an instantly recognisable personality, a queerness ... which at least gives it distinctiveness and can be appealing."[132] Robb uses the term "queerness" in this context to indicate "peculiarity," but the aspect of an interpretation of queerness in MacDonald's fiction from a contemporary theoretical perspective is one that to date remains predominantly unexplored.[133] In the context of the novels, the term serves to indicate a destabilizing of known everyday reality which coincides with the mid to late-nineteenth-century experience of increasing uncertainty. The social critique found in MacDonald's fairy tales is powerful. The influence of Carlyle's cataclysmic thought can be recognized in, for example, *The Princess and Curdie* (1883) where the

130. MacDonald, *From a Northern Window*, 33.
131. Lewis, *George MacDonald*, 14.
132. Robb, *Realism and Fantasy*, 278.
133. Roderick McGillis has addressed this aspect in his article "A Fairy Tale Is Just a Fairy Tale" (2003).

self-destruction inherent in selfish materialism is realized in the collapse of the city of Gwyntystorm.

In MacDonald's critique of his contemporary society he reflected a transformed image back to that society. He writes, "All mirrors are magic mirrors"[134] and as a recurring image in his fiction, the mirror is also a model for his own writing in relation to English society in which he was, "a willing outsider, a conscious and gleeful contradictor of the received and the commonplace, a provider of the alternative."[135]

MacDonald's work also provided an alternative outworking of character to provide a hero figure which the destabilized Victorians of the mid-nineteenth century longed for, a figure to whom they could aspire, at least in the imagination. Carlyle's vision of the hero as "the Great man" who influenced, even saved, "his epoch," [136] is envisioned by MacDonald as morally and spiritually inspiring, speaking against the materialism of his age. MacDonald's depiction of such a Christlike figure reflected both his interpretation of Carlyle's use of the word 'saviour' and his emphasis in Darwinian terms of spiritual growth and development. The heroes in MacDonald's fairy tales and novels, such as Curdie and Robert Falconer, develop into ideal spiritual figures that change society for the better whether they operate in the "real" world of Victorian London or the fairy tale world of Gwyntystorm. This figure is also commensurate with the humanist values espoused by the positivists in their choice of inspirational men and women.

In the years leading up to 1880, George and Louisa MacDonald had lost two of their children and despite regularly spending the winter months in Bordighera, Northern Italy, from 1880 onwards, both Grace, (their third daughter) and Lilia (their first child) died during the next decade. MacDonald's tale *The Princess and Curdie* (1883) carried such a message of destruction that it has been suggested that MacDonald was losing his faith[137] rather than affirming a belief that wickedness carries its own destruction[138] and that "the eternal world of truth" remains

---

134. MacDonald, *Phantastes*, 123.

135. Robb, *Realism and Fantasy*, 286.

136. Carlyle, *On Heroes*, 1.

137. See Carpenter and Pritchard, *The Oxford Companion*, 329 and Wolff, *The Golden Key*, 176.

138. See also *The Light Princess* and *Photogen and Nycteris*, as other examples of this principle demonstrated through MacDonald's stories.

"beyond the abyss."[139] MacDonald's activities beyond his writing for children balance the assertion of pessimism, bitterness, and despair. It was during the decade 1880–90 that MacDonald was a regular contributor to the Broadlands Conference convened by his friends William and Georgina Cowper-Temple. These ecumenical conferences were conceived as times of spiritual renewal. The interest in alternative spiritualities, mentioned above, was a strand growing alongside the deepening doubt in previous certainties. MacDonald perceived doubt and the questioning of belief as a positive sign of spiritual growth, a view he presents in his published sermons[140] and in his adult novels, particularly *Thomas Wingfold, Curate* (1876). He condemns the unquestioning acceptance of received church teaching without a considered underlying faith.

In the last decade of the nineteenth century, MacDonald finished his second adult fantasy, *Lilith* (1895). Apart from two minor novels published in 1897 and 1899, *Lilith* was the last work he produced; thus his two fantasies *Phantastes* and *Lilith* frame his life's work, one mapping the journey of the searching Anodos and the other Mr. Vane's journey to rest in death before his awakening to life. George MacDonald died in 1905, three years after his wife Louisa and five years after lapsing into a profound and unbroken silence during which he neither wrote nor spoke. In using his writing as a vehicle to convey his values, MacDonald established his position as a Christian if not an orthodox writer. The beliefs present in his lectures and sermons were consistent with those in his published work and he defends his conscious construction of the ideal character as protagonist in his novel Sir Gibbie.

The hero figures in the writing of both Henty and MacDonald reflect different aspects of a character, which, put together, construct a complete image. Both physical and spiritual traits are present in their construct of youthful heroism. In the next chapter I review the position which polarizes realism and fantasy as genres by using specific instances from the writing of Henty and MacDonald to challenge such polarization.

---

139. MacDonald, *The Hope of the Gospel*, 206.
140. MacDonald, *Unspoken Sermons*, 355.

3

Genre, Mode, and Ideology

THE HERO FIGURE IN Henty and MacDonald operates in a generic context in which realism and fantasy are combined rather than polarized. A position which categorizes realism and fairy tale or fantasy as purely oppositional ignores the commonalities found in the narratives discussed in this chapter. The narrative structures in the writing of Henty and MacDonald, indicate that the writing of both authors demonstrates, "more than one category, more than one genre."[1]

For clarity, I will begin by considering some definitions of genre. Northrop Frye notes that, "the study of genres has to be founded on the study of convention," and that, "the purpose of genre criticism is to clarify traditions and affinities, to bring out literary relationships."[2] Robert Scholes take this observation a step further in his foreword to Todorov's study *The Fantastic* (1970), when he comments on the difference between the "conventions" and "tradition" which stems from the static Aristotelian generic system, and the willingness of the formalists and their structuralist descendants to acknowledge the inadequacy of categorical generic distinctions. In his method of classification Frye uses the term "mode," a more general term than genre. Since I have chosen to relate the discussion of genre in Henty and MacDonald's work to the hero figure beginning with Frye's discussion of fictional modes I use Frye's terminology. His method of classification for fictional mode begins with "the hero's power of action, which may be greater than ours,

---

1. Todorov, *The Fantastic*, 25.
2. Frye, *Anatomy of Criticism*, 96, 247.

Genre, Mode, and Ideology 53

less, or roughly the same."[3] Frye continues with the analogy of movement between poles, "we may think of our romantic, high mimetic and low mimetic modes as a series of *displaced* myths, mythoi or plot-formulas progressively moving over towards the opposite pole of verisimilitude, and then . . . beginning to move back."[4] The application of continuum[5] to the work of Henty and MacDonald immediately fractures the extant oppositional critical construction of the two writers. Frye also discusses the combination of genre which consequently affects the interpretation of a text."[6] The progression of this argument can therefore be modelled in the following way in order to re-position and re-evaluate Henty and MacDonald in relation to each other and to establish the identity of the hero figure in their work. By starting with Realism and Fairy Tale as the polar opposites, represented as follows,

| Realism | → | Romance | → | Fantasy | → | Fairy Tale |

a transitional stage of simple opposition is demonstrated with the indication that, the elements pass into each other. The next stage in the transitional model is that of the reflection,

| Realism | ⇨ | Romance | ⇨ | Fantasy | ⇨ | Fairy Tale |
| Fairy tale | ⇦ | Fantasy | ⇦ | Romance | ⇦ | Realism |

This model of the combined continuum is still only partially illustrative of my purpose since a central concept of this chapter is the interaction between, for example, realism and fairy tale.

The texts chosen to illustrate this continuum are; *The Tiger of Mysore* (1896) and *Captain Bayley's Heir* (1889) by G. A. Henty and *At the Back of the North Wind* (1871) and *A Rough Shaking* (1891) by George MacDonald. I have chosen these texts for these reasons; *The Tiger of Mysore: A Story of the War with Tippoo Saib* is an historical adventure story based on an event which took place in India in the eighteenth century. It is therefore embedded in a realistic setting and the fictional hero interacts with historical characters. Although the hero

---

3. Ibid., 33.

4. Frye, *Anatomy of Criticism*, 52.

5. Defined by the *Oxford English Dictionary* as "continuous elements passing into each other."

6. Frye, *Anatomy of Criticism*, 312–14.

is fictional, that is, not an historically verifiable person, he is drawn as a typical English boy and could therefore be regarded as potentially any one of his readers, all of whom exist in reality. As a character, he could therefore be regarded as mimetic. However, within the first chapter his story is positioned as quest tale and demonstrates the themes of descent and ascent discussed by Frye as characteristic of the quest tale.[7] The narrative includes elements of the fairy tale and moves into fantasy.

The second text, *Captain Bayley's Heir*, is a lost and found narrative that focuses the reader's attention on characters and motifs that correspond to those present in both the traditional and the literary fairy tale. Set initially in nineteenth-century London, the story moves into an exotic location as the adventure unfolds. The characteristics of the youngest or only son found in the hero operate in tandem with the support of an animal friend and the culmination of the story includes a passage written in the style of a fairy tale.

By contrast, MacDonald's *At the Back of the North Wind* (1872) is not critiqued[8] as mimetic although it begins within the realistic setting of nineteenth-century London. The story slides between realism and fantasy which weave into each other. Embedded in the text is a fairy tale which reflects the host narrative. The difficulty of categorization is clearly demonstrated in *At the Back of the North Wind*. Frye notes the difficulties posed by the presence of a mythical structure in realistic fiction and discusses the devices used to solve the consequent problems of plausibility under the principle of "displacement." Displacement treats a character in romance who is particularly associated with a mythical character (a god, for example) by analogy and metaphor rather than as an actual supernatural character.[9]

MacDonald's novel *A Rough Shaking* (1883) is critiqued as a realistic narrative, but displays elements of the fairy tale in narrative structure, characterization and motif. In common with both *Captain Bayley's Heir* and *The Tiger of Mysore* it is a lost and found narrative, a theme which characterises romance. From this brief introduction to the texts, it is clear that various generic combinations are present in the work of both Henty and MacDonald. The image of the hero in their work provides

---

7. Frye, *The Secular Scripture*, 95–157.

8. See for example, Raeper, *George MacDonald* and Pennington, *Alice at the Back of the North Wind*.

9. Frye, *Anatomy of Criticism*, 136–37.

a focal point for the exploration of the real and the imagined in both authors. The combination of realism and the fantastic in their writing reflects the apparently oppositional or contradictory aspects of Victorian society that Wilson perceived as, "the retreat into fantasy . . . a compulsion of the mid-Victorians."[10] This wider historical context provides the foundation upon which the concept of merger of the real and the fantastic in Henty and MacDonald is built and from which the recognizable and influential figure of the Victorian boy hero emerges.

I noted in the previous chapter that the hero figure in the work of Henty and MacDonald emerges as an ideal. MacDonald defends his construction of an ideal character after his description of Gibbie in the following passage from his novel *Sir Gibbie* (1879). "If anyone thinks I am unfaithful to human fact, and overcharge the description of this child, I on my side doubt the extent of the experience of that man or woman. . . . That for which humanity has the strongest claim upon its workmen, is the representation of its own best; but the loudest demand of the present day is for the representation of that grade of humanity of which men see the most." He continues by interrogating the desire for characters as they are rather than as they might be, and concludes, "It is the noble, not the failure from the noble, that is the true human."[11] MacDonald confronts the concept of "realism" in the depiction of character. He questions the gulf between the real and the imagined at a time when the influence of the "great man" is being held up as an exemplar for emulation[12] whilst fictional realism is regarded as successful when the flawed and imperfect is given prominence. I take my definition of realistic fiction from Maria Nikolajeva who defined realistic fiction as a "conventional generic distinction that does not allow the mixture of fantasy and realism as identified by particular narrative components."[13]

The phrase "realistic fiction" could be regarded as an oxymoron from the point of view of my argument for the mixing of genre in the work of both Henty and MacDonald, in that fiction consists of the imagined even when a contemporary or historical factual event is used as a basis for a story. Henty's work is generally critiqued as "realistic fiction."[14]

10. Wilson, *The Victorians*, 322–23.
11. MacDonald, *Sir Gibbie*, 43.
12. See Carlyle, *On Heroes*, and Harrison, *Autobiographic Memoirs*, vol. 1.
13. Nikolajeva, *From Mythic*, 48.
14. See, for example, Arnold, *Held Fast for England*, Cargill-Thompson, *The Boys Dumas*, Walpole, *Reading*.

Nikolajeva continues, "all children's fiction is essentially, 'mythic', or at least nonmimetic." She explains that her, "point of departure is the concept of literature as a symbolic depiction of a maturation process . . . rather than a strictly mimetic reflection of a concrete 'reality.'"[15] This explanation blows the rigid definition of realistic fiction apart and, when applied to Henty and MacDonald, illuminates their position as authors who trace the journey toward maturation undertaken by their heroes. Their stories reveal the characteristics of nonmimetic narrative, although their points of departure and emphases are different.

The Real and the Imagined in the work of G. A. Henty

Henty began his writing for children with his own experience of journalistic writing. In his capacity as a war correspondent, Henty wrote reports for his papers, reports that were predominantly investigative, and which as Hugo de Burgh notes, "married rational observation with moral empathy," and developed from "the increasing rationalism of intellectual discourse in the period [de Burgh refers to the nineteenth century] and from that scientific approach of finding truths from facts."[16] Although Henty sometimes commented on the events he reported, he rarely analyzed them, leaving such analysis to the editor of the paper. His remit was to send eyewitness copy by telegraph as rapidly as possible to his editor. When Henty began to write novels and stories his emphasis was on telling what happened rather than on analytical or philosophical discussion. His historical stories span a time period from 1250 BC–1900 AD, with almost 50 percent of them based on incidents in the nineteenth century.[17] The majority of Henty's stories begin in England and the circumstances of the hero are defined, locating him in a precise, problematic situation which becomes the springboard for his adventures. The story concludes with the homecoming of the hero. There are of course exceptions and the hero is not always male, but most of the stories follow this pattern. The precise, problematic situation is chiefly, although not exclusively, an historical event, recorded by an historian as having actually happened. Henty records his use of historical sources in an interview on his technique, citing the use of several sources as

---

15. Nikolajeva, *From Mythic* 1.
16. Burgh, *Investigative Journalism*, 26.
17. Information from Pruen and Berlyne, *Henty Companion*, 44–46.

evidence of the historical accuracy of his settings."[18] He assumes that such accuracy is possible even when coupled with the imaginative fiction of the hero's adventure.

In Roger Seamon's discussion on the distinction between history and fiction, he notes that Hayden White, "shifts the idea of history toward the idea of fiction, and this weakens the distinction between them."[19] White himself pushes the concept further when he writes, "individuals can be taught to live a distinctively imaginary relation to their real conditions of existence,"[20] a comment which draws the imagined and the real closer together to meet in the life story of an historical person. The point of connection between the imagined and the historical in a life story is demonstrated in Howe's chapter *Earthly Paradises* in her examination of novels of empire[21] and Tidrick's study of the colonial administrator. Both of these studies demonstrate the indistinct boundary between history and fiction and illustrate Terry Pratchett's observation that, "People think stories are shaped by people. In fact, it's the other way round."[22] The question is therefore raised as to the nature of the real and the imagined, which, when applied to the historical story, accentuates the indistinct nature of the blurred area where the borders of reality and the imagined collide. Henty's historical material came from identified sources frequently cited in his prefaces. For example in the preface to *True to the Old Flag* (1885) he writes, "The whole of the facts and details ... are drawn from the valuable account of the struggle by Major Stedman, ... and from other authentic contemporary sources."[23] Henty's credibility as an historian is discussed in an article by Brown in which Brown cites comments from eminent historians who, "accord him [Henty] respect." Brown also notes a trend in which, "speculation and imagination take the place of facts"[24] in the interests of "modern" historians, an observation which brings to the fore the merging of the real and the imagined in historical writing as percep-

18. Henty, *Writing for Boys*, 105.

19. Seamon, *Narrative Practice*, 207.

20. White, *The Content of Form*, x. This a concept derived from Louis Althusser's discussion *On Ideology*, 307.

21. Howe, *Earthly Paradises*, 123–29.

22. Pratchett, *Witches Abroad*, 8.

23. Henty, *True to the Old Flag*, 5.

24. Brown *Henty and the Historians*, 7.

tions of the nature of facts change to include personal viewpoint and bias. Henty also drew from his own experience as a war correspondent, a source noted by John Ferguson, who writes that, "Henty was a war correspondent who romanticised his experience into boy's adventure stories." [25] Ferguson's terminology emphasizes the indistinct boundaries between experience and romance in his description of Henty's work.

In his first story for young people, *Out on the Pampas* (1871), Henty's style is stilted, giving the impression of a "cut and paste" technique in which historical fact and fictional story are separated. In his later work, history and fiction are interwoven more expertly although descriptive passages in stories drawn from events within Henty's own experience are subject to a change of voice, as though the author slips into reportage. Examples can be found in *By Sheer Pluck* (1884), *The Young Colonists* (1885), *Through the Sikh War* (1894), *The Tiger of Mysore* (1896), and *With Kitchener in the Soudan* (1903). This example from *The Tiger of Mysore* comes about half way through the description of the invasion of Mysore and is representative of the change of voice in the other examples cited, "On the 17th, Tippoo cannonaded the British camp from a distance.... In the meantime the fire of our siege guns was steadily doing its work, ... Tippoo ... placed some heavy guns behind a bank surrounding a large tank and opened some embrasures through which their fire would have taken our trenches." Before and after these passages, the description remains in the third person, told by an extradiegetic narrator as this quotation demonstrates, "The position was a singular one. A small army was undertaking the siege of a strong fortress, while an army vastly outnumbering it was watching them, and was able at any moment to throw large reinforcements into the fort through the Mysore gate ... the efforts of the British being directed against the Delhi gate." Then the first person narrative, part of which is quoted above intervenes, followed by, "The besieged were vigilant, and the instant the leading company sprang from the trenches and, in the bright moonlight, ran forward to the breach, a number of blue lights were lighted all along the ramparts.... The scene was eagerly watched by the troops in the camp, every feature being distinctly visible. The storming party could be seen rushing up the breach and mounting

---

25. Ferguson, *War and the Creative Arts*, 362.

ladders."[26] Genette's distinction between mood and voice in narrative[27] is pertinent to Henty's propensity to change voice from the third to the first person, that is, from "the British" to "our" when his character is engaged in immediate battle. This change of voice accentuates his experience as a journalist in that it discloses a tendency to slip into reportage in his accounts of historical events. Examination of this aspect of his writing reveals a complex approach to narrative, and an authorial engagement with the text that enables a critic to uncover the ideological positioning of an author as differing, or in agreement with, his character. Leon Garfield believes that in the writing of historical fiction "it is the business of the artist to make the commonplace marvellous,"[28] and, despite the realism displayed in passages such as those quoted above, Henty's stories are laced with the marvellous. It is the marvellous elements in the texts chosen for further discussion, *The Tiger of Mysore* (1896) and *Captain Bayley's Heir* (1889) that I aim to substantiate within the context of Henty critiqued as a writer of realistic historical fiction.

The Tiger of Mysore

Henty's historical story *The Tiger of Mysore* is focalized through the boy hero Dick Holland and is an account of his quest for his lost father, imprisoned in India and believed by his mother to be still alive. The story opens with the voice of a minor but significant character, Ben, a sailor, telling his own story to Dick. The reader therefore begins the story at the point where it impinges on the life of Ben's listener, Dick, the hero. Ben and Dick's father were imprisoned together for three months before Captain John Holland, Dick's father, was taken away to another prison in a more remote hill fort. His wife, Dick's mother, the child of an Indian father and an English mother, believes him to be still alive and has raised Dick, in England, with the intention of returning to India in order to give Dick the opportunity to search for his father. She explains her conviction to her brother, now the Rajah, because he is sceptical about this seemingly impossible task and alert to the dangers Dick may encounter as he undertakes his quest, "In my dreams I always see him alive, and I firmly believe that I dream of him so often because he is thinking of me.

---

26. Henty, *Tiger of Mysore*, 151–52.
27. Genette, *Narrative Discourse*, 10.
28. Garfield, *Historical Fiction*, 742.

When he was at sea, several times I felt disturbed and anxious … and each time, on his return, I found, when we compared dates, that his ship was battling with tempest at the time I was so troubled." This explanation is followed by a brief discussion on the gift of second sight and the validity of insights, premonitions and action taken as a result of such intuition, taking the basis on which the story rests into the realms of the supernatural. The Rajah accepts his sister's conviction when he admits, "There are things we do not understand, Margaret. … It may be said that such things seldom happen; but that is no proof that they never do so."[29] Thus Dick is operating in two worlds, the world of the "real," where Tippoo Saib is planning a major uprising in order to expel the British from India following the failed attempt to do so by Tippo's father Hyder Ali and the Maharattas, and the "other" world of the supernatural which is guiding Dick's actions and is the reason for his quest. The prominence of the world of the supernatural is even greater in Henty's story *Rujub the Juggler* (1892). In this story, the action is driven by the agency of Rujub and his daughter, both introduced early in the narrative, and both of whom operate from a supernatural perspective on life, belonging as they do to, "the higher class of jugglers" who, "treat their art as a sort of religious mystery"[30] and whose practice of the mystic arts rests upon a lifetime of esoteric learning. Their actions are enabled by their awareness of future events. This emphasis on the supernatural world is beyond the stereotypical critique of Henty as the archetypal portrayer of imperialist militaristic force focalized through a physically powerful masculine hero to the exclusion of any other consideration. In *The Tiger of Mysore*, Dick sets out on his quest in the company of Surajah, a young officer from the retinue of Dick's uncle the Rajah. Dick's assumption of the position of leader and decision maker, despite Surajah's seniority, establishes his position as agent. The progress of Dick's quest is related by him and the action is initiated by him, thus placing him in the position of heroic leader, since, "Heroic leadership … is mainly or even essentially exemplary; the hero's directive power or force lies in what he does."[31] Dick's "directive power" is confirmed in his response to a tiger attack soon after the undertaking of the quest. Disguised initially as armed retainers of a local rajah, Dick and Surajah attend an event at which Tippoo is pres-

---

29. Henty, *Tiger of Mysore*, 69.
30. Henty, *Rujub*, 114.
31. Miller, *The Epic Hero*, 374.

ent, in order to observe him at close quarters. During the sports, a tiger leaps into the zenana where the ladies of Tippoo's harem are kept. Dick's prompt action results in the rescue of the tiger's victim (who, he later discovers, is an English captive) as well as the death of the tiger as it prepares to attack again. As a reward, Tippoo appoints them as officers in his retinue, enabling them to explore the forts in the surrounding area, a necessary preliminary step towards the discovery of Dick's father. Their disguise reflects their assumed change of allegiance when they are expected to dress in keeping with their positions as Tippoo's officers, "Tippoo likes those around him to be well dressed. . . . You will need two new suits, one for Court ceremonies and the other for ordinary wear in the Palace."[32]

This advice is given by Pertaub, the old man with whom they lodge and who has become, as Dick noted, "a very valuable ally." The old man also advises them to be prepared to, "slip on a disguise," at any time in order to avoid danger.[33] Frye notes the importance of disguise; in the establishment of identity, the shift in identity or the escape from an identity.[34] Dick escapes from his English identity into an Indian identity and repeatedly shifts identity within his initial disguise in response to changing circumstances. As part of the maturation process which Nikolajeva argues is integral to children's literature, the "trying out" of a variety of identities, even though Dick's change is ostensibly undertaken for the sole purpose of his quest for his father, invests the story with the, "cyclical movement"[35] of romance and folk tale that results from the eventual return to the hero's initial identity. *The Tiger of Mysore* demonstrates the, "mingling of modes"[36] as the story shifts from the "realism" of the historical context of the background to the war with Tippoo, complete with maps, (pages 70–92), through the foundational presence of the supernatural world of Dick's mother's second sight, the romance of heroic adventure and quest, to the fairy tale elements of the quest in terms of the "marvellous journey" which is central to romance and fairy

32. Henty, *Tiger of Mysore*, 210.
33. Ibid., 189, 210.
34. Frye, *Secular Scripture*, 106.
35. Ibid., 54.
36. Furst, *Realism*, 6. Furst discusses Auerbach's emphasis "on the flexibility and mingling of modes" in his development of criterion for the identification of realism within a text.

tale. The story progresses through the fairy tales motifs of companion/savior (Surajah), miraculous discovery of aid in the form of Pertaub, the old man who risks his own safety to help Dick and Surajah, the disinterested action of deliverance from the tiger attack, which results in great riches as a gift from the women of the harem, to the recovery of the rescued girl who later becomes Dick's wife on his homecoming after he has recovered his English identity and achieved success in his profession.

Dick's father is eventually discovered and rescued, an achievement made possible by further disguises which not only mask Dick and Surajah's identities but also their age. They become old men, a shift in identity which adds to the impression of uncertainty in the space/time continuum of the story. The perception that the quest spills over into an unspecified timescale is paralleled in MacDonald's *A Rough Shaking* (1891), where the "real" time journey and adventure take months rather than years and also happens in a space outside of time in terms of the inner journey. The space covered in *The Tiger of Mysore*, although vast, unlike *A Rough Shaking*, is specific and geographically named. Frye's classification of fictional mode by the hero's relation to other men and to his environment places *The Tiger of Mysore* in the high mimetic mode of fiction, where the hero is "by degree"[37] superior to the reader and not to the laws of nature. The hero is also on a basis of equality with the reader in his capacity to display the exemplary potential of everyman who is the Carlylean ideal. The analogy of movement between poles, or movement along a continuum which proves to be cyclical, with the supernatural element from the spiritual rather than the physical world and the coincidental provision of aid in extremity, moves towards the fantastic in the portrayal of the co-existence of two worlds as the real and the imaginary come into relationship.[38]

In *The Tiger of Mysore*, the quest takes place in the "other" world of the exotic, which in Henty's stories is frequently, although not exclusively, the world of the colonial east. In this other world, unsolvable problems are solved or rather are therapeutically redefined and consequently, "dissolved through adopting a 'new way of seeing.'"[39] In Dick's situation his

37. Frye, *Anatomy of Criticism*, 33–4.
38. Todorov, *The Fantastic*, 25.
39. Barker, *Making Sense*, 7. Barker's discussion of therapeutic thinking is, he notes, built around "the characteristically Wittgensteinian tactic of 'therapeutic redefinition,'" taken from Wittgenstein's *Philosophical Investigations*, Investigation 309.

new way of seeing involves approaching his quest with a new identity, in a disguise so practised over many months that he sees with the eyes of his alternative, disguised, self. By entering into the exotic location and culture Dick becomes "other." He integrates his culturally divided self, which is a reality since his family is half Indian. Dick is therefore able to accomplish a quest which as a solely English boy he could not attempt, culminating in the "transformation" of his former reality[40] in his homecoming with his father. He creates a "new sort of reality"[41] out of his two worlds, a world which is different from either of them and combines them by merging the space between them.

In my discussion of *Captain Bayley's Heir* (1889) I will concentrate on the narrative patterns and motifs that demonstrate those found in European fairy tale. The only critic to date to note the closeness of the Henty story to the fairy tale narrative is Dennis Butts,[42] who has also noted the closeness of the narrative pattern of the adventure story to that of fairy tale.

The basic pattern of events found in a fairy tale narrative structure, identified by Vladimir Propp in his study *The Morphology of the Folktale* (1958), is quest/journey, struggle/test, success/achievement, triumph/homecoming.[43] The last element, homecoming, Propp interprets in the sense of an actual return or in the sense of coming to a home always sought but only found after the completion of the journey and struggle. Motifs most frequently enter the fairy tale in two types; motifs of place and motifs of character. Examples of motifs of place range from an entire landscape, usually rural, expansive and including mountains; through woods and forests; down to castles, cottages and huts. Motifs of character are found in princes, princesses, the wise woman/fairy godmother, witch or bad fairy, but also in the ordinary person, the woodcutter, the swineherd, the servant girl (who may or may not turn out to be as ordinary as he or she appears), the youngest daughter or, the one I use as a specific example in this discussion, the youngest or only son. This character is one who shows compassion without the expectation of reward. He is one of those general personalities found in the fairy tale who restores order to life in the sense that he puts things right (the rectifying principle) by

40. Jameson, *The Political Unconscious*, 110.
41. Prickett, *The Two Worlds*, 23.
42. Butts, *Henty and the Folk Tale*, 10–17.
43. Propp, *Morphology*, 37–39, 50.

bringing about a just solution to problems, a solution in line with the belief of the ordinary person, in the folk sense that, "the worthy succeed and the unworthy fail."[44] The test of worth is based on action and attitude. In the fairy tale world, worthiness is not based on the same criteria as it is in the everyday world which judges by status and wealth, it is a world in which, as Maria Tatar notes, "compassion counts."[45]

The youngest son's refusal to act from self-interest invites ridicule and he is viewed as a fool and a dreamer. He is categorized with disadvantaged groups and outsiders and consequently ridiculed and despised. Even if he is the youngest son of a king, (usually the third son), he is treated as unable to undertake the same quest as his older brothers because of his perceived stupidity in putting the interests of another person or an animal above his own. Sometimes he is the only son of a poor family and sometimes he is an orphan, but it is his actions and attitudes that show his worth and set him apart whatever his parentage or family's position in the society within which he is placed. His behavior is the ultimate test of his position as hero, because, as I noted above, "the hero's directive power or force lies in what he does." Other motifs from within the fairy tale genre are the faithful companion or friend, often found in the guise of an animal the hero has rescued from cruelty, death, or released from a spell, and the magical object or gift that enables the hero to accomplish tasks which would otherwise be impossible.[46]

Captain Bayley's Heir

In the process of investigating Henty's work I found that the approach of reading his adventure story *Captain Bayley's Heir* (1889) as a fairy tale narrative provoked further thought on the values carried in the text which, I believe, demonstrate the complex positioning of the imperialist viewpoint in nineteenth-century texts for children. Henty's story begins at Westminster School (Henty's old school) where the protagonist, Frank Norris, is shown practising his boxing skills in a serious fight between the "skies" or local boys, and the scholars. The tide turns for Frank, a

---

44. Rohrich, *Folktales and Reality*, 210.
45. Tatar, *Off With Their Heads*, 79.
46. Examples of these motifs can be found in Grimm, *The Queen Bee* and *The Water of Life*.

popular, competent, but not academic boy, when he is wrongly accused of stealing a ten-pound note. He has been framed by his plotting cousin, who hopes to disgrace Frank and by so doing become Captain Bayley's sole heir. Frank runs away to America and makes his fortune in the Californian goldfields. On his journey across America to California he encounters various adventures which test his character, including one in which he rescues and befriends a large and intelligent dog. He eventually returns to England, his name is cleared, and he marries Alice, the girl who has waited for him, always believing him to be innocent.

The subplot is that the real heir is actually a disabled boy, Harry, the son of the Captain's runaway daughter, who had been taken in by a dustman's family when she died, which sad event occurred shortly after she collapsed on their doorstep. This boy is discovered as a result of another self-sacrificial act performed by Frank. Harry describes his own story in the following passage, "Once a good many years ago, ... when he was just a hard-working man, ... a poor woman with a child fell down dying at his door ... they took in the child, and brought it up as one of their own."[47] Beginning with the traditional fairy tale opening style of a timeless past, "Once a good many years ago," the passage continues in the style of a fairy tale and demonstrates Henty's awareness of the fairy tale-like story of his sub-plot but gives no indication that his main plot is also like a fairy tale. The "he" in the first line of the quotation refers to the dustman and Harry tells the tale to the dustman and his wife in order to explain why they have been given their own "fortune." Frank Norris, the boy hero and protagonist of the story and through whom the major part of the text is focalized, is an orphan. Henty frequently made sure his heroes were without parents so that they could pursue their adventure independently, in keeping with Nikolajeva's comment that, "the mythic, nonmimetic approach to literature makes parents superfluous."[48] Frank's progress through a fairy tale trajectory can be traced as follows:

- He is rejected by society after his wrongful accusation and embarks on a journey to seek his fortune.
- He gains an animal friend when he rescues an injured dog.
- He finds his fortune as a result of the compassionate act, which saves two lives.

47. Henty, *Captain Bayley's Heir*, 282.
48. Nikolajeva, *Mythic to Linear*, 23.

- His homecoming is literal, his success assured, and having married Alice, they live "happily ever after."

The story demonstrates Propp's pattern of; journey/quest, to make his fortune; struggle/test, to prove he is able to make his way; success/achievement, as a result of his openness and willingness to help, and his triumph/homecoming. Frank's character is typical of the youngest/only son motif in his willingness to disadvantage himself to help another without the expectation of reward. Frank's animal friend, the dog Turk, whom he saves after his former master has been killed, is invested with magical qualities as stories of his behavior proliferate amongst the miners. One particular episode in the story strongly echoes both Hans Andersen's *The Tinderbox* and parallels an image in MacDonald's tale *The Princess and Curdie*.

Whilst accompanying a convoy of gold which is being conveyed down to the town from the Californian gold fields, Turk is described as guarding the boxes in a small room where the party stopped for the night, "Every week had added to the weight and power of the animal, and he was now a most formidable-looking beast. . . . [H]is low, formidable growl gave a warning which few men would have been inclined to despise. . . . [W]hen they stopped, and the heavy valises were carried from the pack animals . . . Turk always lay down with his head upon them." It was after an attempt had been made to steal the gold that Turk's reputation for ferocity spread, "Turk hurled himself from his recumbent position. . . . The movement was so rapid and unexpected, that before the man could spring back from the window Turk seized him by the shoulder. . . . [T]hey [the men] ran to the window, but their interference was too late. Turk had shifted his hold, and, grasping the man by the throat, was shaking him as a terrier would a rat. . . . This was the only attempt which was ever made on the treasure."[49]

This description of Turk as guardian of the gold is reminiscent of the dog guarding the gold in Hans Christian Andersen's *The Tinderbox* (1836), "That dog was big enough to frighten anyone, even a soldier,"[50] and similar to MacDonald's image of Lina, Curdie's companion, guarding the crown in the palace at Gwyntystorm, "Lina lay at full length . . . her tail stretched out straight behind her and her forelegs before her:

---

49. Henty, *Captain Bayley's Heir*, 331–33.
50. Andersen, *Classic Fairy Tales*, 12.

Genre, Mode, and Ideology 67

between the two paws meeting in front of it, her nose just touching it behind, glowed and flashed the crown." Curdie explains to Irene what would happen if he tried to take the crown as a thief would, "You have no conception with what a roar she would spring at my throat."[51] Turk's rapid despatch of an intruder, bent on stealing the gold, shows his ferocity to be equal to that of either of his fairy tale counterparts, and earns him a reputation that takes him from the ordinary to the marvellous in the image of the supernatural beast guarding treasure. The link to the structure of folk and fairy tales, noted by Butts, and also found in Henty's other stories, may account, in part, for Henty's popularity since this aspect of his stories can be, "seen to satisfy the same human and psychological needs as traditional tales."[52] Henty's story *Captain Bayley's Heir* conveys what Rosemary Haughton, in her discussion on fairy tales, terms, "The tone of positive hopefulness [that] belies the cynical view that cruelty and injustice are somehow more real than love and loyalty."[53]

In her study on realism, Lilian Furst points out that "realism" came to be used primarily as the antonym of "idealism," and associated with "life from the seamy side,"[54] which is the use argued against by George MacDonald in his defence of his ideal character representation. This perception of realism contributed to the perception that the fairy tale values of "positive hopefulness, love and loyalty" are therefore "unreal," or "fantastic" in the popular sense of the word as existing only in the imagination rather than existing in the sense theorized by Todorov as in the place of uncertainty between the real and the imagined, that is, where the two worlds merge.

Henty's "primary" world is that of the historical adventure story, although as both history and fiction they display the "paradoxical ambivalence that is the cornerstone of the [historical novel] genre."[55] Henty exhibits the dominant Victorian political discourse of perpetuating and reinforcing the ideology that justified the continuation of the British Empire, including the benefits of wealth creation and commercial enterprise with which his stories are so closely linked, without appearing to perceive any discrepancy between the two value systems,

51. MacDonald, *The Princess and Curdie*, 235–36.
52. Butts, *Adventure Story*, 74.
53. Haughton, *Tales From Eternity*, 153.
54. Furst, *Realism*, 88.
55. Skyggebjerg, *The History of the Historical Novel*, 1.

that is, those values found in the fairy tale world where "compassion counts" and those values found in the dominant discourse of his immediate historical context. In his discussion on language and ideology in children's literature, Stephens identifies modal difference between fantasy and realism as the difference between the metaphoric and the metonymic mode and notes that, language carrying the "male values permeating the ideology of secular humanism" is found in either mode.[56] Henty's perceived advocacy of and assent to such male values therefore does not exclude the mixing of modes present in Henty's writing.

Both Henty and MacDonald tap into conventions to which the reader readily responds. In this instance the three conventions demonstrated are, the hero, the adventure, and the fairy tale narrative. Henty's construct of an "ordinary" hero helps the reader to recognise his or her own potential for adventure, as he uses the fairy tale narrative pattern of, journey–struggle–success–homecoming. Henty also connects to a structure that satisfies the reader's expectation of familiar patterns of danger and security, even when adjustment is needed to accommodate deviation within this basic pattern. In this way, both Henty and MacDonald are able to use the narrative to "embody values or personal vision."[57] Henty's emphasis is on the world of the physical, on what could be analogized as the body of society; hence his work is critiqued as realism. Ideologically, he wrote imagined realism incorporating the desires of his contemporary culture in the construct of his imagined hero who is an ideal. His imagined narrative which demonstrates the forms of fairy tale and fantasy is embedded in realist historical stories, frequently sourced in historical events. Henty therefore reflects the cultural milieu of his own time back to itself, reinforcing the desired ideal whilst at the same time constructing that ideal. Henty's merging of the real and the imagined in story reflects the merging of the real and the imagined in his historical context. The nineteenth century Darwinian paradigm of progress towards the ideal as encapsulated in Disraeli's idealistic comment that 1862 was, "an age of infinite romance ... like a fairy tale," referred to the opportunities available to "everyman" to reach that ideal. Disraeli's description of the time as holding all possibilities, "like a fairy tale" merged the worlds of the real and the imagined as Henty merged

---

56. Stephens, *Language and Ideology*, 247, 258.
57. Butts, *Adventure Story*, 74.

the real and the imagined in a single narrative. Henty's hero is constructed as if he were a realisable ideal. So is MacDonald's Gibbie. The hero is written into the gap between the real and the imagined, where, according to Todorov, fantasy resides, and according to MacDonald, a potentially transformed character can be realized.[58] In order to achieve his ideal, Henty uses the narrative vehicle of both realism and the imagined in the form of fantasy and fairy tale. Henty notes the failings and complexities of his society, particularly in relation to specific events but he does not often analyze them. His critique remains subliminal whilst overtly he supports the dominant discourse.

My contention is to read Henty and MacDonald as complementary rather than as oppositional in terms of societal values. Consequently the movement of Henty's narrative along the model of the continuum tracks Henty's response to the ideological, historical and cultural desire for the ideal in his construct of the hero, primarily situated in the physical world. Henty's response mirrors MacDonald's response to the same contextual desire for the ideal, which emphasizes the ideal hero primarily situated in the spiritual world.

The Imagined and the Real in the Work of George MacDonald

In Sutherland's discussion on the promulgation of ideology in children's literature as a political act, his third method of promulgation is given as the "politics of attack"[59] which is present in MacDonald's work. He knowingly uses what was by the mid-nineteenth century viewed as a children's genre, the literary fairy tale, as a vehicle to critique serious questions, such as the prevailing values in his society. As Zipes notes, "MacDonald often turned the world upside down and inside out in his fairy tales to demonstrate that society as it existed was based on false and artificial values."[60]

MacDonald's "tone of positive hopefulness" takes the reader beyond the immediacy of a hope for personal wealth and comfort (frequently the reward of Henty heroes) to hope for the whole community. An exception to the hopeful future is found in MacDonald's *The Princess and Curdie*

---

58. MacDonald's Christian position informed his conviction that transformation and renewal in a character is possible. See Romans 12:2.

59. Sutherland, *Hidden Persuaders*, 147.

60. Zipes, *When Dreams*, 125.

(1883), in which the honeycomb of passages carved under the city of Gwyntystorm in order to mine more and more precious stones and metals, causes the destruction of the city as its foundations are increasingly undermined by the underground passages causing the city to collapse. The ending of *The Princess and Curdie* balances the reader expectation of an idealized fairy tale ending and acts not only as a comment on a society driven by greed, but also as a warning of the consequences of such a choice. In Henty's work *For the Temple* (1888), Henty uses the existence of a honeycomb of passages under the city of Jerusalem, which is under siege and on the verge of destruction, as a way for the hero to escape. If MacDonald knew about the existence of such passages, as is likely from his theological studies, it may be that there is a theological interpretive link to be made between his imagined city of Gwyntystorm and the city of Jerusalem which supports a reading of Curdie as a messianic figure. What the possibility of such an interpretation does illustrate however is the predominance of the spiritual and imagined world in MacDonald's work and the prominence of the physical world in Henty's writing. Henty includes real, historical underground passages, MacDonald's imagined passages symbolise the degeneration of the society above them.

When G. K. Chesterton wrote the introduction to MacDonald's biography he was referring to all of George MacDonald's stories when he stated, "the fairy tale was the inside of the ordinary story and not the outside."[61] He emphasized MacDonald's ability to turn the ordinary into the extra-ordinary. By turning the imagined into the real, MacDonald turned fiction inside out, since the creation of fiction is to turn the real into the imagined. Given that MacDonald wrote twenty nine novels not specifically categorized as written for children and all viewed as realistic, Chesterton's statement reinforces the argument for genre boundary erasure found in Nikolajeva's work. Colin Manlove begins his study of MacDonald with the comment that MacDonald's fairy tales "explore relations between fairyland and the 'real' world of everyday existence."[62] This comment is equally applicable if inverted to, "his realistic stories explore relations between the real world of everyday existence and fairyland." MacDonald's stories, viewed as realistic, exhibit "a different

61. Chesterton, *Introduction, George MacDonald*, 11.
62. Manlove, *Modern Fantasy*, 55.

reflection of reality,"⁶³ a reflection that Blanch describes as the world "viewed through the fine gauze of MacDonald's imagination."⁶⁴ The view that, "every literary genre has its distinctive features and conventions. Readers and interpreters need to come to a given text with the right expectation. If they do, they will see more than they would otherwise see, and they would avoid misreadings,"⁶⁵ must be treated with caution. If the reader's expectations are fixed on what they have previously decided is the correct genre of the text studied, they are likely to see less than they would otherwise see and, if not misread, then only read in one dimension. Leland Ryken's statement affirms Nikolajeva's comment that conventional generic distinction does not allow the mixture of fantasy and realism, a convention which she rigorously interrogates. When referring to the whole body of fiction written for adults and children by MacDonald, Chesterton notes, "The novels as novels are uneven, but as fairy tales they are extraordinarily consistent."⁶⁶ Chesterton's observation here recognizes the need for a cautionary approach that does not categorise a text rigidly and therefore misread it.

Frye sums up his discussion on genre by pointing out the rarity of "exclusive concentration"⁶⁷ on one genre alone on the part of the author. He considers the way in which adverse criticism of a novel can sometimes be due to a misunderstanding of the genre(s) represented within it. MacDonald's work provides a number of examples in which such misunderstandings have come into play. One example is his novel *A Rough Shaking* (1893), in which realism, romance and fairy tale are all present in one narrative, they are not exclusive and need not be viewed as oppositional.

A Rough Shaking

The title is both literal and symbolic. It applies to an earthquake, described in chapter 3 of the book, and to the subsequent adventures of Clare Skymer who loses his parents in the disaster. Beginning with the introduction of Clare as a retired gentleman living in England, the

63. Nikolajeva, *From Mythic*, 264.
64. Blanch, *My Personal Debt*. Lecture.
65. Ryken, *The Bible*, 145.
66. Chesterton, *Introduction, George MacDonald*, 12.
67. Frye, *Anatomy of Criticism*, 312.

narrative traces his life from early childhood to the end of his boyhood. The first chapter introduces his extraordinary rapport with animals, a significant thread that runs through the story. Throughout, the story is laced with moral and religious commentary and Clare is presented as the ideal Romantic child, spiritually aware, other worldly, incorruptible and full of goodness to the extent that he is often misunderstood and regarded as simple in the same way that Diamond in *At the Back of the North Wind* is seen to represent the character of the "holy fool." In terms of content, the portrayal of realistic hardship in nineteenth-century rural England, places *A Rough Shaking* in Frye's category of mimetic text, with the hero or protagonist as "everyman," the ordinary person, in this case, a boy. But Clare is anything but ordinary. His character is a pivotal point, swinging the text out of the mimetic and into the non-mimetic, the genre of romance and fairy tale.

I have approached the analysis of *A Rough Shaking* by investigating five distinct phases in which the story of Clare Skymer's early life unfolds and which demonstrate "the salvational logic of romance narrative."[68] Each disaster develops Clare's character and spiritual awareness as he progresses toward the ultimate transformation of the reality through which he moves. Jameson emphasizes that the transformation of ordinary, everyday, reality found in romance does not substitute an ideal realm for that reality. Rather it shows the effect of the hero's inner world on his outer world. Joseph Campbell uses the term "transfiguration" for this progression.[69]

The first phase of Clare's life runs from the loss of his parents to the beginning of his first period of homelessness. The narrative begins with just sufficient information about Clare's parents for the reader to understand his loss when the earthquake leaves him an orphan, or so it seems at the time. The opening of *A Rough Shaking* moves through the non-mimetic characteristic of loss of parents towards what becomes the marvellous journey, which is, as Frye writes in his discussion of the romantic mode, "of all fictions, . . . the one formula that is never exhausted."[70]

Clare's second set of parents provide the care and security he needs as a very young child and prepare him for the next phase of his life. Campbell describes this next stage in the journey towards maturation

---

68. Jameson, *Political Unconscious*, 132.
69. Campbell, *The Hero*, 29.
70. Frye, *Anatomy of Criticism*, 57.

as "the passing of a threshold."⁷¹ In discussing MacDonald's fantasy *Phantastes* (1858) Hein notes that, "the hero ... is brought by his adventures to moral and spiritual maturity."⁷² Clare's journey reflects this developmental aspect as his experience becomes progressively more demanding. During the second phase of his life, disaster follows disaster.

The next section of the story is the most detailed. Although the timescale is unspecified, it is measured in months rather than years. This measurement is implied by the occasional reference to time⁷³ and the state of the weather.⁷⁴ The physical distance covered during Clare's literal journey is equally unspecified since the emphasis is on his moral and spiritual journey through experience, that is, his adventure. The impression given is that the progress in Clare's inner life is vast. There are however, indicators of physical space which tie the narrative into the real world. One of these indicators is the appearance of Nimrod, an enraged bull. Nimrod's escape and return are accomplished in a short space of time, denoting the geographical proximity of the farm from which Clare initially ran away due to mistreatment. Reminders of the reality of locality, such as this episode, place the narrative within a recognizably English rural landscape. Depiction of the harsh poverty which Clare and his companions endure during this second phase of Clare's life reaches its climax in the graphic description of the ravages of rats in the derelict property in which they make their home.

The realistic episodes involving authority figures such as the policeman and the magistrate are predominantly negative, although there is a glimmer of compassion for the plight of the children from the policeman who, the story tells us, "had children of his own."⁷⁵ Apart from this ray of humanity, the antagonism, suspicion, and cruelty of such figures is reminiscent of Oliver Twist's experience in the workhouse described by Charles Dickens. Clare's experience is lifted out of the unmitigated misery of such realism by the appearance of animal friends just as the hero in a fairy tale is helped in extremity, often by animal friends. The animal friend Clare acquires during this phase is Abdiel⁷⁶ the dog, who rescues

71. Campbell, *The Hero*, 51.
72. Hein, *Harmony Within*, 57.
73. For example *Rough Shaking*, chapter 35, 202.
74. For example, ibid., chapter 52, 295.
75. MacDonald, *Rough Shaking*, 208.
76. Note that Abdiel, meaning "servant of God," is named after Abdiel the seraph

the children from the problem of rats attacking the baby and provides Clare with comfort and hope. Jameson comments that nineteenth-century romance indicates a "reaction against social conditions,"[77] a comment which takes the understanding of a narrative beyond realism and towards romance, and which demonstrates the use of romance and fairy tale as a vehicle to expose social injustice and exploitation. MacDonald's other works for children also expose unacceptable social conditions. The purpose of such writing is that it may act as a catalyst for change. This aspect of MacDonald's work has is discussed by (amongst others) Zipes.[78]

The third phase in Clare's life is the short respite he experiences whilst working with an animal caravan. One of the three prominent animal helpers, Nimrod the bull, inadvertently opens this opportunity for Clare, providing him with a period free from hunger and enabling him to encounter his third animal friend, the puma, who rescues him from the violence of Glum Gunn the co-owner of the caravan.

Apart from the early years of his life, the greatest stability is found during the fourth phase of Clare's journey, when he is taken in by Miss Tempest, an elderly lady who discovers Clare, with Abdiel, asleep on the grass opposite her house. Recognizing his innate trustworthiness, she employs him and is rewarded not only by his service but also by his apprehension of burglars who attempt to break into the house. This is one of the episodes which grounds the narrative in reality since the burglars turn out to be Tommy, the boy with whom he had initially run away from the farm, and his previous enemy from the town in the second phase of his life. At the same time the episode instances the marvellous coincidence found in romance and fairy tale. The geographical area covered in his literal journey is once again shown to be small, a chronotopical detail that allies the narrative with that of realism.

Clare reaches the fifth and final phase of his journey from child to youth through the actions of his enemies who unwittingly ensure the transformation of his former reality which Jameson cites as a characteristic of romantic fiction.[79] This episode is an example of the expected resolution or rectification found in the fairy tale narrative. It also provides

appearing in Milton's *Paradise Lost*, Book V and Book VI.
77. Jameson, *Political Unconscious*, 146.
78. Zipes, *Fairy Tales*, 103.
79. Jameson, *Political Unconscious*, 110.

an illustration of Chesterton's comment that all MacDonald's stories are fairy tales on the inside. The transformation of Clare's reality is achieved when he finds his father, the fulfilment of his quest, the "success" or "homecoming" that indicates the conclusion of the fairy tale narrative structure. Steven Cohan and Linda Shires assert that in a romance, the opening and closing of a story mark the events paradigmatically, that is, the initial event (in this case loss of parents) is replaced by the closing event (discovery that father is still alive).[80] The narrative is seen to follow the order of events in the fairy tale described as, "chronological with a forward movement."[81] In Propp's definitive scheme, the story progresses by means of "villainy or lack."[82] This two pronged movement is evident in the progress of Clare and can be mapped in the following way:

Lack—Clare loses both sets of parents.

Villainy—the "black aunt" takes his sister but rejects him.[83]

Lack—Clare is now without a home or protection.

Villainy—the farmer's wife forces his departure.

Lack—Clare lacks all basic necessities.

Villainy—Clare's enemies betray him to the authorities.

Lack—Clare again lacks all basic necessities.

Villainy—violence drives Clare from the work and security of the animal caravan.

Lack—Clare again lacks all basic necessities.

Villainy—Having found a home with Miss Tempest, Clare is kidnapped by his enemies.

Lack—Clare loses his animal friend Abdiel and his identity. His position is serious and potentially life threatening.

   80. Cohan and Shires, *Telling Stories*, 66.
   81. Golden, *Narrative Symbol*, 124.
   82. Propp, *Morphology*, 26–36.
   83. Another example of the belief that boys are inherently bad, see Henty's *Young Buglers* for a comparable reaction.

Restoration—Clare's true identity is restored, his place in society is secure and he is able to restore the fortunes of one of his former companions (the baby).[84]

The narrative progression described here follows the expected hero pattern in a fairy tale narrative which is, according to Joanna Golden, event–action–purpose and destiny. Clare's journey demonstrates this pattern, with the difference that his purpose is to find "something" that "was waiting for him somewhere,"[85] and is commensurate with his destiny, which is to be reunited with his father. Stephens and McCallum provide a comment on the heroic career which is relevant to Clare's position. They note that a shift in the pattern of the hero's progress arose from Franciscan affective piety in which romantic heroes resembling the Christ figure, as Clare does, became less "heroic" in the classical sense and elicit some pity.[86] Mieke Bal clarifies this comment by making the distinction between the active, successful hero and the hero-victim.[87] In *A Rough Shaking* Clare, as the hero-victim, also becomes the active successful hero, fulfilling both romantic and fairy tale expectations. The timescale and spatial locality discussed in the context of realism may be vague in that context, but it is specific enough to take Clare through boyhood with the initial adventures and difficulties curtailed in order to preserve his life and to enable him to reach the end of his boyhood through a series of marvellous coincidences which occur at pivotal points in the story. These incidents occur when Clare has, to use MacDonaldian terminology, "reached the end of himself," just as they occur when a fairy tale hero sits down and wonders what to do next. In the context of fiction viewed as realistic, Pat Pinsent states that excessive coincidences are not the artistic flaws some critics take them to be, but part of the "restoration of the initial order."[88] This order is that referred to by Rohrich in the fairy tale context as the rectifying principle[89] in which, as Clare asks his father, "Don't you think, sir, that everything will

---

84. See *Rough Shaking*, 224.
85. Ibid.
86. Stephens and McCallum, *Retelling Stories*, 92.
87. Bal, *Narratology*, 132.
88. Pinsent, *Paradise Restored*, 103.
89. For more information on the principle of rectification see Rohrich, *Folktales and Reality*.

Genre, Mode, and Ideology

come right one day."⁹⁰ The romantic narrative shows the progression of the hero through destiny, providence, ethical opposition and ultimate transformation,⁹¹ and fairy tale narrative progresses through quest, struggle and success, moving forward via lack and villainy as Propp proposes. The realism of the poverty portrayed in the depiction of the Victorian rural setting merges with romance and fairy tale. Thinking back to the model of the continuum, the position of *A Rough Shaking* is that of moving away from realism, through romance and into fairy tale.

At the Back of the North Wind

The text *At the Back of the North Wind* (1871) could be placed at both ends of the model, where realism and fantasy interpenetrate one another as the story demonstrates the presence of two separate worlds, the real and the imagined. Diamond, the protagonist of the story, displays the attributes of the ideal child hero. His depiction as exceptionally good concurs with MacDonald's comment in *Sir Gibbie*, noted above, justifying his construction of such an ideal. The setting for the story is grounded in the realism and harshness of life in a poor family in Victorian London. The inclusion of the child crossing sweeper, Nanny, as a major character reveals the realities of urban poverty, in the same way as *A Rough Shaking* depicts rural poverty. In his study on fantasy, Todorov notes that it is by means of ambiguity, or uncertainty, that a reader is kept in two worlds at the same time.⁹² In *At the Back of the North Wind*, the characteristic of uncertainty hinges on whether the events experienced by the hero, Diamond, are actually happening to him or are the result of delirium due to his frequent illness. The uncertainty is maintained beyond the end of the story, which transfers the sense of two worlds into the world of the reader as the reader continues to question the uncertainty of the "real."

North Wind, one of MacDonald's supernatural, wise-woman characters, appears in chapter 1 and her ability to shift in shape and size is introduced immediately. Diamond's meetings and journeys with North Wind always occur within the context of his illness, depicting him as

---

90. MacDonald, *Rough Shaking*, 378. Cf. also Anodos' "great good is coming to you Anodos" in MacDonald, *Phantastes*, final page.

91. Jameson, *The Political Unconscious*, 142.

92. Todorov, *The Fantastic*, 31–33.

a vulnerable, if not exactly frail child. His character is in the mold of the Romantic child, supernaturally good and spiritually pure. In the milieu of Victorian London and of the child characters he encounters, he is regarded as the dummling of the fairy tale, and is referred to as "God's baby,"[93] the simpleton who is unfit for the "real" world. Despite this reputation he has a profound impact on those around him and in practical terms acts astutely and decisively. Instances of such actions are provided by his taking over the cab driving when his father is ill; his driving of a "chance" fare, who happens to be Miss Coleman's erstwhile fiancée, missing presumed dead, to the Coleman's diminished residence, and his intervention in the life of the drunken cabbie who subsequently reforms.[94] Following Frye's classification of fictional mode by the hero's relation to other men and to their environment, Diamond as the hero is superior to the other characters but not to the laws of nature in his exceptional spiritual perception. He is set apart from his realistic environment in working class London. He is above the laws of nature in his journeys with North Wind and to the land at her back. Although both of his parents demonstrate a greater degree of spiritual awareness than their peers, they do not reach the level of alternative perception of the world around them that is found in Diamond and recognized as exceptional by Mr Raymond, a gentleman, whose opinion of Diamond is initially formed when he listens to a conversation between Diamond and Nanny the crossing sweeper. Diamond's distinctive voice is established in chapter 1 in the record of his first conversation with North Wind and is developed throughout the story. His extra-ordinary communicative abilities culminate in his rhymes, which as McGillis notes, "connect the natural and the supernatural parts of the book."[95]

In terms of the examination of narrative form, I will focus on the position of the fairy tale *Little Daylight* in relation to the story as a whole. MacDonald's tale *Little Daylight* appears in chapter 28 of *At the Back of the North Wind*. The scene for the tale is set at the close of chapter 27 where the extradiegetic narrator takes over from the internal narrator, Mr Raymond, and provides a brief gloss on Mr Raymond's story told to children in the Children's Hospital. In two sentences towards the end of chapter 27, MacDonald writes, "I don't quite know

---

93. MacDonald, *At the Back*, 187.
94. Ibid., 218–26; 244–49; 177–84.
95. McGillis, *Language and Secret Knowledge*, 154.

how much there was in it [that is the tale] to be understood, for in such a story everyone has just to take what he can get."[96] Adrian Gunther points out that this comment, followed by the observation, "they [that is the children] all listened with apparent satisfaction, and certainly with great attention,"[97] indicates that the story's impact will be on the subconscious and on the imagination rather than on the intellect, in the same manner as the poem Diamond's mother reads to him when they are on the beach and Diamond himself is recovering from illness.[98] The rhymes he subsequently makes to soothe his baby brother operate on this imaginative and subconscious rather than intellectual level, although these rhymes are concerned with rhythm in a musical sense rather than in a verbal sense.[99] Both of the narratorial comments above apply to the wider context of *Little Daylight*, that is, to the main narrative, *At the Back of the North Wind*, as well as to the tale itself. In his introduction to the tale, the extradiegetic narrator makes an intertextual comment drawing the reader's attention to the inspiration of *The Sleeping Beauty* as a possible source for the central idea of Mr Raymond's story. By referring to this fairy tale, the author indicates the genre fairy tale to the listener, creating an expectation that what the listener is about to hear will follow the traditional fairy tale narrative pattern. MacDonald also implies the expectation of change in oral storytelling when he writes, "for a good storyteller tries to make his stories better every time he tells them." He embeds the idea of the genre fairy tale in the mind of the listener/reader, although the earlier comment by the internal narrator Mr Raymond questions strict categorisation. He replies that he will tell, "a sort of a fairy one" in response to the request for a fairy tale when he asks, "What sort of story shall it be?" Mr Raymond's reply, "I suppose, as there is a difference, [between a true story and a fairy tale] I may choose," implies an acceptance of the difference between a true story and a fairy tale, although the phrase "as there is a difference"[100] plants a

96. MacDonald, *At the Back*, 257. This observation presages his discussion on fairy tale in his essay *The Fantastic Imagination* (1893) where he writes, "Everyone, however, who feels the story, will read its meaning after his own nature and development." MacDonald, *Fantastic Imagination*, 316.

97. MacDonald, *At the Back*, 257.

98. Gunther, *Little Daylight*, 107–17. The episode mentioned appears in chapter 13 of *At the Back*.

99. See McGillis, *Language and Secret Knowledge*.

100. MacDonald, *At the Back*, 257, 250.

doubt as to whether that difference might not be as clear or as obvious as the requester assumed. The reader/listener expectation of any genre is culturally learned and therefore it is more difficult for the reader/listener to categorise a narrative when the expected generic pattern is subverted.

Having raised the listeners' expectation of a fairy tale, the narrator begins the story by setting the scene. "On one side of every palace there must be a wood." The first sentence provides two expected fairy tale motifs, the palace and the wood, the one "open to the sun and wind," the other "growing wilder and wilder, until some wild beasts did what they liked in it."[101] The opposition between palace and wood is the first in a series of oppositions which are interwoven throughout the story. These oppositions are indicative of the symbolic code in which oppositions are marked as antithetical.[102] The plight of Daylight as cursed never to see the sun is delineated against the description of her appearance, which is always described in terms of sunshine, blue sky and summer, in which the daylight hours are longer. In Frye's discussion of fictional mode he notes that the typical setting for romance is a forest.[103] Although Daylight's wood is consistently referred to as a wood, the description of its extent and inhabitants satisfy the requirements of a forest, such as wildness, the unknown (fairies), wild beasts and ultimately, the implication of the infinitely unexplored in the note, "nobody had ever yet got to the end of it."[104] Whilst it is clearly stated that this narrative is a fairy tale, Frye's explanation of the combining of fictional forms, one meaning of which can refer to genres, has been demonstrated at the beginning of a narrative viewed as a fairy tale by both editors and critics,[105] although the author paves the way for this flexibility by referring to the story as "a sort of a fairy one." In the mixing of genre, the tale reflects in a minor way the major combination of fantasy and realism in *At the Back of the North Wind* of which it is a part. The reference to Barthes' symbolic code in connection with binary opposition invites a symbolic meaning for the wood, which, described as "trim and nice" near the palace and getting progressively wilder and uncomprehended the further from civilization it stretches, is interpreted by Gunther as representing the subconscious mind, which

---

101. Ibid., *At the Back*, 258.
102. Barthes, *S/Z*, 27.
103. Frye, *Anatomy of Criticism*, 36.
104. MacDonald, *At the Back*, 258.
105. See for example Sadler, *The Gifts* and Gunther, *Little Daylight*.

Daylight explores more deeply as she grows older and as her physical and emotional conditions change. Manlove notes that everything wild has been excluded from the palace and that Daylight is, "forced to wake only by night because only the sunlight of mental life has been given first place at the palace."[106] The concept of exploration of the subconscious mind in terms of place foreshadows Joseph Conrad's examination of the same concept in the novel *Heart of Darkness* (1902), an account of Marlow's actual journey into the Congo reflected by the depiction of the increasingly wild reaches of the mind of Kurtz. MacDonald's statement that, "The world is the human being turned inside out. All that moves in the mind is symbolised in nature,"[107] provides a rationale for his creation of mindscapes in landscapes throughout his fiction.[108] His perception and demonstration of mind/place symbolism situates MacDonald within Modernism.[109]

At the beginning of the tale, the attention given to the wood indicates its prominence as the scene of action. As a fairy tale motif, the wood or forest is an essential part of the background. The emphasis given to it in the opening paragraph of the tale reinforces the conscious inclusion of the expected motifs of a fairy tale. The birth of Little Daylight is announced against the background of a description of the elements, "when the wind and the sun were out together . . . she made her appearance from somewhere."[110] The statement, "she made her appearance from somewhere," equates her looks and character with the sun and the wind and establishes the basis for her elemental, mysterious presence in the wood later in the story. The "bright eyes" and "lively ways" associated with her name, Daylight, and implying daylight as her natural element, provide the second opposition, that of day and night or light and darkness. The contrast between her looks and her enforced place of waking existence prepares the listener for the same startling discrepancy as she dances in the moonlight at night and, in her weakened state at the waning of the moon, when her hair remained "the sunniest" and her eyes, a "heavenly blue, brilliant and profound as the

106. Manlove, *MacDonald.s Shorter Fairy Tales*, 19.

107. MacDonald, *Dish of Orts*, 9.

108. See for example Chesterton, *Introduction*.

109. For a further note on MacDonald's placement within Modernism see for example Manlove, *MacDonald.s Shorter Fairy Tales*.

110. MacDonald, *At the Back*, 258.

sky of a June day," giving her an "unnatural appearance."[111] The fairies are introduced through their connection with the wood and as part of the natural world, linking them to Daylight's elemental character. They live in trees, "one, a hollow oak; another, a birch tree . . ." By characterizing the fairies as elementally connected to their environment the narrator deviates from the traditional, oral, fairy tale convention in two ways. The first is by placing them in the history of the country by connecting them to the history of its inhabitants as this quote demonstrates, "fairies live so much longer than we, that they can have business with a good many generations of human mortals."[112] The second is by drawing into the story the image of the dryad from Greek mythology. The inclusion of a mythical element is another example of the co-existence of generic modes. The image of the dryad is usually associated with youth, so the depiction of them as ageless not only links them to the youthfulness of Daylight, but with the ageless wise woman of MacDonald's tales *The Golden Key* (1867), *The Wise Woman* (1875), *The Princess and the Goblin* (1872), and *The Princess and Curdie* (1883). It also sets up the third opposition, that of youth and age, in preparation for the contrast between Daylight's condition and appearance at the waxing and waning of the moon. "[T]he more beautiful she was in the full moon, the more withered and worn did she become as the moon waned . . . she looked, . . . like an old woman exhausted with suffering."[113]

The wicked fairy is referred to in terms of age and is defined by mud and swamp, parts of the natural world associated in the Victorian mind with ill-health and disease.[114] The remote, unexplored place where she lives and the description of mud and swamp also equates with those parts of the British Empire associated with disease, ignorance, and spiritual darkness, providing a connection within the story to the wider nineteenth-century imperial context.[115] This thematic link also points forward to Conrad's *Heart of Darkness* where the concept is explored in depth.

111. Ibid., 258, 259, 265.
112. Ibid., 260, 259–60.
113. MacDonald, *At the Back*, 265.
114. See information on damp, sanitation and swamp miasmas in Wilson, *The Victorians*, 157.
115. See for example Laurence, *Rise and Fall*, and Ferguson, *Empire*.

Genre, Mode, and Ideology 83

The next traditional fairy tale motif, the occasion of the christening, describes the invitations and who is forgotten in a similar way to the same event in MacDonald's fairy tale *The Light Princess* (1867). The narrator's commentary on narrative expectation draws attention to the fairy tale convention of the christening and giving of gifts by fairies when he says, "In all history we find that fairies give their remarkable gifts to prince or princess . . . always at the christening." This assertion draws in the fourth opposition, that of goodness and wickedness as he continues, "wicked fairies choose the same time to do unkind things." The narrator's commentary continues as he introduces a brief theology of suffering into the tale, "But I never knew of any interference on the part of a wicked fairy that did not turn out a good thing in the end."[116] He immediately lightens the allusion by giving *The Sleeping Beauty* as a proven example of such interference and its benefit, which is, that Sleeping Beauty is spared the "plague of young men" and wakes up "when the right prince kissed her." The narrator concludes, "For my part I cannot help wishing a good many girls would sleep until just the same fate overtook them. It would be happier for them, and more agreeable for their friends."[117] This situation is of course debatable in terms of the maturation process, male dominance and female independence. In the context of *Little Daylight*, the brief interpolation of theology echoes an earlier, fuller discussion in chapters 6 and 7 of *At the Back of the North Wind* as North Wind takes Diamond out in a storm. Her task is to sink a ship. North Wind voices MacDonald's views on divine providence through an episode that constitutes the basis for a theology of suffering. After several pages of discussion between Diamond and North Wind as Diamond attempts to reconcile his firm belief in the goodness of North Wind with her mission to sink a ship with people on board, North Wind herself tries to explain how she hears, "the sound of a far off song . . . it tells me that all is right; that it is coming to swallow up all cries."[118] In the last chapter of *Phantastes* (1858), MacDonald writes, "What we call evil, is only the best shape, which, for the person and his condition at the time, could be assumed by the best good."[119] I have used the phrase theology of

116. MacDonald, *At the Back*, 260.
117. Ibid.
118. Ibid., 77.
119. MacDonald, *Phantastes*, 320. A biblical example of this line of thought can be found in Genesis 50:20, at the end of the story of Joseph. Joseph speaks to his brothers,

suffering and not theodicy in these contexts, to reflect MacDonald's belief that whatever the situation, God is in it with the sufferer rather than acting as a distant, impersonal agent. Commentaries on MacDonald's theology[120] discuss his theology of suffering in depth but in the present context of fairy tale it is an unexpected departure from generic convention. The spell placed upon Daylight, despite the best efforts of the two good fairies "kept in reserve,"[121] means that she will not know what daylight is, will fall asleep as soon as the sun appears and, although awake at night, will wax and wane with the moon. The rearrangement of the household to accommodate this pattern is glossed over, except for the effect of the waning moon on the princess, "She was wan and withered like the poorest, sickliest child you might come upon in the streets of a great city in the arms of a homeless mother."[122] This tragic condition is close to that of Nanny when Diamond finds her ill and before she is brought to the children's hospital. (Nanny has no mother, she lives with a gin drinking grandmother.) The short description is an unexpected jolt back to into wider context of the fairy tale, which is the immediate realism of Diamond's London as it is presented in *At the Back of the North Wind*. The story continues, "And thus things went on until she was nearly seventeen years of Age."[123] Seventeen is the age at which the princess in MacDonald's fairy tale *The Light Princess'* (1864) discovers water as Daylight discovers the element "moonlight." Just as in *The Light Princess*, the princess swims in the lake, so Daylight dances in the moonlight. By performing these actions, both gain independence and freedom. Gunther writes, "the active agent in his [MacDonald's] fairy tales is almost always Female."[124] She contrasts Daylight with the passive heroine of traditional tales, particularly Sleeping Beauty. Gunther's view ignores both the high proportion of traditional fairy tale heroines who are the propelling force of the tale and the unavoidable fact that Daylight still has to await her prince before she can be freed from the spell which binds her. It is at the time when Daylight is reaching "the zenith of her

---

"you meant evil against me; but God meant it for good."

    120. For example Hein, *Harmony Within*, and Raeper, *George MacDonald*.

    121. MacDonald, *Little Daylight*, 263.

    122. MacDonald, *At the Back*, 264.

    123. Ibid., 265.

    124. Gunther, *Little Daylight*, 111.

loveliness," as the moon is "nearer the full,"[125] that the prince discovers her. One paragraph explains how the prince came to be deep in the wood. This paragraph reads like a potted version of a boy's adventure story and includes political rebellion, violence, flight, disguise and hardship of the kind that toughens the prince and brings out the essential "decency" and thoughtfulness of his character, characteristics which are present in the ideal Victorian hero examined in a later chapter. The only unexpected trait is his passivity. His action is portrayed in terms of lack of choice. He has been, "compelled to flee for his life". He has not abandoned his peasant disguise because, "he had no other clothes to put on and . . . very little money." He tells no-one he is a prince, "For he felt a prince ought to be able to get on like other people," and he has set out on his quest through necessity. MacDonald continues to parody the fairy tale narrative when he says of the prince, "He had read of princes setting out upon adventure; and here he was in similar case, only without having had a choice in the matter."[126] The prince is following a passive destiny, but his destiny is still that of the fairy tale figure, the youngest or only son, and the outcome will depend upon an act of spontaneous compassion.

From the point of the prince's appearance, the expected fairy tale motifs gather around him. Although he does not realize it, he receives supernatural help from the good fairy and from her gifts, which he has with him precisely when they are needed. These gifts are the tinder box and a small bottle of cordial, both gifts that resonate with former fairy tale appearances, such as Hans Christian Andersen's *The Tinderbox* (1836) and John Ruskin's *King of the Golden River* (1841). The hospitality of the good fairy reinforces her parallels with the wise women already cited from MacDonald's tales. The food she gives him and the rest he has in her cottage have an extra-ordinary restorative effect, in the same way that the food and rest offered by the wise woman in *The Wise Woman*, *The Golden Key*, and *The Princess and the Goblin* restores Rosamond, Tangle and Irene respectively.

At the point when the prince first sees her, Daylight is living in her own house deep in the wood. As she grows older, she retreats further into the darker, wilder parts of the wood until she settles at the edge of an open glade, "for here the full moon shone free and glorious."[127] In

---

125. MacDonald, *At the Back*, 273.
126. Ibid., 267.
127. Ibid., 266.

MacDonald's stories, both those critiqued as realist as well as the fairy tales; the moon and the night time are the place of mystery and revelation. From the Greek Artemis and the Roman Diana, goddess of the moon and patrons of virginity and hunting, the mythical association of women with the moon is overt in *Little Daylight* and in MacDonald's tale *Photogen and Nycteris*. In both these tales, the female attributes of intuition and mystery symbolized by night and the muted light of the moon are complemented rather than overshadowed by the male attributes of rationality and order symbolized by the day and the clarity of the sun. The prince, "wandered and wandered, and got nowhere," before he reaches this open glade. "Somewhere" is defined in the prince's terms as anywhere not in the wood, so anywhere still in the wood he feels to be nowhere. The paradox is that he has reached the only place where he needs to be in order to fulfil his destiny. In her retreat into the wood, Daylight, still described in terms of the sun and the summer sky, is, in the process of maturation, taming the unknown, taking her daylight character into the dark unexplored recesses of the wood, even while she wanes with the moon. The prince first observes Daylight dancing and singing in the glade, when she appears to him as "some strange being of the wood,"[128] an elemental creature rather than a human.

Daylight's dance graphically illustrates Nikolajeva's concept of "a symbolic depiction of a maturation process"[129] in terms of cyclical motion and a continual movement from the circular to the linear as Daylight progresses around the glade and also towards the completion of her character as she approaches adulthood. Her dance is inspired by the fullness of the moon and "the exuberance of her delight."[130] Fairy tale, romance and myth, the three genres that "co-exist," to use Jameson's term, in this story, all exist in mythical time, emphasizing the importance of the cycles of nature. In this story the cyclical nature of the phases of the moon are, at the point of the prince's entry, intersected by the linearity of his story up to the point of his meeting with Daylight. At the point of intersection he breaks into the dance and joins her to complete the transformation of both their realities which is characteristic of both romance and fairy tale. When the bad fairy realizes the prince has "seen Daylight," "she contrives by her deceitful spells, that the next

128. Ibid., 268, 269.
129. Nikolajeva, *From Mythic*, 1.
130. MacDonald, *At the Back*, 274.

night the prince could not by any endeavour find his way to the glade." Here the narrator vigorously breaks into the story to reinforce the theological commentary he had inserted earlier, "it is all of no consequence, for what they [the wicked fairies] do never succeeds; nay, in the end it brings about the very thing they are trying to prevent. . . . [F]rom the beginning of the world they have really helped instead of thwarting the good fairies."

The princess, "dancing like an embodied sunbeam" has already taken control of what might have been a relationship, "for, however much she might desire to be set free, she was dreadfully afraid of the wrong prince."[131] In this respect, Daylight is, as Gunther writes, "the active agent," in the progression of the story. By preventing the prince from finding Daylight again until she is in her "waned" condition, the wicked fairy has ruled out any possibility of the spell being broken because she has ruled out compassion, not having any herself. I have already mentioned the importance of compassion within fairy tales, and, true to the compassionate act performed by the youngest or only son in traditional fairy tales, the prince kisses the princess when she appears old and ill, purely out of compassion and without knowing that in doing this act, he is fulfilling his destiny and freeing Daylight from the spell which binds her.

The seven days and nights when the prince is wandering in the wood equate within the fairy tale narrative structure with the struggle or test, which continues until his action towards the supposedly old and sick woman is confirmed as impartial. Searching for the princess, whom he has only seen "at the zenith of her loveliness," his behavior toward the person he finds at the foot of a great birch tree is entirely disinterested. It is at this point that the two gifts from the good fairy are needed; the tinderbox to light a fire and the cordial which revives the princess sufficiently for her to open her eyes and look at the prince. It is worth noting that this is the second time the princess has been found at the foot of a birch tree. One of the good fairies lives in a birch tree and may have been helping the princess more than she realizes. The prince's compassionate kiss completes the fairy tale cycle of quest, test and success, by freeing the princess. The final expectation in a fairy tale narrative is that of success, or homecoming, which in this case does not happen. As with so many of MacDonald's stories, there is no conclusive ending. I have

131. Ibid., 276, 278.

already noted the point made by Cohan and Shires that the opening and closing of a story mark events paradigmatically, that is, the initial event is replaced or transformed by the closing event. Although *Little Daylight* follows this pattern, the story departs from the expected "happy ever after" ending and finishes with the prince and princess still in the wood facing "the first gleam of morning."[132] As Gunther states, "the ending is the beginning, a new stage in the process, a new birth."[133]

The reader is returned to the host story, *At the Back of the North Wind*, which ends with what appears to be the death of Diamond. The hypodiegetic narrator, Mr Raymond, articulates one of MacDonald's key ideas when he says, "they thought he was dead. I knew he had gone to the back of the north wind,"[134] indicating that the dimension at the back of the north wind is more real than the "real" world, and that reaching it is a movement into more life. This indication is fully articulated in *The Golden Key* when the old man of the sea says to Mossy, "You have tasted death now," said the Old Man. "Is it good?" "It is good," said Mossy. "It is better than life." "No," said the Old Man: "it is only more life."[135]

The fairy tale pattern of journey, test, success, interwoven with the romance pattern of destiny, providence, ethical opposition and transformation, encompasses the progress of the prince and Daylight both within and outside of their expected fairy tale roles. The "reliance on antecedents for parodic effects,"[136] is so overt as to prepare the listener for the subversion of narrative and character and the oppositions found in setting, character, characteristics, time, and ethics. The narrator leaves the Prince and Daylight as the sun rises on the next phase of their lives, at the same time as the reader is pulled back into the hospital ward, with the words, "The children in the hospital were delighted"[137] with the story. The tale ends with the expectation that daily life in the world of the palace with its consequent responsibilities and practicalities will resume, whilst Diamond and Mr Raymond are led back into the "real" practicalities of their responsibility for the recovering Nanny.

132. Ibid., 281.
133. Gunther, *Little Daylight*, 116.
134. MacDonald, *At the Back*, 378.
135. MacDonald, *Golden Key*, 210, 211.
136. Knoepflmacher, *Ventures into Childhood*, 257.
137. MacDonald, *At the Back*, 282.

The tale *Little Daylight* is a pivotal point in *At the Back of the North Wind* as the lives of Diamond's family, Nanny and Mr Raymond, hitherto touching only occasionally, become inextricably linked. Romance and fairy tale leak into the realistic aspects of *At the Back of the North Wind*, transforming "ordinary reality" or "the commonplace." If, as Todorov theorizes, fantasy resides in the hiatus between the two worlds of the physical and the spiritual, the "real" and the "unreal,"[138] then the place of the fantastic is the only true "reality," where the two worlds merge, the twilight zone, "the outskirts of fairyland."[139] Living in the world of fantasy is therefore the only "realistic" place to be, the only place where a perspective on reality can be gained since it is the only place that takes account of the space between the two worlds. Hence the closing statement "they thought he was dead. I knew he had gone to the back of the north wind," is not an oppositional statement but an instance of a different way of seeing, in which a statement is viewed from a different angle, or perhaps, as a complementary image, rearranging perceived reality.

The Place of the Hero in Relation to the Investigation of Genre and Form

In the previous section I gave examples of Henty's work as a narrative vehicle for both realism and the imagined in order to resolve the desire for an ideal hero. MacDonald's work demonstrates the converse of Henty's merging of the real and the imagined. MacDonald merges the imagined and the real. His emphasis on the imagined emphasizes the spiritual element in his desire for an ideal hero just as Henty places the physical and moral element in the dominant position. In MacDonald's work, "the imagination plays between the real and the imaginary in a see-saw manner that remains highly instructive, even indispensable, for mastering the real in depth, for reshaping it."[140] MacDonald's reshaping of the real succeeds in making "all the ordinary ... magical ... ."[141] He uses the literary fairy tale as a vehicle for his critique of society by embedding contemporary social and political reality in the overtly imagined forms

---

138. Todorov, *The Fantastic*, 25.
139. MacDonald, *Golden Key*, 173.
140. Rodari, *Grammar*, 56.
141. Chesterton, *Introduction*, 10.

of fairy tale and fantasy and in so doing creates "two worlds co-existing in time and space, superimposed upon one another."[142] MacDonald's critique of society co-exists with his own interpellation into the dominant discourse of his time since he does not critique his own position. He therefore demonstrates the contradictions of his historical context, discussed in chapter 2, by writing critically and at the same time subliminally reinforcing the existing hegemonic principles. The work of Henty and MacDonald does not demonstrate "the irreducible opposition between the real and the unreal,"[143] but rather the irreducible valency of the real and the imagined. As Bal observes, "the choice of a hero and of the features attributed to him or her betrays an ideological position."[144] The apparently contradictory ideological positions of Henty and MacDonald, investigated in terms of emphases on the physical and the spiritual, are seen to converge when categories of the rational and the intuitive, the conscious and the unconscious, theorized by George Levine is applied to their work. Levine links the concept of "unselfconscious authority" to "heroic action" in "the spaces beyond the domestic–in the wilderness of empire."[145] This wilderness is the place where the Henty hero has his physical adventure. The internal or unconscious space is the place where the MacDonald hero has his or her adventure. The correlation between the exotic spaces of empire and the "exotic" spaces of the mind has already been noted and is discussed further in chapter 6.

In the next chapter I examine the construct of the child in the second half of the nineteenth century, beginning with an investigation of the influences which support the formation of this construct. These influences form an integral part of the construct of the youthful hero.

---

142. Prickett, *Two Worlds*, 14.
143. Todorov, *The Fantastic*, 167.
144. Bal, *Narratology*, 132.
145. Levine, *Not Like My Lancelot*, 56.

4

Child and Hero

The Construct of the Child 1850–1900

"Children . . . they are both 'us' and 'the other'"[1]

G. A. HENTY AND GEORGE MacDonald continued and developed an emerging construct of both child and hero with the educational purpose of encouraging their readers to emulation, a purpose that is explicit in Henty and implicit in MacDonald. I begin this chapter by tracing the background to the construct of the child between 1850 and 1900.

A link between the construct of the child and the cultural view of the hero is found in the political emphasis on colonial expansion in the second half of the nineteenth century. Joseph Zornado states, "the adult invents the child and constructs the world"[2] and in nineteenth century England the invention of both "child" and "world" not only applied to the domestic world but also to the global world of imperial expansion. An increasing colonization of childhood by an adult society whose emphasis is on an education that became ever more controlling, and the representation of the colonized subject as child, (for example the Irish, the African, and the Indian) identifies the child as "both 'us' and

---

1. Steward, *An Interview*, 1.
2. Zornado, *Inventing the Child*, 3.

the 'other.'" Also, the cultural view of the hero in the second half of the nineteenth century is directly related to a construct of the child derived from the "foundational fiction" of the Romantic child.[3] James Steward's comment quoted at the beginning of this chapter was made in the context of the representation of the child in the eighteenth century, at a time when the realization of the child as "both 'us' and 'the other'" was in the process of being theorized. European philosophers and educationalists such as Jean-Jacques Rousseau (1712–78) in France, and the artists who pictorialized the child, for example Joshua Reynolds (1723–92) and Henry Raeburn (1756–1823) in England, contributed to this theoretical construct.

The concept of the child in his natural state, existing closer to nature and therefore, it was assumed, closer to God, was posited in the seventeenth century and expanded by both the German and English Romantics. During the eighteenth-century Enlightenment this attention culminated in Rousseau's theory of education recorded in *Emile* (1762). Rousseau disagreed with systems of education that treated the child as if he were an adult and believed in "childhood under the guidance of nature," following the theories of Bernadin de Saint Pierre (1737–1814) who believed that, "Whoever follows nature will be happy and virtuous, whoever departs from her rule will be miserable."[4] This theoretical position permeated middle and upper class English society and became the popular view of the ideal child in the second half of the nineteenth century. Nevertheless, the outworking of such a view in the treatment of children living in extreme poverty led in practice to hardship, exploitation, abuse and illness in many cases, as Gillian Wagner reveals in her study *Children of the Empire* (1982). Although an emphasis on the child as an especially privileged species developed, especially in wealthy families, orphaned children and those children whose parents were unable to care for them were viewed as not only social, but also moral problems. The solution to send children to the colonies was formalized after 1869, when the development of charitable missions and other voluntary organizations following the evangelical revival accentuated the need to address social conditions and poverty, particularly in urban areas. Earlier in nineteenth century, Wagner notes that "the numbers of children sent overseas were relatively small," and the

3. Thacker and Webb, *Introducing Children's Literature*, 13.
4. Boas, *The Cult of Childhood*, 35.

reason was, "because they were unwanted: they might have committed a crime or merely have become public nuisances through destitution."[5] Following American Independence, children were sent to Australia, South Africa, and Canada. After the evangelical revival of 1859, the rationale for promoting child emigration changed. Influential figures such as Lord Shaftesbury raised the profile of social concern and the organizations that grew up in the wake of such awareness and desire for action believed that the good of the child and the social problems caused by poverty could both be met by providing children with the opportunity for a new life and alleviating the need for a workforce in recently established colonies. Consequently the discrepancy between the child's unique and cherished position in a better off family and his position as a destitute orphan destined for emigration lay in his treatment and not in a differentiated view of the child. Both positions derived from an enhanced focus on the child as "an embodied individual defined as non-adult."[6] The mistreatment and distress caused by uprooting the child from his familiar surroundings was not an intended outcome; the intended outcome of a new and better life for the child lay in the idealized view of the child, who, it was believed, would become "Stronger in body and mind, pure in thought, with aspirations to good"[7] if exposed to the beneficent influences of nature. Both Wagner and the records of organizations such as Barnardo's and Quarrier's homes show that a few children may indeed have found a better life, but the underlying fictionalization of the reality faced by the majority of child emigrants was consistent with the Victorian tendency to "live a distinctively imaginary relation to their real conditions of existence."[8]

Both Henty and MacDonald demonstrate a focus on the place of the child within the family congruent with the emphasis in their contemporary context. In his story *For the Temple* (1887), an historical story of the fall of Jerusalem in AD 70, not only does Henty demonstrate the nineteenth-century focus on the child but does so in the historical setting of another time and culture. John, the hero, frequently comments upon his responsibility not to throw away his life needlessly because he knows how important he is to his parents. He articulates this

---

5. Wagner, *Children*, xiv, xiii.
6. Gittins, *Historical Construction*, 26.
7. Woodsworth, *Motto*.
8. White, *Content of the Form*.

responsibility in a conversation with his father before he sets out to form a band of resistance fighters, "I do not intend . . . to throw away my life, though I care little for it except for the sake of you and my mother and Mary."[9] MacDonald's character Diamond in *At the Back of the North Wind* (1871) is the loved child of a poor but not destitute family. His position within the family indicates that the child focus was not limited to the wealthy whilst also implying that his parents were exceptional representatives of their stratum of society. For example, when Diamond explains to his mother what constitutes possession, he says, "Love makes the only myness." His phrase articulates the way his family functions from day to day and enables them to act in such a way that they do not regard their own advantage as the most important factor in any decision. When Diamond's father and mother are discussing whether they should take up Mr. Raymond's proposal to look after his horse Ruby whilst he is away, Diamond's father comments that "he did not think there was much advantage to be got out of it," but his mother, Martha, explains, "but there would be an advantage, and what matter who gets it!"[10] Her reasoning prevails, indicating a value structure that is oppositional to the prevailing materialism critiqued by MacDonald in his adult novels, such as *Robert Falconer* (1868) and *What's Mine's Mine* (1886) and in his longer fairy tale *The Princess and Curdie* (1883).

Diana Gittins posits a definition of the child as "an embodied individual defined as non-adult," as distinct from childhood which "rather than a material state of being, is more an adult construction."[11] This distinction differentiates between the child as an individual and what he might become, and an abstract term used to describe status. Theorized constructs of the child interact with an historically constructed concept of childhood, which, Gittins notes, "needs to be understood in relation to ideas about what children should be."[12] Phillipe Ariès (1962) traces such a concept of childhood through artistic representation drawn from western European culture. Ariès demonstrates that the idea of childhood developed at the same time as the concept of the nuclear family and structured schooling, both of which "removed the child from adult

---

9. Henty, *For the Temple*, 111.
10. MacDonald, *At the Back*, 325, 288.
11. Gittins, *Historical Construction*, 26.
12. Ibid., 27.

society [and] shut up childhood."[13] Likewise, George Boas, in his book *The Cult of Childhood* (1966), traces the growth of the idea of childhood from antiquity to the twentieth century by examining views of the child found in literature and art. Boas identifies two major themes in these parallel developments, both grounded in oppositional theological views of the child; that of innocent sinlessness and that of innate wickedness. The *speculum naturae* (mirror of nature) and the Romantic development of the concept of childhood theorized by Rousseau are based upon the first view, that of innocence. The teaching that the child is innocent, or sinless, derives from Pelagius, a British lay monk of the fourth and fifth centuries. The pathway from Pelagius' teaching that humanity is capable of good without divine grace, leads towards the concept of the child as a *tabula rasa*, a blank sheet, which needs only to be written into goodness by education. The theories investigated here feed into the composite construct of the child which informs the heroic construct in the work of both Henty and MacDonald.

The Innocent Child: A Link to the Youthful Hero

The ancient idea of the child as *speculum naturae*, the mirror of nature, his initial goodness untarnished until he comes into contact with adult society, is found as early as the work of Cicero (106–43 BC). Boas writes, "When the child has been seen as a replica of Adam before the fall, he has been praised as the possessor of all virtues."[14] Ariès locates the child within a community in his discussion of the increasing importance of the family unit as a single entity and the visual representation of children within the family during the fifteenth and sixteenth centuries. The two concepts of childhood identified by Ariès as emerging during this period focus on the child as different from the adult, but both remain within the domain of the innocent child. The first concept is what he terms, "coddling", the sentimental view of the child and his actions as fascinating and amusing in their difference from adult behavior. The second is, an "interest and moral solicitude,"[15] focusing on the need for a particular education suited to the status of "'childness." This term, which aptly describes the state of being a child, is used

---

13. Ariès, *Centuries*, 397.
14. Boas, *The Cult of Childhood*, 11.
15. Ariès, *Centuries*, 125.

by MacDonald in his theological work *The Hope of the Gospel* (1892).[16] These parallel concepts do not follow separate linear paths in their progression through the seventeenth to the nineteenth century but both diverge and intersect without losing their particular emphases.

During the eighteenth century, visual representation of the child changed from the child included as part of the family group to the child alone as the main focus of a painting. The change is traced by Anne Higonnet, who notes the rapid progression towards, "an invented cultural ideal,"[17] culminating in the "Romantic child," whose literary and visual representation became pervasive during the nineteenth century. "That brilliant error known as the Romantic School"[18] developed in Germany, France, and England during the late eighteenth and early nineteenth centuries. Represented in Germany by, for example, Ludwig Tieck (1773-1854) and Novalis (Friedrich von Hardenberg, 1772-1801), in France by Victor Hugo (1802-85), Alexander Dumas (1802-70), and Alfred de Vigny (1797-1863), and in England by William Blake (1757-1827), Samuel Taylor Coleridge (1772-1834), and William Wordsworth (1770-1850); the Romantics believed in a reality deeper than that immediately observable, and valued the ancient and medieval in art. George Lewes commented, "The desire to get deeper than Life itself led to a disdain of reality and the present. Hence the selection of the Middle Ages and the East as regions for the ideal."[19]

Later in the nineteenth century, as Romantic ideas and ideals became culturally current, the fascination with unknown regions became associated with the expanses of colonial space, which existed as much in the imagination as in reality. Henty's adventure stories set in geographically remote but real countries enabled his hero to demonstrate the ideals of physical and spiritual character and to experience a freedom of action impossible in a known social environment with his family close at hand. Such a setting took the history included in his writing into the realms of romance. MacDonald's fairy tales provided the same freedom by locating characters in the past. As Jean Webb notes, "Both the physical and imagined landscapes are those which satisfy the

---

16. MacDonald, *Hope of the Gospel*, 58.
17. Higgonet, *Pictures*, 8.
18. Lewes, *Life*, 417.
19. Ibid.

cultural imagination."[20] The Romantic emphasis on the importance of the imagination and spiritual awareness provided a balance to the growing emphasis on the narrow empiricism of scientific investigation. Samuel Taylor Coleridge voiced a need for the metaphysical which resonated within a society entering a period of spiritual uncertainty and grasping at scientific truth to stem the tide of doubt. Coleridge writes, "For the writings of these mystics, (Fox [1625–91], Boehme [1575–1624], and Law [1686–1761]) acted in no slight degree to prevent my mind from being imprisoned within the outline of any simple dogmatic system. They contributed to keep alive the heart in the head."[21]

MacDonald was influenced by the German Romantics and translated the poetry of Goethe, Schiller, and the work of Novalis. This influence has been explored elsewhere, for example in the work of Dierdre Hayward.[22] Roderick McGillis categorically states, "his [MacDonald's] imagination is a product of their [the Romantics] theories and practices."[23] MacDonald's fellow Scot, Thomas Carlyle, was equally inspired by the same German thinkers and developed his social philosophy, so pervasive throughout the nineteenth century, from his earlier immersion in their work. It is possible that MacDonald was familiar with Victor Hugo's thought in Hugo's exposition of the child's pre-existence before birth. MacDonald would certainly have been aware of Origen of Alexandria's (AD 185/6–254/55) doctrine of the pre-existence of souls, following his theological studies. MacDonald incorporated the idea the of the child's pre-existence before birth into his story *At the Back of the North Wind* in the form of a dream that comes to Diamond after he had been nursing his baby brother.[24]

The major contribution to the concept of the Romantic child in England came through the work of William Blake and William Wordsworth. MacDonald notes the centrality of the beneficent influence of nature as a teacher in Wordsworth's thought when he says, "The very element in which the mind of Wordsworth lived and moved was a Christian pantheism." MacDonald cites Wordsworth as, "the High Priest of nature [who], saw God present everywhere . . . to Wordsworth, God,

20. Webb, *Conceptualising Childhood*, 365.
21. Coleridge, *Collected Works*, 152.
22. Hayward, *George MacDonald*.
23. McGillis, *Childhood and Growth*, 150.
24. MacDonald, *At the Back*, 233–42.

as the Spirit of Truth, was manifested through the forms of the external world, [including] the face of a little child."[25]

In the first half of the nineteenth century (1815-48) in Germany, the notion "Biedermeier"[26] in art and literature reflected both the nostalgia of a lost pastoral age and the concept of the ideal family. Amongst the foremost proponents of this harmonious rural construct were the illustrator Ludwig Richter (1803-84) and the writer Christoph von Schmid (1768-1854). The centrality of the concept of the child within the family, lay in the child's closeness to nature and therefore to God. This position enabled the child to act as bridge between the physical and spiritual world and embodied the concept of the child as victim and the redemptive child. A key to the child's position on the borderland between the physical and spiritual world lay in his sense of wonder and his ability to "read" the book of nature in which, "there is no animal or plant which cannot serve as God's messenger."[27] This notion holds echoes of the doctrine of correspondences developed by the Swedish philosopher Emmanuel Swedenborg (1688-1772) and is incorporated into the Romantic vision. Swedenborg believed that everything in the physical world had a corresponding counterpart in the spiritual world. Adelheid Kegler explains, "'According to Swedenborg . . . all the things and qualities in our world—rocks, plants and animals; colors, sounds and scents—really do exist, independent of their seeming, since they are the outward manifestations of a spiritual life. Every physical thing is an image of eternity."[28]

MacDonald's lecture on Wordsworth demonstrates the influence of Swedenborg on MacDonald's thought. Discussing Swedenborg's influence on MacDonald, Kegler notes Swedenborg's teaching on the Grand Human Being and explains the aspect of the timelessness of the Grand Human Being in relation to the human being. She writes, "This aspect, pointing beyond the element of time–as it were 'backward' to the origin . . . is symbolised by MacDonald in the figure of the child. In the rather

---

25. MacDonald, *Wordsworth's Poetry*, 245, 247.

26. The literal translation of "Biedermeier" is "honest", or "trusty farmer." Ute Dettmar notes that the term was coined by A. Kussmaul and L. Eichrodt in 1855 after the name of a fictitious character. The term was used to characterize specific tendencies in the field of art and literature 1815-1848. Dettmar, *19th Century Children's Literature*.

27. Dettmar, *19th Century Children's Literature*, 4.

28. Kegler, *Sleep of the Soul*, 27.

theoretical picture-language of *The Golden Key* it is the oldest of all human beings: "the old man of the fire," a naked playing child."[29] In this imagery, the child is the meeting place of the Grand Human Being and the ordinary and can be linked to Carlyle's "great man," described in *On Heroes, Hero-Worship and the Heroic in History* (1841), and to Carlyle's concept of the heroic as latent in "everyman" whose heroism is demonstrated in Henty's and MacDonald's idealized youthful hero.

In MacDonald's writing the notion of the borderland between the physical and the spiritual frequently appears as an image, and is associated with the process of maturation from childhood to adulthood, for example in *Phantastes* (1858), *The Golden Key* (1867), *Little Daylight* (1871), *The Carasoyn* (1871), *At the Back of the North Wind* (1871), and *The Princess and the Goblin* (1872). The notion of borderland is discussed by Marion Lochhead in her study *The Renaissance of Wonder in Children's Literature* (1977) where Lochhead places MacDonald in the forefront of authors creating what she terms, "the alternative world of faery" and cites the development of such literature as a reaction to, "a hard and artificial industrialism."[30] Conversely, the notion of Biedermeier was less a reaction to the present than a desire to preserve a constructed ideal past in the face of imminent political unrest and social upheaval.

The child as naturally innocent and good was balanced by the view that education was needed to inculcate a "good" moral character. The content of such education was dependent upon gender since the feminine capacity for goodness was constructed as greater than the masculine, a concept impressed, so he felt, upon MacDonald's eldest son Greville, who wrote "That girls were far above boys in goodness was always impressed upon me."[31]

Innate Wickedness: Gendered Expectations and the Need for Education

The quotation above, from Greville MacDonald showed a cultural emphasis on the second theological view, dominant amongst Protestant communities and originating in Psalm 51:5, "I have been evil from the time I was born; from the day of my birth I have been sinful." Zornado

---

29. Ibid., 33–34.
30. Lochhead, *Renaissance*, vii.
31. MacDonald, *Reminiscences*, 28, 29.

discusses the implications of such a theological view within the theory of Daniel Gottlob Moritz Schreber's (1808–61) black pedagogy, noting that the most important aspect of the black pedagogy is the cult of the personality instituted by the father, "in which he is always right."[32] Zornado observes that the black pedagogy assumes the child to be "the other." In the nineteenth-century evangelical movement this theological view matured into a strict code of behavior encompassing every aspect of the child's life, girls as well as boys, including the child's reading material.

Nineteenth-century Western education until the 1860s primarily focused on the education of boys, so the emphasis on punishment in order to inculcate good behavior and ultimately to "civilize" the child into the prevailing cultural norms deflected the doctrine of innate wickedness away from girls. Greville recalls, "I do not know that my sisters were ever punished."[33] The implication here is that they did not need to be punished, being innately morally superior to boys. The assumption that girls were not as innately wicked as boys placed an expectation upon them that rebounded if they did not perform as a girl should. Charlotte Brontë's *Jane Eyre* (1847) records the response to what was regarded as inappropriate behavior in Mr Brocklehurst's words, "No sight so sad as that of a naughty child, . . . especially a naughty little girl."[34] Despite the atmosphere of female superiority felt by Greville in the MacDonald household, MacDonald produced a story in which the heroine performs against these expectations of goodness. In *The Giant's Heart* (1867), a disturbing story which, as Raeper observes, "paints an uncomfortable picture of a giant who gorges himself on vegetable-like children,"[35] the heroine begins the adventure in which she and her brother find themselves, by teasing her brother "till he could not bear it any longer."[36] Realistic as this behavior might be amongst siblings, it does not conform to the nineteenth century expectation, rather, it epitomizes Brontë's "naughty little girl." The underlying cultural norms are compounded in her brother's response. He "gave her a box on the ear," but was, "so sorry and ashamed that he . . . ran off into the wood."[37]

32. Zornado, *Inventing the child*, 89.
33. Ibid., 28.
34. Bronte, *Jane Eyre*, 26.
35. Raeper, *George MacDonald*, 315.
36. MacDonald, *Giant's Heart*, 67.
37. Ibid., 67.

That her brother should have such a reaction to this action, provoked as he was, runs with the accepted norms of middle-class behavior in England in the nineteenth century. To strike a woman was regarded as a cowardly act, a premise inculcated into middle-class boys from a young age. Henty articulates the cultural norm in his story *By Sheer Pluck* (1884), when the hero, Frank Hargate expresses horror at the thought of fighting against the women warriors of Dahomey (West Africa). His mentor, Mr Goodenough, explains, "That is merely an idea of civilization, Frank.... Among the middle and upper classes throughout Europe a man is considered a brute and a coward who lifts his hand against a woman.... You won't see much difference between women and men when the fight begins, Frank. These female furies will slay all who fall into their hands, and therefore in self-defence you will have to assist in slaying them."[38] Henty takes the opportunity in this conversation between Mr Goodenough and Frank to put forward a view on women's rights and women "who leave their proper sphere," which in this instance is, to "employ themselves in domestic duties and in brightening the lives of men."[39] Like MacDonald's female characters, none of Henty's fictional female heroes conform to this sphere, except by implication on the last page of his stories when they step metaphorically out of their story and into the "reality" of English middle or upper class marriage.

The two children in *The Giant's Heart* inadvertently enter Giantland and eventually outwit the giant by stealing his heart, dropping poisonous spider-juice on it to torture him and eventually killing him by burying a knife into the heart, "'up to the hilt.'"[40] This little girl may have started off behaving badly, but she is the heroine. She takes control throughout the story, masterminds the discovery of the giant's heart and shows no mercy when the children capture it. She is one of MacDonald's female heroines who defy the image of the superior goodness of girls by behaving independently. In this she reflects MacDonald's intellectual view of women and his circle of friends recorded by Greville who writes "My parents' intimacy with such protagonists of the feminist movement as... Josephine Butler, Madame Bodichon,... Mrs Reid, Principal of Bedford College,... Anna Sidgwick, Miss Buss and Miss Beale, no doubt made

---

38. Henty, *By Sheer Pluck*, 212.
39. Ibid.
40. MacDonald, *Giant's Heart*, 96.

deep . . . impression upon me."[41] (Miss Buss and Miss Beale were in the forefront of promoting women's education.)

Associated with the representation of boys as innately more wicked than girls is the image of the boy as wild and in need of civilization. This image is closely linked to the construction of the male as pursuing physical outdoor activities, a construction noted by Alison Lurie as persisting into the twentieth century[42] and which continues into the twenty-first as children's toys, games, and advertised activities become ever more polarized. The boy as "savage," holds connotations of both the wild and the naturally noble and once again relates boyhood (childhood) with colonized peoples.

"The Little Savage": Boys and Primitivism, the Need for Civilization

"does she think . . . we should come in like wild Indians . . ."[43]

This quotation is taken from Henty's story *The Young Buglers* and makes the psychological link between the natural behavior of the boy and that of the contemporary nineteenth-century concept of the savage, epitomized by the use of the word "wild" with its implication of difference to nineteenth-century middle-class mores. In Captain Marryat's children's novel *The Little Savage* (1848–49), a Robinsonade in which the orphaned Frank Henniker grows up on an island with an old seaman, the title itself indicates the consequences of growing up far from "civilization", that is, without the parameters of Western society. The equation of uncivilized behavior and barbarism can be demonstrated from Henty's *The Young Buglers*.

The orphaned Scudamore children are sent to live with a maiden aunt who is convinced that the two boys will be beyond control. Tom comments, "Poor aunt. . . . What does she think of us that she can suppose that, upon our very first arrival, we should come in like wild Indians, throwing stones at her pigeons, and frightening her Minnie [the cat] into fits."[44] That Henty condones the subsequent behavior of

41. MacDonald, *Reminiscences*, 29.
42. Lurie, *Language*, 215.
43. Henty, *Young Buglers*, 9.
44. Ibid., 9.

his heroes can, on occasion, stretch the twenty-first century reader's credulity. The Scudamores terrorize the local, tyrannous schoolmaster, by perpetrating acts of violence upon his person and his house until he is forced to leave. When his new watch is "requisitioned" by the boys, who are disguised as "a gigantic footpad" (one standing on the shoulders of the other), it is smashed and thrown through the schoolmaster's window, "The head-constable was sent for, and after examining the relics of the case, he came to the same conclusion at which the rest had already arrived, namely, that the watch could not have been stolen by an ordinary footpad, but by some personal enemy of the schoolmaster's, whose object was not plunder, but annoyance and injury. . . . For the next month Mr. Jones' life was rendered a burden to him." When their behavior includes actions such as, "the chimney-pots were shut up with sods placed on them. . . . Night after night the windows of his bedroom were smashed; cats were let down the chimney; his water-butts were filled with mud, the cord of the bucket of his well was cut time after time; the flowers in his garden were dug up . . . ," the boys behavior, from a contemporary twenty-first-century point of view, goes beyond the usual run of practical joke, but when questioned, Tom Scudamore responds, "You never do believe me Mr. Jones, so it is no use my saying I didn't do it; but if you ask Miss Scudamore [the boys' aunt], she will bear witness that we were in bed hours before and that there are bars on our windows through which a cat could hardly get."[45] This statement is, taken literally, the truth, for Henty heroes never lie. Also note that it is their younger sister, the good girl, who has allowed the boys out through her window. It is notable that the child in MacDonald's stories does not display the ambivalence of character demonstrated in *The Young Buglers*.

The convention of "the bad boy" in children's literature continued into the twentieth century. The American convention is charted from Mark Twain and Thomas Bailey Aldrich in the nineteenth century, through to the twentieth century by Lorinda Cohoon who writes, "'Naturally bad' boyhoods seem to be one of the most prevalent late twentieth-century constructions of boyhood,"[46] but the ambiguity contained in the term is evident in Henty's construct of the boy. In Henty's work, the boy who can answer "yes" to the questions, "Can you thrash most fellows your own age? Can you run as far and as fast as most

---

45. Henty, *Young Buglers*, 31, 33, 34.
46. Cohoon, *Necessary Badness*, 5.

of them? Can you take a caning without whimpering? . . . Are you good at planning a piece of mischief, and ready to take the lead in carrying it out?"[47] is not perceived as a threat to the stability of society, rather he is perceived as model material for the continuation of imperial activity in his demonstration of leadership and independence. Here lies the ambiguity. The underlying decency of these boys stemming, generally but not exclusively, from a middle-class upbringing and an English public school education, disqualifies them from being categorized as delinquents, whatever their behavior. Conversely, similar "spirited" behavior in a girl is condemned as "wicked, violent" and "most headstrong," from the point of view of a conventional status-conscious mother, depicted in Henty's *Rujub the Juggler*[48] and in the citation from *Jane Eyre* above. In the passage from *The Young Buglers*, "savagery" is synonymous with wildness and violent aggressive behavior, but the connection of "child" to "savage" began with Rousseau's emphasis on the child state as closest to the state of nature. In human development the child state was related to Rousseau's view of primitive man, a concept he developed from the idea of the noble savage found in Michel de Montaigne (1533–92) who, "suggested in 1580 that cannibals live in an Edenic state of purity and simplicity."[49]

MacDonald's fictional boys, such as Diamond (*At the Back of the North Wind*), Clare Skymer (*A Rough Shaking*), and Gilbert Galbraith (*Sir Gibbie*), all ideally good characters, display both masculine and feminine characteristics. Arguably their androgyny demonstrates Greville's perception (quoted at the beginning of this section) that to be good it was necessary to be feminine. Curdie, the miner boy in MacDonald's *The Princess and the Goblin* and *The Princess and Curdie*, although a masculine character, reconnects with his perceptions of goodness in terms of spiritual awareness after contact with Irene and her Great-Great-Grandmother. This instance also supports Greville's perception of MacDonald's attitude to the masculine nature as inferior to the feminine in goodness.

In the twentieth century, the trend towards the child living close to nature was subsumed into the concept of the well-behaved middle class child operating with the minimum of intervention from adults. These

---

47. Henty, *Through the Sikh War*, 19.
48. Henty, *Rujub*, 35, 37.
49. Ashcroft, *Primitive and Wingless*, 188.

children may *live* like primitives, but they maintain the politeness and "decent" behavior inculcated by their education. Outstanding examples can be found in, for example, Edith Nesbit's Bastables, Arthur Ransome's Walker family and Enid Blyton's Famous Five or Secret Seven. At the end of the story the children step out of their "natural," or "native," primitive existence and revert to "civilization," which is once more populated by adults. The unquestioned understanding is that "real" life, outside of the holidays, in which children inevitably reach adulthood, gives parameters to the children's primitivism, reducing it to the level of a game or at best, an extended holiday camping expedition. The primitivism of Henty's boys is part of their actual lives, manifesting itself in "uncivilized" behavior, whereas the manifestation of primitive simplicity in MacDonald's stories emphasizes the state of ideal purity.

The Childlike: Innocence and Experience

The term "child," interpreted as "an embodied individual defined as non-adult," came to be used in relation to other groups perceived by the dominant discourse to be socially inferior such as women, foreigners and the colonized. This relation is common to both the concepts of innocence and of innate wickedness, despite their oppositional positions. In the context of Rousseauian theory, the developing representation of the innocent child was towards feminization. Higonnet adds to the explanation for this trend as follows; not only was the natural purity of the child associated with the female as socially and intellectually inferior, but in terms of artistic representation, "the image of the Romantic child spread to popular genre paintings,"[50] which became predominantly the province of female painters because of their exclusion from the dominant male art world. Steps toward an increasingly idealistic representation of children throughout the nineteenth century by artists such as Kate Greenaway (1846–1901) and Jessie Wilcox Smith (1863–1935) were mirrored in children's literature, which was also a primarily female domain in the early nineteenth century (1800–1850) and included, for example, the authors Mrs Sherwood (1775–1851) and Hannah More (1745–1833). This predominantly austere period of literature produced for children, inclined theologically towards the concept

---

50. Higonnet, *Pictures of Innocence*, 9.

of the innate wickedness of the child, and was written with the conscious purpose of moral education.

The discrepancy between the artistic visual representation of the ideal child by the celebrated male artists of the late eighteenth and early nineteenth centuries and the literary representation of the child in need of strict moral education and correction, mirrored the dichotomy running through nineteenth-century society discussed in the previous chapter, that of the "astonishing capacity (of nineteenth-century society) to mask its own contradictions."[51] Idealization of the child in later nineteenth-century children's literature culminated in the creation of characters such as Cedric Errol in Frances Hodgson Burnett's *Little Lord Fauntleroy* (1886) and Johann Spyri's *Heidi* (1881 English translation 1884). Illustrated editions of *Little Lord Fauntleroy* unite the visual and the literary concept of the Romantic child and demonstrate the feminization of the image. Reginald Birch's illustrations for the first edition of the book (1886) represent Cedric with long wavy blond hair and wearing a velvet knickerbocker suit. This is the figure satirized by Ronald Searle in the character of Fotherington Thomas, in a post-Freudian age when the validity of such angelic goodness in a child was no longer an accepted construct.[52] One area in which the feminization of the young child was apparent amongst the middle and upper classes in the nineteenth century was in the development of children's clothes which rendered gender indistinguishable. A later manifestation of the continuing connection between clothes and the innocence of childhood can be found in Mary Wesley's *The Camomile Lawn* (1984). The story is set in 1939, against the backdrop of imminent war. Sophy accompanies her older cousins who are going swimming. They wait for her to catch up and one of them swings her up onto his shoulders, "The child's gingham dress flew up and Richard (her uncle) saw that she was wearing no knickers." He calls to his wife,

"Helena . . . That child Sophy is wearing no knickers."
"How on earth do you know?" Anxiety showed in Helena's eyes.
"I saw Oliver pick her up."
"Is that all?"
"All?" He was nonplussed. "It's indecent. I ask you."

---

51. Ashcroft, *Primitive and Wingless*, 84.
52. Willans and Searle, *The Compleet Molesworth*, 12.

"Richard," Helena laughed, "she's only ten, she never wears knickers if it's hot. . . . A little girl of Sophy's age can't be indecent."[53]

This brief passage demonstrates an ambiguity and growing confusion about the position of the child in an adult world that had experienced a societal paradigm shift since the turn of the century and particularly since World War I. The war veteran Richard shows an innate apprehension that childhood innocence can no longer be as certain as it once was, whilst his wife Helena has no such qualms and still views Sophy as a little girl who therefore "can't be indecent." Higonnet discusses the subtleties of such ambiguity in her study on the history of the visual representation of children. Whilst the child was viewed as untouched by adult sexuality, the trend of innocent neutrality continued and it is evidence of Higonnet's premise that the concept of the child is currently (late twentieth and early twenty-first centuries) undergoing a cultural change and that distinctive differentiation between boys and girls in terms of clothing, toys and other consumables is increasing. The feminine qualities of child characters in the children's writing of George MacDonald can be demonstrated in the figures of Diamond (*At the Back of the North Wind*), the supernaturally good child located in the working class environment of nineteenth-century London, and Clare Skymer *(A Rough Shaking)*, whose name initially raises the question of ambiguity and who exemplifies other worldly goodness in the face of extreme hardship and mistreatment in a nineteenth-century English rural context.

I have established that in the capacity of "other" the concept of "child" is extended to the foreigner, the female and the colonized, with the cult of personality instituted by the father as the dominant authority represented by the imperialist ruler. An example of such use can be found in Henty's *The Young Buglers* (1880) where the regimental drummer Sam, a black character, sometimes a figure of fun or ridicule, relates his escape from the French camp to Tom Scudamore, one of the two boy heroes, "Why, Massa Tom" Sam said "you didn't think dat dis chile was going to stop prisoner with dose French chaps . . ."[54] Sam uses the epithet "chile" for himself three times in the course of his story of capture and escape. Although Henty's use of parodied language grates in the twenty-first-century ear, throughout the narrative, Henty subverts his own stereotype in the character of Sam. Despite the superficial portrayal

---

53. Wesley, *Camomile Lawn*, 24, 25.
54. Henty, *Young Buglers*, 230.

of Sam as the traditional figure of fun, he rescues the boys from every difficult situation they get into; he nurses them back to health after being wounded and looks after their interests in practical ways. In relation to character and behavior, Sam conforms to the construct of the ideal hero. Reading against the text, Sam emerges as the single hero of the story. This example is one of many where Henty writes-in a non-English hero without acknowledging him as such. By reading such "gaps in the text as significant omissions,"[55] we have an appropriate way of interpreting these occurrences. In *The Young Buglers* the hierarchical nature of the French army is also depicted in terms of the parent/child binary. Tom and Peter Scudamore, fighting in the Peninsular War against the French, rescue a French general's wife and child from Spanish bandits whilst scouting disguised as Spanish boys. When they return the captives to the French camp, it is imperative that the boys are not discovered to be English. After the French colonel has heard the account of the rescue from the general's wife, he places the boys under the protection of his soldiers with the words, "so I leave them to you; you will take care of them, my children, will you not?"[56] In this passage, the French colonel is placing himself in the position of parent to his soldiers as an authority figure within the microcosmic society of the regiment, just as the father has authority over the children in the microcosmic society of the family.

Ashcroft notes that the concept of race developed at the same time as the concept of child and that both became "mutually important concepts in the imperial discourse."[57] The development of the idea of racial hierarchy and implied superiority therefore cannot be separated from the growth of control over the child. The two concepts operate within the parent/child binary creating a "natural" hierarchy of authority. In the context of empire this familial relationship ensured the acceptance of authority by the colonized "children" which enabled the "white fathers" to govern. Acceptance of the dominant civilization by the colonized enables the imperialist to "invent" the colonized just as the concept of the child was invented to conform to the ideals of the dominant nineteenth-century discourse. Zornado maintains that moral authority vested in such adult or imperial power was seen as so inevitable as to cause subordination to be accepted without question and "made empire

55. Rice and Waugh, *Modern Literary Theory*, 14.
56. Henty, *Young Buglers*, 166.
57. Ashcroft, *Primitive and Wingless*, 185.

durable."[58] This pervasive rationale was reinforced in Henty's stories by "native" characters such as Abu (*With Kitchener in the Soudan*), Rujub (*Rujub the Juggler*), and the old chief (*By Sheer Pluck*). In the story *With Kitchener in the Soudan* (1903) Abu, son of the Emir, says to Gregory, the hero, "I begin to see, Mudil, that we are very ignorant. We can fight, but that is all we are good for. How much better it would be if, instead of regarding you white men as enemies, we could get some of you to live here and teach us the wonderful things you know!"[59] Similarly, Rujub talks to the hero Ralph Bathurst after his daughter has been rescued from a tiger by Ralph. Rujub discusses his reasons for hating the whites. Following his surprise that anyone would risk his own life to save that of a stranger he concludes, "I had to think it all out again. Then I saw things in another light. Other conquerors, many of them, India has had, but none who have made it their first object to care for the welfare of the people at large. . . . I cannot love those I have been taught to hate, but I can see the benefit their rule has given to India."[60]

By putting these speeches in the mouths of colonized people as a result of actions done by an Englishman, Henty presents their changed perception of their situation as the logical conclusion of their experience. This changed perception is always and only contingent upon the hero behaving as the ideal nineteenth century hero should in terms of moral values. Margery Hourihan notes, "It makes the values inherent in the structure and narrative point of view seem to "go without saying," to be simply natural."[61] The subjects expressing these views (Abu and Rujub) are shown, in their new realization, to live "spontaneously" or "naturally"[62] within the value structure demonstrated by their English colonizers. In this way the ideology of the benefits of empire became accepted by a process of interpellation.

The Childlike "Other": Ruled and Ruler

The two opposing theological views, of innocent sinlessness and innate wickedness, applied to the concept of the child and also transferred to

---

58. Zornado, *Inventing the Child*, 103.
59. Henty, *With Kitchener*, 306.
60. Henty, *Rujub*, 241.
61. Hourihan, *Deconstructing the Hero*, 52.
62. Althusser, *On Ideology*, 309.

those other groups regarded as inferior, such as women and the colonized. These two additional groups were perceived as dependent and unable to negotiate the white male discourse of power in order to penetrate the powerbase. Subsequent developments in terms of the Romantic construct of the child and theories of education drew the concept of the child as *speculum naturae* and *tabula rasa* closer together. The work of Henty and MacDonald exhibits concepts of the child which incorporate both ideas. In Henty's boy characters, this composite construct is implicit and deeply embedded in his contemporary cultural emphasis on character education. MacDonald's child characters demonstrate the same composite construct accompanied by MacDonald's own interpretation of educational theory. The implication of the idea of the child as *tabula rasa*, the blank slate, whose development is dependent upon education and guidance from an adult source is that the child could, in theory, choose goodness or wickedness dependent upon education. Humanist thought continues this emphasis on education, found in the philosophy of John Locke (1632–1704), who viewed the child as a blank slate in need of the appropriate education to enable him to become a rational human being, that is, an adult, a responsible mature citizen, in the mold of the society into which he is born. Avery notes that from the beginning of the concept of the child as a separate entity until the late eighteenth century, the ideal was the industrious child,[63] an ideal that gave priority to character education as educational theory developed drawing in both theological viewpoints. In France the early dominance of the Jesuits in the field of education, provided the basis for the view that education and training were of primary importance in molding the child's character. Their premise was based on Proverbs 22:6, "Train up a child in the way he should go; and when he is old, he will not depart from it."

The *tabula rasa*, or blank slate or space, also described colonial space when viewed by the colonizer. Ashcroft notes that Henry Morton Stanley recorded his impression as he looked west toward the Congo in 1877 as "The largest half of Africa one wide enormous blank . . ."[64] The "wide enormous blank" also applied to the history and culture of the people who lived in it. In imperial terms, the myth of the virgin or vacant land was as a space waiting to be "written" in the image of the colonizer, whose

63. Avery, *Childhood's Pattern*, preface.
64. Ashcroft, *Primitive and Wingless*, 187.

superiority was thought to consist in his civilization born of education. This assumed superiority was precisely the same hold as the adult had over the child, the adult possessed the knowledge which he imparted to the child in order that he become civilized, since "literacy and education create the divide between civilization and barbarism."[65] In his history of character formation, James Arthur records that Locke believed character education to be more important than intellectual development."[66] On this point he was in agreement with Jesuit and Puritan educational theory, despite his rejection of their biblical rationale. Both Henty and MacDonald wrote this tenet into their stories. Henty in particular took an anti-academic stance. In *Condemned as a Nihilist* (1893), Godfrey's father protests, "According to my idea it is perfectly scandalous that at the great schools such an essential as writing is altogether neglected, while years are spent over Greek, which is of no earthly use when you have once left school."[67] The opinion that classical languages were "of no earthly use when you have once left school" is echoed throughout his writing, although later on in the same story, Godfrey, imprisoned as a suspected Nihilist and in solitary confinement, "did his best to keep up his spirits. He had learnt by heart . . . the first two books of the Iliad, and these he daily repeated to himself, . . . repeated the dates in Greek history . . ."[68] In this passage, Henty appears to be poking fun at this own view by pointing out that at least Greek comes in useful in an extreme situation. In the wider imperialistic sense, Godfrey's ability to "keep up his spirits" by using his education and literacy establishes his superiority over both his jailor and the prison official (both Russian and therefore "other"), by the controlled coolness of his behavior. George MacDonald's parable *The Wise Woman* (1875) also provides an example of the control and poise that places the educated middle or upper class protagonist in a position of superiority. In chapter 14, after her period under the tuition of the Wise Woman, Rosamond returns to the palace and only gains entry by her dignified reasoning with the sentry, remembering that the Wise Woman had told her, "Nobody can be a real princess . . . until she is a princess over herself, that is, until, when she finds herself unwilling to do the thing that is right, she makes herself do it. For instance, if you should

65. Ibid., 186.
66. Arthur, *Education With character*, 10.
67. Henty, *Condemned as a Nihilist*, 18.
68. Ibid., 78.

be cross and angry, you are not a whit the less bound to be just."[69] That both Godfrey Bullen and Princess Rosamond hold positions in society that rank them in the middle and upper class respectively places their stories in the wider context of romance, which, as Northrop Frye notes, features "pervasive social snobbery." He states, "Naïve romance confines itself largely to royal families; sentimental romance gives us patterns of aristocratic courage and courtesy." These patterns of behavior reach beyond the confines of royalty and aristocracy (nobility) and develop into the concept of "noble" behavior. Both Henty and MacDonald extend the link with behavior. Frye notes that the "blood will tell" convention associates "moral virtue and social rank."[70] The word "noble" therefore takes on a double meaning, on the one hand referring to a person's position in the hierarchy of society and on the other referring to a form of behavior that has become associated with that rank but not necessarily performed by a person of rank. Henty remains almost, with two exceptions, exclusively within the "blood will tell" convention. His heroes may on occasion appear to come from a humble background but are in the end revealed to be gentlemen. An example is William Gale in *For Name and Fame* (1886). Willie is stolen from his parents, and abandoned outside a Cambridgeshire Workhouse. The gatekeeper's wife takes a special interest in Willie. She refuses to believe that the woman, subsequently discovered, who had left him there, is his real mother. "I believe, Billy," she said over and over again, "that your parents were gentlefolk . . . and it is for you to bear in mind, and to act so as, if you were to meet them, they need not be ashamed of you."[71]

MacDonald takes the possibility of nobility as revealed by behavior further. In his tale *Cross Purposes* (1862), two children, Richard and Alice are enticed into fairyland and given guides, a goblin for Richard and a fairy for Alice, to take them to the fairy queen. As the only humans in fairyland at the time, they are thrown together, but Alice is at first reluctant to have anything to do with a poor boy like Richard, despite his "gentlemanly" manners. As they travel together they grow closer, but their friendship cannot survive outside of fairyland since the class division between them in their own world is too great. Richard, the poor boy, demonstrates "noble" characteristics in terms of moral virtue

69. MacDonald, *The Wise Woman*, 109.
70. Frye, *Secular Scripture*, 161.
71. Henty, *For Name and Fame*, 33.

throughout the story. Despite this consistency, he is unable to cross the social divide. On his return from fairyland he remains distanced from Alice despite their mutual attachment and shared journey. Richard does not conform to the "blood will tell" convention noted by Frye,[72] since he is genuinely poor and remains in the lower social strata where he was at the beginning of the story. MacDonald does retain the "blood will tell" convention in stories such as *Sir Gibbie* (1879) and *A Rough Shaking* (1891).

Writing on character education James Arthur cites the theory of David Fordyce (1711–51) which emphasized the need to develop the child's imagination with the purpose of enabling the child to consciously take responsibility for his own moral decisions. By doing so, the child could, theoretically, act on his own initiative without supervision or by a set of superficial rules.[73] MacDonald's approach chimes well with Fordyce's theory and his character Diamond in *At the Back of the North Wind* (1871), demonstrates innate understanding of this argument when he acts to do the right thing on his own initiative. As North Wind points out to him, "what's the use of knowing a thing only because you're told it?"[74] Fordyce's theory of character education by imaginative development was added to Locke's concept of the need to educate the child into responsible citizenship, by Robert Owen (1771–1858). Owen's educational experiment in New Lanarkshire was based on his development of a model community. Owen believed education should be available to anyone in the community. Adults were therefore able to learn alongside children, positioning education and literacy as the source of empowerment. The theories of Paolo Freire, writing in the second half of the twentieth century, politicized this position in a contemporary situation enabling people previously disempowered by lack of education to take decisions and initiate actions they would not have been able to envisage whilst in the subordinate position caused by illiteracy. Owen's experiment ran from 1800–1825 in New Lanarkshire and from 1824–29 in New Harmony, Indiana. His emphasis on education for personal development and responsibility was accepted by nineteenth-century

---

72. Frye, *Secular Scripture*, 161.
73. Arthur, *Education With Character*, 10.
74. MacDonald, *At the Back*, 57.

theorists such as John Ruskin, Thomas Carlyle, and John Stuart Mill who regarded character development as, "the solution to social problems."[75]

In the mid-nineteenth century, the concepts of the ideal child and the need for children to be educated either to release their "naturally good" qualities or to correct their "innately" wicked state drew ever closer as the emphasis in children's literature began to move from a position of didacticism towards imaginative fiction and fantasy. Sarah Maier notes that, "MacDonald had his own vision of the child and of the imagination which combined the idealization of the child by the Romantics and the educational purposes of Locke and Rousseau."[76] This statement recognizes the development of the construct of the child in the work of the Victorian fantasists and in George MacDonald in particular. An examination of the difference between the concepts of character maturation and education in MacDonald's fairy tales demonstrates the complementary nature of these two processes. Dieter Petzold defines the concepts as follows, "maturation is . . . the unfolding of inherent qualities, even though this may be influenced by certain external conditions. Education . . . implies a conscious manipulation of the process. While maturation seems natural, education aims at cultivation. . . . Humans . . . need to be taught to internalise the values and norms of society."[77] How complementary these concepts are is dependent upon the nature of the education offered in order to effect the result required by any given societal norms. Petzold concludes that MacDonald's fairy tales are primarily tales of maturation, but the education encountered in the process of maturation is more overt in some than in others. For example, *The Wise Woman* is cited by critics as one of MacDonald's most didactic works. Reis believes that the story is "marred by the sort of non-functional sermonizing which . . . weakens many of the novels but is usually absent from the imaginative works."[78] This view is dependent upon the critical criteria applied to the story by the reader.

The merging of two concepts previously viewed as oppositional to create a third construct within the context of children's literature demonstrates another instance of the contradictions evident in the Victorian milieu. This third construct provided an impetus for the para-

75. Arthur, *Education With Character*, 12.
76. Maier, *Romanticising and Fantasising*, 111.
77. Petzold, *Maturation and Education*, 11.
78. Reis, *George MacDonald's Fiction*, 84–85.

digm shift in emphasis which propelled writing for children out of the morally didactic course in which it was embedded. The impetus for the mid-century revival of fantastic tales came from Germany and whereas the earlier Victorians used the literary fairy tale as a vehicle for moral education, the emphatic change in children's literature is epitomized by the publication of Lewis Carroll's *Alice's Adventures in Wonderland* (1865). Avery observes that MacDonald, "restructured" the form of the fairy tale, to provide moral vision, but allowed children to think for themselves.[79] Discussing the fairy tale in his essay *The Fantastic Imagination* (1893), MacDonald explains his intention when he writes "Everyone, however, who feels the story, will read its meaning after his own nature and development."[80] This statement indicates his view that the polysemous nature of the tales encouraged personal growth and application. In his book entitled *The Child's Inheritance: Its Scientific and Imaginative Meaning* (1910), MacDonald's son Greville interprets MacDonald's theory of education. He explains MacDonald's main premise as, "the means and purpose of education are to bring into germination, flowering and fruit-bearing the child's sleeping inheritance."[81] Put succinctly, education is, "leading forth and not stuffing in."[82] George MacDonald applied his theory to adults as well as to children when he wrote, "The best thing you can do for your fellow, next to rousing his conscience, is—not to give him things to think about, but to wake up things that are in him; or say, to make him think things for himself."[83]

MacDonald did not view the child as *tabula rasa*, but as one whose perceptions could be awakened by the world of nature around him. This view correlates with the Romantic vision. Referring to MacDonald's essay entitled *Wordsworth's Poetry* (1893)"[84] John Pridmore writes, "MacDonald claims that for Wordsworth nature is 'a world of teaching.'" Pridmore explains MacDonald's thinking that such teaching is given progressively, nature engaging with the human spirit at successively

79. Avery, *Childhood's Pattern*, 313.
80. MacDonald, *Fantastic Imagination*, 316.
81. MacDonald, *Child's Inheritance*, 272.
82. MacDonald, *Fairy Tale*, 14.
83. MacDonald, *Fantastic Imagination*, 319.
84. This essay is included in MacDonald, *A Dish of Orts*, 245–63.

higher levels.[85] McGillis' criticism agrees with this observation when he notes, "Childhood is separate from nature. . . . Despite this, MacDonald follows Wordsworth in endowing nature with a formative influence on the growing child."[86] In his story *The Wise Woman* (1875) MacDonald includes natural forces in his account of the wise woman's education of Rosamond, the princess, who "never thought of there being more than one Somebody—and that was herself." While Rosamond reflects, "how very good she had grown, and how very good she was to have grown good and how extremely good she must always have been that she was able to grow so very good as she now felt she had grown. . . . Suddenly, a great wind came roaring down the chimney, and scattered ashes about the floor; a tremendous rain followed, and fell hissing on the embers; the moon was swallowed up, and there was darkness all about her. Then a flash of lightening, followed by a peal of thunder."[87] Melba Battin comments, "As so often happens in MacDonald, this storm on the outside reflects the chaos or nightmare going on inside Rosamond."[88] The experiences Rosamond has in the care of the wise woman lead her through a process of self-discovery which enables her to choose to change. This is not an inevitable process. Her counterpart Agnes, an equally self-absorbed girl, has not made this choice by the end of the book, although MacDonald implies that the story is not yet finished for Agnes and her parents, or for Rosamond, who faces the prospect of re-educating her own misguided parents. MacDonald writes, "If you think it is not finished—I never knew a story that was. I could tell you a great deal more concerning them all, but I have already told more than is good for those who read but with their foreheads, and enough for those whom it has made look a little solemn, and sigh as they close the book."[89] McGillis continues, "This is the basic pattern of nearly all of MacDonald's novels and fantasies. It is also paradigmatic of much Romantic narrative, the circuitous yet progressive self-education and self-discovery."[90]

In the course of her adventure, whether aligned with the fairy tale struggle or with the romantic quest tale, the choices made by the hero

85. Pridmore, *Nature and Fantasy*, 2.
86. McGillis, *Childhood and Growth*, 156.
87. MacDonald, *Wise Woman*, 4, 29.
88. Battin, *Duality*, 212.
89. MacDonald, *Wise Woman*, 142.
90. McGillis, *Childhood and Growth*, 159.

determine the direction of her character development. In terms of the education she receives from within her societal context, her imaginative application, or rejection, of this education, affects her journey toward maturity. This choice is demonstrated by the disparate reactions of Rosamond and Agnes to the teaching of the Wise Woman, and by both the application of received education and personal initiative in the unexpected situations in which Godfrey Bullen finds himself in Henty's story *Condemned as a Nihilist*, cited above. The phrase "finds himself" indicates the self-discovery implicit in the romantic narrative, even whilst he (the child/hero) remains dependent on taught social construct, an aspect of the hero figure discussed in the next chapter.

The Child as Victim: Hero as Protector

One manifestation of the innocent child is the representation of the child as victim, a representation that "enables the imagining of a version of selfhood in which the subject may be taken as self-determining and individualized, but inextricably dependent upon social formations, especially institutions, outside the self."[91] Children (and the colonized) are therefore viewed as "little citizens" in need of support from the state. Laura Berry contends that perceived danger to them reflects an unspoken perceived danger to the adult self and that the focus on the child's welfare and dependency on the state deflects potential social conflict by constructing the state as the solution to social problems. This contention relates back to Locke's emphasis on education for responsibility and enables the educators to remain in a position of power. Berry notes the significance of the motif of hunger in connection with what she terms, "revolution anxiety,"[92] the fear of being "devoured" by the masses. Hunger is a key motif in the portrayal of child poverty and understood at all levels of society. At a time when the French Revolution was overthrowing the established ruling class in France, political unrest was changing the face of Germany, the Chartists were becoming vocal in England, and the numbers of working class people were growing exponentially in England's major cities, with attendant housing and employment pressures and accompanying social unrest, "revolution anxiety" was a reality to both the increasing middle classes and the governing class.

91. Berry, *The Child*, 4.
92. Ibid., 8.

Growing awareness of the child as victim engendered the growth of a public discourse focused on the need to protect children. Arguably, there is a correlation within the twenty-first-century context which confers a necessarily high profile to the protection of children from adult abuse and the need to protect adult society from terrorist attack. In the context of nineteenth-century empire, the colonized become those in need of protection and education. Walvin records that in 1841, one third of the entire population in England were under the age of fourteen. In the cities, homeless children congregated together. They became increasingly difficult to ignore as their numbers grew.[93] Ashcroft maintains that the trope of the child both, "absorbed and suppressed the contradiction of the imperial discourse,"[94] referring to the equation of the child as colonial subject, but his comment is equally applicable to the contradiction in representations of the child in the domestic context. The contrast between the child within the wealthy family and the orphan who was shipped to the colonies forms a concrete example of "the contradiction of imperial discourse." Walvin notes another connection between the concept of the child as victim and the exploited colonial subject in his observation that the factory child was often compared to the slave of the New World.[95] The purity of the Romantic child illustrated visually and verbally as clean, healthy, innocent, and in need of protection from the adult world, represents the binary opposite to the construction of the child as victim. The reality of child poverty and child exploitation discussed by James Kincaid in his examination of the complexity of adult responses to the child, addresses this opposition, emphasizing the place of adult power and control over the child.[96] In terms of literary representation, an example of the knowing child can be found in MacDonald's depiction of Nanny, the crossing sweeper befriended by Diamond during his first journey with North Wind. Nanny addresses Diamond, "What *do* you do, then? ... You ain't big enough for most things" and continues, "I can't think how a kid like you comes to be out all alone this time o' the night." The narrator commentates, "She had called him a *kid*, but she was not really a month older than he was; only she had to work for her bread, and that so soon makes

93. Walvin, *A Child's World*, 18–19.
94. Ashcroft, *Primitive and Wingless*, 184.
95. Walvin, *A Child's World*, 52.
96. Kincaid, *Child-Loving*, 71–95.

people older."⁹⁷ Walvin observes, "For poor children the innocence of infancy—of not knowing—was soon stripped away by exposure to the realities of their crowded, exploited and often sordid environment."⁹⁸ Significantly, Nanny's precocity imposes a limitation on her imagination. She cannot comprehend what Diamond is talking about when he tells her about North Wind and responds, "I think you must ha' got out o' one o' them Hidget Asylums."⁹⁹ Diamond, although working class himself, comes from a home where he is valued as a child and allowed a childhood. He symbolizes the Romantic child who is in touch with the divine, in touch with the world of the imagination and is able to integrate both the spiritual and the imaginative into his own world and the world of the adults whose lives he touches.

Boas notes that the educational theorist Johann Pestalozzi (1746–1827) believed that one of the most significant innate traits of the child was faith and that the existence of God was listed by both the English Platonists and René Descartes (1596–1650) as one of the primary unlearned ideas of the soul.¹⁰⁰ MacDonald's representation of the Romantic child, for example in the characters of Diamond, Clare Skymer and Gilbert Galbraith, always displays a higher level of faith than any of the adults around him. Paradoxically, these "poetic children," represented as being spiritually and imaginatively aware, are also regarded as being, "wise beyond their years," but instead of being in need of corrective education from the adult world, they have, "'something to teach the adult.'"¹⁰¹ There are occasions when such children teach the adult world by their manner of sickness and dying. Higonnet notes, "the image of the Romantic child is haunted by death . . . (they) have something profoundly in common with Madonna and Child images, though secular. . . . Both image types lament the sacrifice of the child."¹⁰² The character of Diamond is an example of this haunting. His death at the end of *At the Back of the North Wind* is an inevitability, since his tenuous hold on the physical world is precisely what enables his understanding of the reality of the spiritual and imaginative world. Sarah Maier cites

97. MacDonald, *At the Back*, 45, 49.
98. Walvin, *A Child's World*, 15.
99. MacDonald, *At the Back*, 49
100. Boas, *The Cult of Childhood*, 36.
101. McGillis, *Childhood and Growth*, 164.
102. Higgonet, *Pictures of Innocence*, 30.

the death of Diamond as, "a clear indication of MacDonald's belief in death as more life,"[103] a central concept derived from Dante Alighieri (1265–1321) and stated clearly in MacDonald's shorter tale *The Golden Key* (1867). In Mossy's encounter with the Old Man of the Sea, the Old Man asks Mossy a question, "You have tasted death now," said the Old Man. "Is it good?" "It is good," said Mossy. "It is better than life." "No," said the Old Man: "it is only more life."[104]

Both the construct of the child as victim in need of protection and that of the Romantic child engendered the artistic representation of the child with "messianic potential."[105]

The Redemptive Child: the Hero who Saves

"The child is not meant to die but to be forever fresh-born."[106]

In MacDonald's collection of sermons *The Hope of the Gospel* (1892) he writes, "For God is not only the Father of the child, but of the childhood that constitutes him a child, therefore the childness is of the divine nature."[107] MacDonald's exposition of the divine in the child takes this concept beyond the Romantic view of the ideal child who is closer to God and molds it into a cohesive theology of the child that can be traced through MacDonald's imaginative stories. Characters who achieve and retain this childlikeness can be found in George MacDonald's Clare Skymer (*A Rough Shaking*) whose spirituality matures through suffering; Gilbert Galbraith (*Sir Gibbie*) who retains his purity of motive throughout the story; Rosamond (*The Wise Woman*), who rediscovers her child self under the tutelage of the Wise Woman and thereby "saves" her parents; Diamond (*At the Back of the North Wind*), who dies before he reaches youth and adulthood; and ultimately, in the child who is "the oldest man of all", the Old Man of the Fire (*The Golden Key*). In MacDonald's adult novel, *Paul Faber: Surgeon* (1879), the Polwarths retain their childlike goodness despite deformity and also retain their physical link to childhood in their diminutive stature. In the eyes of Juliet, Faber's wife, who

103. Maier, *Romanticising and Fantasising*, 121.
104. MacDonald, *Golden Key*, 211.
105. Vloeberghs, *Constructions*, 72.
106. MacDonald, *Princess and Curdie*, 23.
107. MacDonald, *Hope of the Gospel*, 58.

is initially unable to see beyond appearances, Polwarth, "appeared one of the kobolds of German legend." Finding that Polwarth's conversation is deeply thoughtful and spiritually insightful, her response is, "What a peculiar goblin it is!"[108] Juliet is unable to reconcile Polwarth's appearance with his childlike nature. The contradiction she perceives between his internal and external self, echoes the confusion of Victorian society in its anxiety about the possibility of downward evolution, or degeneration. The fear of a degenerating underclass identified particularly with the urban poor is graphically depicted in MacDonald's *The Princess and the Goblin* (1883) and is discussed more fully in chapter 6. In his novel *Paul Faber: Surgeon*, MacDonald clouds the evolutionary issue in the characters of Polwarth and his niece, who, appearing physically goblin-like to Juliet, are mentally and spiritually more highly evolved than those people around them who are not only better educated but also of a higher social standing and more physically beautiful by the standards of their contemporary society. By introducing characters such as the Polwarths who chime with contemporary Darwinian preoccupations, MacDonald creates questions that turn accepted societal norms upside down as he "demonstrates that society as it existed was based on false and artificial values."[109] In so doing, MacDonald elevates childlike goodness to a redemptive level. Characters who possess such goodness unwittingly bring redemption into the lives of those with whom they came into contact. The reform of the drunken cabman after an encounter with Diamond at night provides an example of such redemptive activity.[110]

In the context of empire, the childlike hero is represented as able to elevate the understanding of the colonized. Both MacDonald and Henty contain examples which illustrate this point. In MacDonald's novel *David Elginbrod* (1863), David's daughter Margaret represents the role of redeeming women, who, by their hold on the childlike retain their hold on the divine and thereby "save" their men by bringing them into touch with the divine.[111] In *The Princess and the Goblin* and *The Princess and Curdie*, the inspiration for Irene's retention of, and Curdie's return to, childlike goodness, finds its source in the ageless Grandmother. She echoes the Old Man of the Fire in her ancient goodness and has

108. MacDonald, *Paul Faber*, 295, 97.
109. Zipes, *When Dreams*, 125.
110. MacDonald, *At the Back*, 177–84.
111. See Elliott, *The Angel*.

been variously interpreted as, for example, God, Nature and Wisdom.[112] The relation of the young child to extreme age in MacDonald's stories demonstrates the cyclical nature of mythical time,[113] even whilst it intersects with linear time, as it does in MacDonald's adult novels.

The child as savior to the parent is also present in Henty's work. This child's youthful activities are primarily literal and physical but include such abstract concepts as the re-ignition of hope and re-introduction into life after a "burying" or "death" in prison. Dick Holland (*The Tiger of Mysore*) exemplifies this redemptive quality. Henty's stories, narrated in linear historical time also demonstrate cyclical, mythical time in their repeated pattern of "success" and "homecoming." Both Rosamond (*The Wise Woman*) and Dick (*The Tiger of Mysore*) are entrusted with a mission to save their respective parents. The extension of situational redemption brought to the adult via the ideal child demonstrates a progression in the nineteenth-century concept of the child. Juliet Carron expands the idea, in her study *The Role of the Child as a Route to Spiritual Reality: A Jungian Approach*. Carron situates the child as an archetype rather than as a construct so that the child is the "bringer of protection and salvation." She concludes that although the child is a construct of adults, this construct stems from the unconscious process which regards the image of the child as, "an inherent and necessary ingredient for adult wholeness,"[114] or, as McGillis notes, "For MacDonald, . . . childhood is a state of being which everyone must aspire to."[115] Don King defines George MacDonald's meaning of the word "childlike" more specifically, as including traits of humility or innocence which lead to selflessness and unpretentiousness, awe in the sense of not being dismissive of the seemingly impossible but being delighted by it; and longing, . . . a yearning for something more, a something beyond ourselves and everyday experience, [116]something that in G. K. Chesterton's terms would make, "all existence a fairy tale."[117] Novalis, whose work influenced MacDonald, personifies the undefined awareness of a longing for goodness beyond oneself in Heinrich von Ofterdingen's search for

---

112. See for example Hayward, *The Mystical Sophia*.
113. Discussed in Nikolajeva, *From Mythic*.
114. Carron, *Role of the Child*, 13, 494.
115. McGillis, *Childhood and Growth*, 152.
116. King, *The Childlike*, 17–18.
117. Chesterton, *Introduction*, 9.

the blue flower[118] and C. S. Lewis, in his autobiography, defines this longing as "joy,"[119] demonstrating a chain of influence from Novalis through MacDonald to Lewis[120] deriving from the Romantic emphasis on the imaginative and the spiritual. MacDonald's non-fiction writing consistently records his thinking on the connection between the childlike and the divine.[121]

The character North Wind, a female figure who also exhibits the childlike qualities MacDonald associates with the agelessness of eternity, demonstrates her "childlike" faith in her unquestioning obedience. In the passage including the storm at sea, already mentioned in chapter 3, MacDonald expands on a tenet of Bernadin de Saint Pierre that states, "whoever follows nature will be happy and virtuous, a tenet commented on by Boas, who writes, 'Should one object that a storm at sea is as natural as a sunny day, the answer I suppose, would be that the word "natural" includes the meaning "beneficent.""[122] MacDonald locates the redemptive qualities of the child, both Diamond and the childlike in North Wind herself, within a divine context that transcends both of them. When North Wind tells Diamond, "I do not exactly know where it [the song she hears] is, or what it means"[123] she locates the sound of the song in the context of agelessness and timelessness, that is, eternity, and her hearing it is dependent upon her obedience to do the work she is given in her character as North Wind. The eventual outcome of her work she must leave in the eternal dimension. This is the same mystery found by Tangle in her encounter with the Old Man of the Earth who constantly rearranges a set of colored balls and thereby links the earth to eternity. In *The Golden Key*, the Old Man of the Earth, the oldest and wisest man of all, appears to Tangle in the shape of a small child, for as MacDonald writes, "He who will be a man, and will not be a child, must–he cannot help himself–become a little man, that is, a dwarf. He

---

118. See note in Novalis and Versluis, *Pollen and Fragments*, 14. See also the novel based on the life of Friedrich von Hardenberg (1772–1801) before he became known as Novalis, Fitzgerald, *The Blue Flower*.

119. Lewis, *Surprised by Joy*.

120. The influence of Novalis on MacDonald is well documented by for example, MacDonald, Raeper and Hein. Lewis himself acknowledged his debt to MacDonald in *Surprised by Joy* (1959) and in *George MacDonald: an Anthology* (1946).

121. MacDonald, *Unspoken Sermons*, 13, for example.

122. Boas, *Cult of Childhood*, 35.

123. MacDonald, *At the Back*, 77.

will however, need no consolation, for he is sure to think himself a very large creature indeed."[124] As ever, MacDonald measured the stature of a person in spiritual terms. The development of the position of the child, both internal and external, in this chapter is integral to the emergence of the hero figure located in the writing of Henty and MacDonald. Their interpretation of the construct of the hero is discussed in the next chapter.

---

124. MacDonald, *Fantastic Imagination*, 322,

5

The Construct of the Hero 1850–1900

"The history of heroes is the history of Youth"[1]

THIS QUOTATION FROM BENJAMIN Disraeli's *Coningsby* indicates the connection between the cultural view of the child and the cultural view of the hero through the construct of the adolescent boy in the nineteenth century. The youthful hero served to bridge the gap between the domestic scene and the "wide world." In Victorian England (1837–1900), the "wide world" correlated with colonial interests, and "Heroes have their importance for the history of culture because they . . . provide a useful index of [an age's] values."[2] Also, in Walter Houghton's discussion on hero-worship, he observes that hero-worship, "answered, or it promised to answer, some of the deepest needs and problems of the age."[3] Houghton's discussion defines "the age" as 1830–70, but includes the last thirty years of the nineteenth century since they fell within the reign of Queen Victoria. His reference to, "the needs and problems of the age" relates to the uncertainty created by the rapid change induced by industrial development and its impact on the external environment, and the doubt engendered by new theological and scientific thinking in the internal, the spiritual and intellectual, environment. These upheavals have been appraised in chapter 2 on historical context. The loss of familiar

---

1. Disraeli, *Coningsby*, 99.
2. Burns and Reagan, *Concepts of the Hero*, 120.
3. Houghton, *Victorian Frame*, 310.

certainties in every area of life, including the loss of religious belief, led to a loss of confidence and a tendency to view the concept of "hero" as a source of "inspiration and escape."[4] The image of the hero held the Victorian imagination, acting as an example for emulation and as an inspirational ideal. The ambiguity of the concepts "inspiration" and "escape," used together, reflects the paradoxes of the period and demonstrates that interweaving of fantasy and reality which prompted Disraeli to describe the period as one of "fairy tale."

The renewed interest in medievalism preoccupying the Pre-Raphaelites produced art and literature that not only reinvented an idealized version of a past age, but also believed a version of it could be created in the present. As a protest against the perceived disintegration of contemporary society the concept of the ideal hero found expression in, for example, the reprinting of the Arthurian legends and other stories of warrior heroes such as Roland and Beowulf. The "traditional heroic values," meaning in this context, those values found in the persona of the medieval knight, who represented "personal strength and achievement," values which, as Burns and Reagan understatedly note, "imperfectly agreed with Christian values."[5] The movement away from the medieval warrior hero towards the concept of the Miles Christianus, the warrior-saint, unites the later medieval concept of devotion to Christ, found in the fictional account of Sir Gawain, with the earlier warrior, and points forward towards the humanist concept of the hero which emphasizes the public man who incorporates the classical virtue of service and domesticity into his persona. The addition of the characteristic of Christian devotion rather than the loss of warrior attributes indicates a change of focus in the hero, a greater spiritual awareness. The Victorians perceived such heroism in the person of, for example, General Gordon (1833–85).[6]

A fusion of the physical and the spiritual is a key to the hero figure in both Henty and MacDonald. Their work creates a complementary image of two emphases which reflect the preoccupation with colonial power and devotion to service which focused attention on social and spiritual improvement, and education. These two emphases, the one complementing the other, can be illustrated by the figure of an image in

---

4. Ibid., 332.
5. Burns and Reagan, *Concepts of the Hero*, vii, 125.
6. For information on General Gordon see Waller, *Gordon of Khartoum*.

a mirror. The figure is one and the same but the aspect is different. For example, the classical and adventure hero (physical) is complemented by the fairy tale hero (the imagined/spiritual). These two images meet in the contextual construction of the "Victorian" hero who displays characteristics both physical and spiritual, and who, as an ideal, is in the realm of the imagined. The constructed hero occupies, "the space of fantasy in which cultural contradictions reside."[7] From "the space of fantasy," the hero is positioned to occupy both physical and psychological spaces represented as exotic, domestic and internal landscapes.

Writing in the late fifteenth and early sixteenth centuries, Erasmus (1466–1536), constructed the hero figure incorporating both humanist and Christian, or "saintly," characteristics. The consequent hero emerges as, "the unromantic private citizen,"[8] concerned with the betterment of society in terms of social involvement. In contrast to the medieval concept of the warrior-hero, he appears anti-heroic, a peace-time hero condemning war as destructive to the public/domestic sphere of life. This "unromantic private citizen" is later resurrected in Thomas Carlyle's "sincere man," who is the hero as "everyman." He is both human and ideal, both real and imagined.

This overview shows that the Victorians constructed their hero figure against a background of medievalism and classicism. Whilst emphasizing progress in terms of the role of the period in the evolution of society and human development in Darwinian language, the Victorians reach back to earlier ages, seeking inspiration to bring meaning to their contemporary situation. Whilst rejecting so many traditional beliefs and values, they clung to the concept of heroism as a source of stability and a focus for action, and published Augustus Comte's *New Calendar of Great Men* (1892) as a values reference. In his article on the disappearing Victorian hero, George Levine includes discussion on the different views of Carlyle and John Stuart Mill. Levine concludes that although they are coming from opposite directions, Carlyle and Mill meet on the point of the importance of individual character and individual development,

> ... denying fashionable conventions, yet accepting the best authority. Such acceptance depends upon strong individual personality and deep feelings and desires. To get in touch with the better self, buried in Arnoldian manner in the midst of the ordinary

7. Marshall, *Psychoanalyzing*, 1212.
8. Burns and Reagan, *Concepts of the Hero*, 136.

and the banal, to achieve the Goethean ideal of self-development, self-culture, self-expression, one needs to be stronger than most. ... Mill ... seeks the strongest possible self. ... But for Carlyle, too, the development of individuality, the unfolding of each person's intrinsic nature, seems to be the primary aim of life.[9]

I note here that "the best authority" is not defined by Levine in this passage, but the values implied by "best" in this context form another avenue of exploration and follow the pattern of those values implicit in the Victorian construct of the hero in a leadership role. Romance and folk tale convention produced an interweaving of narrative expectation which supported the hierarchical structure of society whilst potentially subverting it by a literary reflection of the upheavals and possible class mobility that characterized nineteenth-century England. Carlyle's theory that everyman can be a hero, translated into practice by Smilesian self-help, and was directly linked to imperialist intent by Smiles when he wrote, "the unflinching self-reliance and dormant heroism of the English race [was demonstrated in the response to the rebellion in India]. In that terrible trial, all proved almost equally great–women, civilians, and soldiers ..."[10] The emphasis on individualism points to another paradox in the construct of the hero, that of Smilesian "unflinching self-reliance" and the emphasis within the concept of the Arnoldian public school boy on the team player.

The Hero-Figure as Exemplar in G. A. Henty and George MacDonald

The hero, theorized by Thomas Carlyle, was a dominant influence on the nineteenth-century English mind-set but the constructs of the heroes he presented were drawn from wider, if mainly western, sources. His lecture series *On Heroes and Hero Worship* fuelled the propensity of the Victorians to focus their need for stability on both historical and contemporary figures whom they could elevate to ideals. It is as though the rationale for virtue written by Sir Philip Sidney in 1581 became the rationale for the Victorian emphasis on the efficacy of emulation, "For as the image of each action styrreth and instructeth the mind, so the loftie image of such worthies most inflameth the mind with the desire to be

---

9. Levine, *Not Like My Lancelot*, 59.
10. Smiles, *Self-Help*, 21.

worthy."[11] This anticipated emulation, as much as his stated intention to teach history, was Henty's motivation for writing his stories.

Henty's two major purposes for his writing were stated in the prefaces to his books. Henty's first purpose was to "interest the reader because of the characteristic English pluck and daring of its hero"[12] and the second was to interest his readers in history. I will focus on the first purpose in examining Henty's construct of the Victorian hero. As is the case with other such general descriptive terms, the term "Victorian hero" is popularly understood to portray a character or concept. In the same way as the term "Victorian" is used to portray a number of undefined characteristics, the term "Victorian hero" is simplistic, but it is a starting point for discussion. Henty addresses his readers directly, as the following examples from *Condemned as a Nihilist* (1893), and *Sturdy and Strong* (1888) show. In the preface to *Condemned as a Nihilist* (1893) he writes, "There are few difficulties that cannot be surmounted by patience, resolution and pluck,"[13] and in *Sturdy and Strong* (1888), "for success in life it is necessary not only to be earnest, steadfast, and true, but to have the faculty of turning every opportunity to the best advantage; ... steadiness, perseverance, and determination to get on would assuredly have made their way in the long run. If similar qualities and similar determination are yours, you need not despair of similar success in life."[14] The heroes of these stories demonstrate such qualities. That Henty anticipated reader identification with his hero is supported by an article in *Answers*, Christmas Double Number, December 13th, 1902 in which he notes, "of course the hero must be British," and he points out that his stories with non-English heroes had not sold as well as his other books."[15] "The ethically formative power of story" is discussed by Marshall Gregory, in an article in which he asserts that "identifying with characters in stories can exert a powerful influence on the quality and content of our own lives."[16]

In the nineteenth century, the view that regarded emulation as beneficial accorded with the intellectual influence of positivist thought

11. Sidney, *Defence of Poesie*, 73.
12. Henty, *Young Colonists*, Preface.
13. Henty, *Condemned as a Nihilist* Preface.
14. Henty, *Sturdy and Strong*, 3, iv.
15. Henty, *Writing for Boys*, 105.
16. Gregory, *Ethical Criticism*, 206, 194.

and with Carlyle's emphasis on the hero as "great man." Henty assumes reader identification with a character and consciously endeavors to create a protagonist in his stories with whom his intended audience can identify. In this way Henty's emphasis on and encouragement of identification with the hero figure is embedded in his historical context and the need of Victorian society for hero figures. Maria Nikolajeva challenges the assumption that readers will identify with a character, usually the protagonist. Citing the "literary-didactic split", Nikolajeva argues that readers who reject "the fixed subject position imposed on them by the text," display a higher degree of literary competence than those who unquestioningly identify with the protagonist. Nikolajeva supplies instances where conclusive and singular identification of the protagonist may be open to question where, for example, "the text allows a variety of subject positions," or where a complex single character, displaying contradictory traits, requires the reader to empathise without the need to identify. The position of the reader in relation to both the narrator and the main character, or characters where there are "a variety of subject positions," is as observer. As a mature reader he is able to adopt a position that allows examination of the character rather than identification. Nikolajeva states that the reader's "subject position will thus be neither tied to [the character] nor to the narrator, but rather emerge from an active, dialogical response to what the narrator tells [the reader] and what [he] can infer [himself or herself]."[17]

In the majority of Henty's stories, the hero holds a prominent position within the text and demonstrates subjectivity and agency in that he is both acted on and he acts. In the initial chapters of those stories critiqued as "typically' Henty,"[18] by, for example Guy Arnold (1980), Patrick Dunae (1975), Martin Green (1980), Marjorie Hourihan (1997), Robert Huttenback (1965), and Hugh Walpole (1926), the hero is constructed as subject by circumstances outside of his control but which place him in the position of agent, in which his own choice of action dictates his subsequent progress. This pattern fits both the adventure and the fairy tale hero. Henty indicates that he is also aiming to fill a

---

17. Nikolajeva, *The Identification Fallacy*, 2, 6.

18. "Typically Henty" in the sense that they demonstrate the formulaic structure of the orphaned (or apparently orphaned) hero who travels to an exotic location to meet adventure and make his fortune. Examples include *By Sheer Pluck* (1884), *For Name and Fame* (1886), and *Through the Sikh War* (1894).

gap by providing more adventure and less moralizing than, according to Bernard Davin, writing in 1932, "the earlier pioneers," of adventure stories.[19] In the Preface to *The Young Buglers* (1880) Henty writes, "I remember that, as a boy, I regarded any attempt to mix instruction with amusement as being as objectionable a practice as the administration of powder in jam; but I think this feeling arose from the fact that in those days books contained a very small share of amusement and a very large share of instruction." He continues, "I have endeavoured to avoid this."[20] Whilst Henty's educative purpose was conscious and overt, he recognized that enjoyment was an important part of successful education.

Writing in the periodical *Boys of Our Empire* in praise of Henty just after his death, Robert Leighton[21] states, "He was a teacher as well as an influence."[22] Despite their popularity, both Henty and MacDonald sought to avoid personal adulation. An article on Henty in *The Gem*, December 16, 1899, states, "No living writer of books for boys and girls is more widely popular.... His [Henty's] sympathy with the young and earnest desire to inspire them with noble aims ... is apparent in all he writes."[23] MacDonald, faced with two adult autograph collectors following one of his lectures, also "firmly declined" to supply their request for the famous autograph.[24] That both authors refused to encourage a focus on themselves supports their construct of heroism that stems from behavior, and not perceived status.

George MacDonald was less explicit in his purpose to provide a protagonist for emulation, but everything he wrote depicted the journey of a person or persons towards maturity. Although MacDonald, "said nothing of *mission* nor of *message*," his second son Ronald cites his awareness that "having been driven ... to give up the professional pulpit, he was no less impelled than compelled to use unceasingly the new platform whence he had found his voice could carry so far."[25] This educative

19. Davin, *School for Heroes*, 11–12.

20. Henty, *Young Buglers*, Preface.

21. Robert Leighton (1858–1934) was a prolific story writer and the father of Clare Leighton (1899–1989) wood engraver. I am indebted to Dr. Nicholas Hawkes for this information.

22. Leighton, *George Alfred Henty*, 224.

23. *A Favourite*, 209.

24. *George MacDonald*, 25.

25. MacDonald, *From a Northern*, 23, 33.

intention applied equally to his adult and to his children's writing. In MacDonald's work the emphasis is on moral and spiritual maturity. The development of a character towards "goodness" is described by Naomi Lewis as, "the shining power of innocence,"[26] and in a brief discussion of MacDonald's novels, C. S. Lewis noted, "One rare, and all but unique, merit these novels must be allowed. The 'good' characters are always the best and most convincing. His saints live; his villains are stagey."[27]

I have already noted, from an educational point of view, MacDonald's philosophy was one of "leading forth and not stuffing in," a line of thought which derives from Romantic theories of the child. When MacDonald writes "Everyone, however, who feels the story, will read it after his own nature and development,"[28] he demonstrates a process towards maturation and the exercise of the developing imagination. Frye describes this process in his discussion on the movement of a child toward critiquing his own experience in his reading. Frye notes, "the child should not 'believe' the story he is told; he should not disbelieve it either, but send out imaginative roots into that mysterious world between the 'is' and the 'is not' which is where his own ultimate freedom lies."[29]

In MacDonald's terms this process applies to, "the child of five or fifty or seventy-five,"[30] since the reader's process of maturation is leading toward the ultimate goal of childlikeness, or "childness," found in God. In his story *Gutta Percha Willie* (1873) MacDonald discusses the discovery approach to education through his account of Willie's learning style in chapter 2, acknowledging after his description of how Willie learnt to read, "Now I am not very sure how this would work with some boys and girls. . . . But it worked well in Willie's case, who was neither lazy nor idle."[31] MacDonald indicates the need for a particular attitude within the individual before intellectual education can properly begin. In his published essay *The Fairy Tale in Education* (n.d.) Greville MacDonald expands on the need for a fundamentally imaginative attitude to the world since, he argues, imaginative hope and wonder are kept alive by

---

26. Lewis, *Children's Books*, 693.
27. Lewis, *George MacDonald*, 18.
28. MacDonald, *Fantastic Imagination*, 316.
29. Frye, *Secular Scripture*, 166.
30. MacDonald, *Fantastic Imagination*, 317.
31. MacDonald, *Gutta Percha Willie*, 7–8.

fairy tale in the face of educational systems which encourage, "the very antithesis of that spontaneity, . . . which, . . . finds expression in art for the hidden mystic life."[32] Greville's emphasis on the priority of imaginative, moral and spiritual development reflects that of his father, George MacDonald, and echoes Samuel Coleridge's appeal to the imaginative and spiritual.

Both Henty and MacDonald regarded experience as a better educator than study in the molding of character, a position noted by McGillis in a discussion of *The Princess and Curdie* (1883), "Curdie, like all of MacDonald's protagonists, learns more through experience than through book learning."[33] MacDonald's story *The Wise Woman* (1875), critiqued by Reis as too overtly didactic, demonstrates the values towards which the protagonists may work, should they so choose, in order to become fit for emulation. *The Wise Woman* establishes MacDonald's position on character formation, with the implication that his child readers (of any age) should aspire to the reformed Rosamond. For example MacDonald writes, "Nobody can be a real princess . . . until she is a princess over herself, that is, until, when she finds herself unwilling to do the thing that is right, she makes herself do it."[34] According to Gerard Genette's theoretical terms of narratorial position[35] MacDonald's narrative commentary in *The Wise Woman* (1875) demonstrates the extradiegetic-heterodiegetic pattern of narration in his interpretation of the Wise Woman's treatment of Rosamond and Agnes. Joanna Golden comments, "these interpretations are necessary because the hero needs them as a lesson for his development; he requires chastisement and guidance if he is to become a hero."[36] MacDonald's narratorial comments to the reader explain the element of choice open to both Rosamond and Agnes. The Wise Woman provides both chastisement and guidance. The choice as to whether the chastisement and guidance are accepted lies with Rosamond and Agnes, just as Carlyle and Smiles place the choice of progression toward heroic behaviour with the individual. By including such commentary as the quotation above on one of the characteristics of a real princess, MacDonald broadens his commentary to include the

32. MacDonald, *The Fairy Tale*, 7.
33. McGillis, *George MacDonald's Princess Books*, 157.
34. MacDonald, *Wise Woman*, 109.
35. Genette, *Narrative Discourse*, 248.
36. Golden, *Narrative Symbol*, 61.

reader. The comment is not only directly linked to Rosamond but in its use of the word "nobody" extends its range of application to "anybody," to "everyman" or in this case, "everywoman." It is applicable to Carlyle's "dullest day drudge" who "longs . . . to do true and noble things."[37]

Henty frequently emphasizes the superiority of experience over study in the development of his hero's character even when his hero makes use of his study to help him through a difficult situation. An example of this self-subversion has already been noted and is expanded in the passage from *Condemned as a Nihilist*. Whilst in solitary confinement in prison, "Godfrey did his best to keep up his spirits. He had learnt by heart at Shrewsbury the first two books of the Iliad, and these he daily repeated aloud, set himself equations to do, and solved them in his head, repeated dates in Greek history, and went through everything he could remember as having learned."[38]

The Henty hero begins his story from a morally advantaged position compared to Rosamond and Agnes in MacDonald's *The Wise Woman*. His early upbringing always includes at least one parent or other significant adult who teaches him to "act right and straight and honourable . . . to be a good man and a gentleman."[39] Both Henty and MacDonald consciously construct heroes from a Christian moral base, heroes who provide leadership within their social context from a moral perspective. I use the word moral here as defined by Geoffrey Galt Harpham as, "some rule that overrides the confusion of customs, habits, norms, some principle that legitimates action even in the absence of clear rules or unanimous consensus." Harpham continues, "without morality, one could never be a hero, just a dissenter, a loner, and oddball."[40] Harpham's observation places the hero figure within his societal norm but also encompasses the Carlylean concept of the leader as set apart in his ability to act from a position of principle even when it is not in step with the prevailing behavior. The perceived innate superiority of the hero figure reflects the Victorian need for morally upright heroes to emulate. The time has come to discuss the influences that feed into the makeup of this hero.

---

37. Carlyle, *On Heroes*, 70.
38. Henty, *Condemned as a Nihilist*, 78.
39. Henty, *For Name and Fame*, 33.
40. Harpham, *Shadows of Ethics*, 259.

Influences on the Nineteenth-Century Construct of the Hero

In his novel *Westward Ho!* (1855), Charles Kingsley addresses the dedication to The Rajah Sir James Brooke, K.C.B. and George Augustus Selwyn, Bishop of New Zealand. He offers a story, in which he aims to present, "That type of English virtue, at once manful and godly, practical and enthusiastic, prudent and self-sacrificing."[41] Kinglsey's implication here is that Brooke and Selwyn embody the virtues mentioned. Kingsley also links these qualities to the Elizabethan worthies in whose time his story is set, but Kingsley's character is a Victorian construct drawn from a wider range of sources. Kingsley's dedication encapsulates a number of characteristics included in the ideal Victorian hero. I approach these characteristics by investigating the classical, active, adventure, flawed, gendered, and fairy tale hero, categories chosen for the following reasons. The classical, active, adventure and fairy tale represent constructs from history and literature that influenced the Victorian construct of the hero. The category of flawed hero is not expected in the hero figure of the nineteenth century boy's adventure story, particularly in the stereotypical Henty hero, although he is a recognizable figure in MacDonald's adult writing. In order to present a balanced view of the stereotypical boy hero, instances of female heroism in Henty's work are included and characteristics of MacDonald's female heroes are mapped to the characteristics of the Victorian construct of heroism. The hero as victim or outsider is not prominent in Henty's stories, although MacDonald's Diamond in *At the Back of the North Wind* (1871) and Claire Skymer in *A Rough Shaking* (1893) partially demonstrate this character's position.

The Classical Hero

"In those cultures where moral thinking and action is structured according to some version of the scheme I have called classical, the chief means of moral education is the telling of stories."[42]

In this quotation Alistair MacIntyre refers to Greek, medieval, and Renaissance cultures, all of which have influenced the development of Western thought and were part of Henty's and MacDonald's mental landscape. Having studied Latin and Greek at school, as did all pub-

---

41. Kingsley, *Westward Ho!*, Dedication.
42. MacIntyre, *After Virtue*, 121.

lic school boys of his time, Henty was familiar with the classical hero as he is represented in classical literature. MacDonald, educated in Scotland, still needed tuition which would familiarize him with classical languages and literature in order to progress to Aberdeen University. In MacIntyre's discussion of Aristotelian ethics, he notes that in classical, heroic societies, morality and the social structure cannot be divided.[43] Since there is no discrimination between the social and the political, the heroic is inextricably linked with activity in the public sphere of life, that is, how a person lives in society. According to MacIntyre, the foundation of all other virtues in this context is courage. Linked to courage are reliability, faithfulness, honesty, friendship, self-restraint, wisdom, and justice, without which the fifth-century Greeks believed public order could not be sustained. In Henty's story *By Sheer Pluck* (1884), the protagonist Frank Hargate chooses to take his place in society as a doctor even though he has made his fortune and "He worked hard and steadily and passed with high honours."[44] Other heroes, such as Percy Groves (*Through the Sikh War*, 1894) pursue careers as members of parliament. Both Henty and MacDonald emphasize the need for courage in any situation, whether in the martial or the public sphere of life. "Courage," wrote Harvey S. Ford, "was (Henty's) keynote." Ford quotes Henty's assertion, "that if not in itself the very highest of virtues, courage is the parent of almost all the others, since but a few of them can be practiced without it."[45]

MacDonald regarded courage as essentially a spiritual virtue, a statement confirmed in the last paragraph of *Phantastes* (1858) where his protagonist Anodos observes, "Yet I know that good is coming to me—that good is always coming; though few have at all times the simplicity and the courage to believe it."[46] In his inclusion of "simplicity" in this comment, MacDonald links the virtue of courage with childlike belief and thence to the ideal spirituality of the child displayed in his construct of the hero. The importance of courage and spirituality in MacDonald's thought is illustrated in the design of his bookplate which includes the motto, "Corage, God mend al" (Courage, God mend all), an anagram on his name.

43. Ibid., 123.
44. Henty, *By Sheer Pluck*, 352.
45. Ford, *G. A. Henty*, 269.
46. MacDonald, *Phantastes*, 320.

Figure 1: George MacDonald's bookplate[47]

In addition to the need for courage to live well in the public sphere, Plutarch's concept of the "great man" influenced the view of the heroic which has "directly helped to shape the concept of the heroic in European thinking," and Homer used the word "heroes" in reference to warriors who play a part in the action: their honour was, Russell notes, "the yardstick of every action." They were fully human, had leadership qualities and, "won contests of skill and bravery."[48] An example of this type of warrior hero can be found in Henty's *The Young Carthaginian* (1887). Malchus was the son of a soldier who trained him from boyhood to be ready for an anticipated war with Rome. Henty writes, "Malchus had been an apt pupil. . . . He could wield the arms of a man, could

---

47. Taken from personal copy of : MacDonald, *George MacDonald*, flyleaf.
48. Russell, *Plutarch*, 24.

swim the coldest river, endure hardship and want of food, traverse long distances at the top of his speed, could throw a javelin with unerring aim . . ."[49] Clearly physical prowess is an important component of the Henty hero figure, found not only in this example of Malchus, but in other works such as *The Tiger of Mysore* (1896), where Dick Holland's mother takes particular care to provide him with opportunities to become physically strong and active. Similarly in *With Kitchener in the Soudan* (1903), Gregory's mother encourages him to exercise in order to develop muscular strength, and in *A Soldier's Daughter* (1906) in which Nita's father ensures her ability to behave like a soldier when the need arises partly by developing her physical strength with boxing lessons. The character of Malchus includes all the attributes of the "Victorian" hero even though his story is set in ancient Carthage. Hugh Pruen notes, Henty heroes "are always the same–from Ancient Egypt to the Boxer Rebellion."[50] This statement is simplistic but holds for the majority of Henty protagonists. When A. S. Byatt observed that historical novelists "are trying to find historical paradigms for contemporary situations"[51] she could not have found a clearer example than that of Henty's presentation of Victorian England in the guise of ancient Carthage. Whilst Byatt's assertion refers to a conscious decision on the part of twentieth century historical novelists, Henty's depiction of the past was always in terms of his present. In Henty's story, Malchus' father Hamilcar comments on the decline of Carthage, but Hamilcar's observation reverberates with the contemporary Victorian fear that a similar decline could be observed in late Victorian Britain and reads as a warning of future events. Hamilcar comments, "It seems to be the fate of all nations, that as they grow in wealth so they lose their manly virtues. With wealth comes corruption, indolence, a reluctance to make sacrifices, and a weakening of the feeling of patriotism."[52] At the end of the story Malchus settles in his wife Clotilde's homeland, referred to by Henty both as Cisalpine Gaul and as Germany[53] another example of Henty's contemporizing of history. Since the political corruption of Carthage had prevented Malchus from returning to Carthage, his preferred option is to settle permanently

49. Henty, *Young Carthaginian*, 14.
50. Pruen, *Henty Companion*, 2.
51. Byatt, *On Histories*, 11.
52. Henty, *Young Carthaginian*, 38.
53. Ibid., 379, 83.

elsewhere, propagating the best of Carthaginian culture, including the virtues outlined above, in his new context. Malchus recreates an ideal homeland when the real one fails. Henty echoes the potential for such an outcome for the British Empire when he writes in the preface to *St. George for England* (1885), "The courage of our forefathers has created the greatest empire in the world around a small and in itself insignificant island; if this empire is ever lost, it will be by the cowardice of their descendants."[54]

Henty's connection of wealth and the decline of manly virtues which he depicts in terms of national greatness is echoed by MacDonald's relation of wealth and spiritual decline. In *The Princess and Curdie* (1883), MacDonald launches a powerful attack on his contemporary society in the form of a satirical "discourse" delivered by "the first priest of the great temple," a member of the clergy, to the people of Gwyntystorm, exposing attitudes commensurate with the materialism and preoccupation with wealth creation which MacDonald continually attacked in his adult novels. He writes, "the first priest chose his text; and his text was, *Honesty is the best policy*. . . . The main proof of the verity of their religion, he said, was, that things went well with those who professed it; and its first fundamental principle, grounded inborn invariable instinct, was that every One should take care of that One. . . . If everyone would but obey this law, number one, then would everyone be perfectly cared for—one being always equal to one." The "discourse" continues for another page until the legserpent, one of Curdie's animals, seized the first priest and, "dropped him into the dusthole amongst the remnants of a library whose age had destroyed its value in the eyes of the chapter. They found him burrowing in it, a lunatic henceforth—whose madness presented the peculiar feature, that in its paroxysms he jabbered sense."[55] Throughout the process of "cleansing" undertaken by Curdie and his helpers, both human and animal, Curdie displays the same characteristics found in the Henty hero in terms of leadership, courage, initiative, and physical strength.

A facet of character lacking in the classical hero, but present in the Victorian hero, is captured succinctly by D. A. Russell when he states that the Homeric hero is not "an officer and a gentleman."[56] The hero

54. Henty, *St George*, preface.
55. MacDonald, *Princess and Curdie*, 274–75, 276.
56. Russell, *Plutarch*, 25.

found in Henty's stories is "an officer and a gentleman," qualities which derive primarily from his middle or upper class position in society and his English public school education. The Henty hero adds the characteristics of "an officer and a gentleman" to those of the Homeric hero.

The Active hero

In her study *Deconstructing the Hero* (1997), Margery Hourihan states that the hero is above all things, "a man of action." The active hero whom Hourihan cites as representative of, "the intrepid British lad" found in the "flood of adventure stories" produced by "the age of imperialism."[57] Henty's stories are critically perceived[58] as prime contributions to this "flood." Hourihan associates the active hero (always male) exclusively with the glorification of violence as the definition of manhood. The active hero may be the most clearly analogous with the "Victorian hero" depicted by Michael Brander in his biography of Samuel White Baker, but the Victorian hero is too simplistic a description since the Victorians, although pre-occupied with heroism, held a variety of views, some of which have been discussed in a previous chapter. The composite construct of the Victorian hero renders him more complex than the simplistic description allows. The active hero of the Henty story includes the concepts of the muscular Christian, the Arnoldian boy, the English gentleman, everyman, and the leader of men. Masculinity, as advocated by F. D. Maurice and Charles Kingsley in the form of "'muscular Christianity," promoted physical exercise, "as a means of bodily purification and practical Christianity."[59] Kingsley advocated cricket on the basis that it encouraged respect, discipline and obedience to rules, but the Henty hero, although a competent games player, demonstrated by Frank Hargate in *By Sheer Pluck* (1884), showed his physical dominance when necessary, through the skill of boxing, an individual sport. MacDonald recognized the importance of physical fitness and his second son Ronald MacDonald notes MacDonald's personal competence as a boxer, "he was fond of boxing, a very quick hitter and clever with the gloves."[60] Ronald MacDonald's sentence reads like a description by Henty of one

57. Hourihan, *Deconsturcting the Hero*, 2–3.
58. For examples of critical assessment of Henty see Arnold, *Held Fast for England*, Carpenter and Pritchard, *Oxford Companion*, and Fisher, *Bright Face*.
59. Hignell, *Rain Stops Play*, 49.
60. MacDonald, *From a Northern Window*, 40.

of his own heroes, for example, "boxing gives quickness of thought, and doubtless improves the pose and figure."[61] Henty's observation appears in his story *A Soldier's Daughter* (1906) and refers to the heroine Nita's competency in boxing. This story also provides an instance of Henty subverting what is perceived as his stereotypical attitude to women. In *With the Allies to Pekin* (1904) Henty writes, "(boxing) develops self-reliance and quickness of eye . . . an Englishman who can box well is a match for any two foreigners knowing nothing of the art."[62] This premise is demonstrated in *Condemned as a Nihilist* (1893) when Godfrey fights with a Russian much bigger than himself but who does not have his skill in boxing.

There is some discrepancy between the active Victorian hero and the muscular Christian games player which needs clarification in relation to the construct of the Arnoldian boy, since the Victorian hero is noted for his initiative and independence of thought rather than his homogeneity. In his discussion on ideology, Dani Cavallaro notes Louis Althusser's theory that the "individual is transformed into a social being by ideology,"[63] with particular reference to cultural institutions. In the nineteenth century, one of those institutions was the English public school system developed by Thomas Arnold. The concept of the Arnoldian boy is recognizably present in the image of the Henty hero. He demonstrates "manly virtues" not only in terms of physical prowess but also by his truthfulness and unselfishness."[64] These two characteristics are always present in the persona of the Henty hero and are found in Frank Hargate of *By Sheer Pluck* (1884), who is noted as a cricketer who "played a steady rather than a brilliant game,"[65] and whose integrity and selflessness are unquestioned.[66]

In the ethos of the public school, the Arnoldian boy was trained to act in a team situation, to obey the team captain and present a united front. The embryonic hero present in the ideal Arnoldian team player was the character accused by Luigi Barzini of operating by a limited set of fixed ideas, inculcated by his schooling and from which he did not

61. Henty, *Soldier's Daughter*, 12.
62. Henty, *With the Allies*, 15.
63. Cavallaro, *Critical and Cultural theory*, 84.
64. Henty, *True Heroism*, 54.
65. Henty, *By Sheer Pluck*, 10.
66. See for example the episode described on pp. 54–64.

have the imagination to deviate.⁶⁷ This limited character does not correlate with the fundamental resourcefulness and the ability to act on his own initiative found in the Henty hero.

Samuel White Baker's biographer Michael Brander specifies, "he [S.W.B.] was always an individualist and never a team man."⁶⁸ The characteristics emphasized in this context are those of individualism, leadership in the sense of acting decisively on one's own initiative, and the ability to behave calmly in dangerous situations. The correlation Brander draws between Baker and the Henty hero demonstrates the versatility of that hero. He cannot be easily categorized because, as Arnold comments, "he is an ideal."⁶⁹ Henty's stated intention was to create a boy hero who could be "everyman" as well as the "conspicuous leader" cited by Niemeyer as integral to Carlyle's construct.⁷⁰ Henty's young heroes are, in Victorian terms, always gentlemen, a position that is revealed as the story progresses in those instances where the birth of the heroes is either surrounded by mystery or they are "lost" as young children. (The working class heroes, Jack Simpson, *Facing Death*, and George Andrews, *Sturdy and Strong*, become gentleman.) Hourihan comments, "the notoriously unstable signifier 'gentleman' usually suggests education and polite manners, but often implies an intellectual and moral superiority..."⁷¹ Henty's heroes incorporate all of these attributes. In MacDonald's heroes, such as Curdie, and Richard, the protagonist of *Cross Purposes* (1862), the characteristics of intellectual and moral superiority are emphasized. Both of them originate from a lower social class although they display the "middle class" characteristic of "polite manners," noted by Hourihan. I use the term Henty's "young" heroes in this instance since Henty frequently subverts his expected stereotype by casting the actual hero of the story in an unexpected role. By "actual" hero I refer to one who has shown the characteristics noted in this chapter consistently throughout the story but whose heroism is hidden within a secondary character, usually non-English. Examples can be found in Sam (*The Young Buglers*, 1880), Luka (*Condemned as a Nihilist*, 1893) and Stanislas (*A Jacobite Exile*, 1894). The technique of distributing

67. Barzini, *Impossible Europeans*, 53–54.
68. Brander, *Perfect Victorian Hero*, preface.
69. Arnold, *Held Fast for England*, 41.
70. Carlyle, *On Heroes*, xi.
71. Hourihan, *Deconsturcting the Hero*, 63.

characteristics across a number of characters differing in age, race and social position, "allows a variety of subject positions,"[72] and is a technique that focalizes a problem from different subjective viewpoints. In a Henty story, the solution to a problem can appear as the result of a discussion between the hero and another character, a situation which enables the hero to take the credit even when his companion has made most of the suggestions or even initiated the action. In Henty's work this other character is often the protagonist's companion in adventure or his servant, frequently one and the same. The examples given above in Sam, Luka and Stanislas, all of whom take the servant role, demonstrate the position of the alternative hero. Surajah in *The Tiger of Mysore* (1896), in his position as companion to Dick Holland, the Anglo-Indian hero, is not his social inferior.

The statement "The school as a place to explicitly train character was what came to distinguish the English public school from all other Western school systems"[73] is sweeping and general. Later educationalists, such as Erik Erikson (1902-94), a psychoanalyst whose work focused on social and emotional growth, emphasise the impossibility of mass producing a character type. Nevertheless, in the nineteenth century, a distinctive character type was associated with the English public school system and parodied by Barzini. The imperialist intent of the period 1850-1900 needed the construct of the youthful hero both to win and to administer the empire. The English focus on character in the development of educational opportunities outside of the public school system, allayed the fear of losing the empire through the degeneration of the nation's youth, and the production of literary heroes was founded on the belief that, "The young need to be prepared for life by being brought into contact with a world of exemplary characters in literature and culture."[74] Throughout her study, Hourihan notes the youthfulness of the hero in the context of the adventure story, designating adventure as a youthful activity and pursued in tandem with the adolescent process of self-discovery. MacDonald's emphasis on the process of individual spiritual and moral development is aptly described by John Pennington as "muscular spirituality,"[75] a theory, Pennington argues, developed in

72. Nikolajeva, *Identification Fallacy*, 5.
73. Arthur, *Education*, 14.
74. Ibid., 33.
75. Pennington, *Muscular Spirituality*, 133.

MacDonald's fiction in response to Darwinian theory and as an extension to the muscular Christian activism advocated by Maurice and Kingsley. MacDonald's emphasis on the need for inner, spiritual strength in order to undertake and fulfil one's journey and "adventure" is demonstrated in all of his work, but is most clearly exemplified in the Princess books in which Curdie conquers his inner wilderness of disbelief in Irene's Grandmother and gains the ability to discern the positions of other people on the evolutionary ladder of spiritual progress. MacDonald's emphasis on the spiritual, and Henty's emphasis on the physical journey, is not mutually exclusive. The "two realms" critiqued as parallel in the writing of MacDonald[76] are integral to the Victorian historical context. The spiritual dimension, encompassing the unconscious mind, the irrational or inexplicable in empiricist terms, and the providential in terms of fictional coincidence, is "the world of the heroic"[77] in MacDonald's work. Both authors provide heroes that, put together, create the longed-for ideal hero of Victorian aspiration, the physical complemented by the spiritual and vice versa.

The attributes of the culturally constructed Victorian boy hero, such as courage, truthfulness, support for the weak, and physical strength are equally present in MacDonald's Ranald in *Ranald Bannerman's Boyhood* (1871) and can be illustrated by specific episodes in the story. In *Ranald Bannerman's Boyhood* the emphasis lies in the hero as "everyman." William Raeper refers to this text as, "George MacDonald's boyhood translated into English." Raeper also notes that the Scottish character displays a dualism that enables the Scotsman to function within an English context without losing his Scottish cultural identity. He comments, "The Scots speak not one language but two—a refined English and a 'natural' Scots, for Scots remains the language of emotion and ancestry."[78] Having established the "everyman" emphasis, I will immediately qualify it by noting Ranald Bannerman's particular response to literature and the encouragement given to him by his teacher as a direct parallel to MacDonald's own experience.[79] MacDonald's detailed comment on the reading of poetry[80] presages responses to his own read-

76. Prickett, *Two Worlds*, 2.
77. Levine, *Not Like My Lancelot*, 64.
78. Raeper, *George MacDonald*, 192.
79. MacDonald, *George MacDonald*, 63.
80. MacDonald, *Ranald Bannerman*, 229.

ings, demonstrated in contemporary reviews,[81] and MacDonald's later development as a writer places him in the position of Carlyle's hero as both poet and man of letters, both of whom Carlyle regards as "set apart" and able to present, "the reality which lies at the bottom of all appearance."[82] In this passage Carlyle quotes Fichte's philosophy. As a reader of Carlyle and influenced by Fichte[83] and Swedenborg,[84] MacDonald's work demonstrates the concept of the spiritual reality behind appearances. In his lecture on *The Hero as Poet* (1840), Carlyle states, "we are all poets when we read a poem well," and follows this observation with "even the commonest speech, has something of song in it."[85] Carlyle moves from the hero as "great man" to the hero as "everyman" within a few pages.

First published in serial form in *Good Words for the Young* Nov. 1869–Oct. 1870, *Ranald Bannerman's Boyhood* presages MacDonald's later books such as *The Princess and the Goblin* (1872) and *The Princess and Curdie* (1883) (see, for example, passages in *Ranald Bannerman's Boyhood*, pp. 137, 216). Indicators of MacDonald's views on, for example, education and allusions to political changes, such as his comments on the Poor Laws,[86] make *Ranald Bannerman's Boyhood* as much a story for adults as for children. Set in the North East of Scotland, MacDonald's home, the story begins with Ranald's earliest memory and ends with his departure to school and university. In between are all the agonies of growing up, punctuated by vivid episodes that act as stepping stones toward maturity. At the time of publication, MacDonald had been living in England for approximately twenty years. His biographers Greville MacDonald, William Raeper, Rolland Hein, Elizabeth Saintsbury, and Kathy Triggs all allude to *Ranald Bannerman's Boyhood* in order to illustrate incidents in MacDonald's early life, and Saintsbury in particular blurs the boundary between biography and fiction in her use of quotation from this text. As in Henty's historical stories, *Ranald Bannerman's Boyhood* allows "the reality of the facts to yield sometimes

---

81. Records of MacDonald's responses to poetry can be found in, for example, the journal *Wingfold* 45 (2004) and 56 (2006).
82. Carlyle, *On Heroes*, 79.
83. See Hayward, *George MacDonald*.
84. Raeper, *George MacDonald*, 183, 370.
85. Carlyle, *On Heroes*, 83.
86. MacDonald, *Ranald Bannerman*, 56, 186.

to the idea which each of them must represent in the eyes of posterity."[87] *Ranald Bannerman's Boyhood* is a subjective account, focalized predominantly through Ranald. He is presented by MacDonald as a "real" boy, although he is portrayed with intimations of the ideal that are more fully developed in works such as *At the Back of the North Wind* (1871), published in the same year, *The Princess and the Goblin* (1872), *The Princess and Curdie* (1883) and the adult novel *Robert Falconer* (1868). Although *Ranald Bannerman's Boyhood* does not take Ranald beyond youth, there are indications that he has ability as a writer. The implication is that as the fictional narrator of his own boyhood experiences written at a later date, he continues to write, as did George MacDonald. Even as a young child, Ranald displays resourcefulness and daring set against a background of peer conformity, such as in his escape from Dame Shand's school. At the age of six, he recalls, "I found myself led by the ungentle hand of Mrs. Mitchell [the housekeeper] towards a little school on the outside of the village. . . . Mrs Mitchell opened the door and led me in. It was an awful experience." No doubt the last five words echo generations of young children's experience. There follows a description of Dame Shand's school, the room, the other children and the dog, which is guarding a child tied to the table leg. Ranald resolves to escape. The account continues, "And I soon had my first experience of how those are helped who will help themselves," a direct Smilesian precept. Ranald runs away but faces an even greater difficulty than escape when he is pursued by the dog, "For one moment I felt as if I should sink to the earth for sheer terror. The next moment a wholesome rage sent the blood to my brain. From abject cowardice to wild attack . . . was the change of an instant." Ranald attacks the dog, and escapes. Reflecting on this episode, he refers to the action as prompted by "rage," with the observation, "I cannot call it courage."[88] The discussion on the flawed hero and the nature of courage later in this chapter contains the citation of an incident in Henty's *Rujub the Juggler* (1895), in which the hero, Ralph Bathurst, analyzes his behaviour as the result of rage in a reflection similar to that of Ranald. Bathurst responds to the statement, "you have shown today that you have plenty of courage," with the response, "The courage of a Malay running amuck . . . , that is not courage, it is madness."[89] Bathurst

---

87. Lukacs, *Historical Novel*, 76.
88. MacDonald, *Ranald Bannerman*, 33–34, 36, 38.
89. Henty, Rujub, 224.

cannot accept that he has "fought nobly," only that he might have fought "desperately or madly." Ranald faced the danger and escaped, whilst the other children remain tyrannized by Dame Shand. His resourcefulness, a key quality in the active hero, continues as he finds a hiding place. The next day, Ranald's father steps in to prevent his being taken back to the school. At this point in the story a character is introduced with whom Ranald has most of his remaining boyhood adventures and who, apart from his origin, fits the mold of the Victorian hero not only as a boy, but in his later becoming a "well-known 'General.'" Turkey, the herd boy, is "a hero" to Ranald and his two younger brothers. Apart from his ability to control cattle, including bulls, Turkey knows everything about the natural world and in this respect closely resembles Dickon from Frances Hodgson Burnett's *The Secret Garden* (1911). Ranald recalls, "Short of flying, we believed him capable of everything imaginable."[90] Turkey is also portrayed as "real boy", but is not represented as having the faults depicted in Ranald. His character presents a blending of the real and the ideal such as is found in Henty's stories. Had he been English rather than Scottish, Turkey's low position in the strata of society would have made his rising to become a General prohibitively difficult in the context of a Henty story. Henty's heroes are, with two exceptions, of upper or middle class origin. In England, position in society created a barrier to advancement in the army in the days when a commission had to be purchased rather than earned. As a Scottish Highlander Turkey's origin was less of a barrier to advancement. His impoverished position as a fatherless cow herd, and his care for those around him, also qualify him as fairy tale hero, whilst his soldierly accomplishments demonstrate the characteristics of the classical hero. His qualities of leadership, resourcefulness and courage are typical of the active hero and are displayed to the full in the episode involving Wandering Willie. Wandering Willie is described as, a "half-witted" person "commonly styled Foolish Willie. His approach is announced by a wailful strain upon the bagpipes . . ." His dress is, "the agglomeration of ill-supplied necessity and superfluous whim," since he attaches colored ribbon and bits of rag to his clothes and his pipes. "When he danced he was like a whirlwind that had caught up the contents of an old clothes shop." His figure engenders both fascination and fear in the children and is used as a threat by Mrs Mitchell, the housekeeper, who maintains that if Ranald and his brothers do not

90. MacDonald, *Ranald Bannerman*, 335, 66, 67.

behave, "she would give this one or that one to Foolish Willie to take away with him." Although this never happens, "One day, in early summer . . . wee Davie disappeared."[91] Ranald soon discovers that Willie has carried Davie off and whilst the adults are debating what to do, he runs straight to Turkey, who, Ranald felt sure, would know how to rescue Davie. The result was that, "[Turkey] set off at a swinging trot in the direction of a little rocky knoll in a hollow . . . which he knew to be a favourite haunt of Wandering Willie." Willie is there, with Davie, but it takes all Turkey's resourcefulness and coolness to retrieve Davie. Willie is strong, unpredictable and beyond reason. Turkey manages to steal his pipes while Ranald rescues Davie.

Turkey treats the pipes in such a way that, "the pipes cried out at every kick," and Willie, who "was more attached to them than to any living creature," turns from his pursuit of Ranald and Davie, "and once again pursued his pipes."[92] The details of this adventure demonstrate Turkey's finely balanced timing in the execution of his tactics to achieve the rescue in what is a genuinely dangerous situation. Ranald of course plays a major role in Davie's rescue, but without Turkey's strategy it could never have been achieved. I noted earlier that in his novel *Sir Gibbie* (1879), MacDonald defends his depiction of ideal characters against what he perceives as the demand for, "the representation of that grade of humanity of which men see the most." MacDonald's position on character representation echoes that of Carlyle's description of everyman as hero and reflects the aspirational ideals found in the Comtean *New Calendar of Great Men* (1892). MacDonald's graphic use of the term commonplace, referred to below in relation to Curdie, encapsulates his rejection of the demand for less than the ideal.

As Ranald matures, episodes such as the rescue of Davie extend to incorporate that element of spiritual growth so integral to MacDonald's work. The inclusion of failure, in the chapter *I Go Down Hill* is paralleled by Curdie's experience in *The Princess and Curdie* (1883) when, as Curdie grew older, "he was gradually changing into a commonplace man."[93] Realization of his degeneration comes to Ranald, as it does to Curdie, in a crisis precipitated by his own destructive action, at which point, he is able to initiate the process of growth and renewal.

91. MacDonald, *Ranald Bannerman*, 100, 102, 103.
92. Ibid., 104, 108, 101, 110.
93. MacDonald, *Princess and Curdie*, 22.

My reason for examining the progress of Ranald Bannerman in some depth is to demonstrate the development of characteristics paralleled in and associated with the Henty boy. Incorporating the classical virtues of courage and honour and combining the active virtues of physical fitness with the muscular Christian virtues of truthfulness and unselfishness, the Victorian hero is building into a more complex character than the stereotypical construct can accommodate.

The Adventure Hero

According to Mikhail Bakhtin, the adventure hero is one who reacts in the correct way to further his fortunes when the opportunity arises.[94] He specializes in being in the right place at the right time. This opportunity is not just a matter of coincidence, action has to be taken. Abundant examples of such an opportune coincidence can be found in Henty's work. *By Sheer Pluck* (1884) demonstrates one instance, when Frank Hargate grasps an opportunity to offer his skill as a taxidermist after he has overheard a conversation whilst seeking work. Frank's offer leads to an association which provides travel, adventure, a profession and a secure future.

MacDonald includes opportune coincidences in his story *A Rough Shaking* (1891), when Clare Skymer meets with Nimrod the bull, with Miss Temple his benefactress, and when he discovers his lost father. In *At the Back of the North Wind* (1871), Diamond's meeting with Mr. Raymond, with Miss Coleman the daughter of his father's employer and, later in the story, his meeting with her fiancé are moments of providential coincidence which create opportunities for him to act in a way that will make something good happen for his family, his friends and consequently for himself.

The second characteristic of Bakhtin's adventure hero is that he is not significantly changed by his experiences. The Henty hero displays the same virtues as a boy that he displays at the culmination of the story. The majority of Henty's stories end as the hero reaches maturity and returns to England after his adventure, although there are exceptions such as *The Young Buglers* (1880) and *The Young Franc-Tireurs* (1872). In most of the stories the hero has gained experience and expertise through his adventures, but his character, although strengthened, is essentially

---

94. Bakhtin, *Dialogic Imagination*, 116.

the same. In *Condemned as a Nihilist* (1893), the hero is described at the end of the story, "His spirits were as high and he was as full of fun as of old; But the experience he had gone through had ... given him self-reliance and confidence."[95] This statement refers to Godfrey Bullen who has just spent three years escaping from a Siberian prison. His character has matured rather than changed. Clare Skymer and Diamond also demonstrate essentially unchanged characters. The MacDonaldian emphasis on spiritual and emotional stamina constructs Clare and Diamond as ideals of goodness rather than ideals of the English boy character, with exceptional physical stamina, although Clare in particular also possesses physical strength and stamina. As I have already proposed, in the work of Henty and MacDonald the physical and the spiritual ideal can be envisaged as two characters facing each other in a mirror. The same physical and spiritual characteristics exist in both but with a different emphasis. In the work of MacDonald, Ranald Bannerman and Turkey, characters in *Ranald Bannerman's Boyhood* (1871) can be correlated with the Henty hero in terms of their growing capacity for initiative, action and leadership. Their story typifies linear time and a mimetic approach to literature, characteristics associated with realism in fiction. The blending of realism and fantasy in both Henty and MacDonald demonstrates non-mimesis in its depiction of progress toward maturation, a progress in which cyclical or "mythic" time and linear time intersect one another. The diagrammatic illustration of the hero's progress along a continuum can be by taken further in the character of Clare Skymer, who, in *A Rough Shaking* (1893) includes the essential elements of the Henty hero in terms of perseverance, survival skills, honesty and integrity, but also displays the other worldly goodness of Diamond from *At the Back of the North Wind* (1871), which places him in the position of the hero as victim, and as an example of the character of the holy fool whose goodness is perceived as rendering him unfit for the real world. The references to Clare's adult life, however, belie this perceived unfitness, since the story of his childhood stops with the implication that he will become the captain of an English gunboat, following in the footsteps of his father. Such a position of leadership in a masculine profession places him on the same level of operation as Henty's Nat Glover who serves as Commander of an English frigate in the story *A Roving Commission* (1900). Following the

---

95. Henty, *Condemned as a Nihilist*, 349.

continuum through Diamond to other characters from MacDonald's work such as Richard (*Cross Purposes* 1862), Curdie and Irene (*The Princess* books, 1872 and 1883) and Mossy and Tangle (*The Golden Key* 1867), establishes that the merging of realism into fantasy and fairy tale, does not essentially change the heroic characteristics.

The Flawed Hero

I have not yet discussed the existence of weakness as an element of the hero figure but it is one which enables the possibility of reader identification with the hero, facilitating the process of emulation. I have already noted the intention of both Henty and MacDonald to encourage emulation. If the readers of Henty or MacDonald took the position of non-identification, they would still be in a position to observe the values employed by the hero and so make a choice as to whether or not to act upon them within or outside of the hero's skin. In Carlyle's second lecture (*The Hero as Prophet*, 1840) he states, "Is not a man's walking, in truth, always "a succession of falls?" Carlyle's exposition follows in terms of how the hero reacts to his "falls," which Carlyle views as necessary to the hero's "struggle . . . onwards."[96] More recently, Erica Jong writes, "a hero must be imperfect or how can she be tested?"[97] In this way the concept of the hero as everyman is reinforced. The unexpected appearance of an explicitly imperfect Victorian hero in Henty's *Rujub the Juggler* (1893) illustrates this assertion. Ralph Bathurst, a colonial administrator in India, is literally paralysed with fear at the sound of loud noises, especially gunfire. He is about to set off to investigate a dispute amongst villagers when he is informed that the area has been troubled by a man-eating tiger. His informant advises him,

> "Well, if I were you I would put a pair of pistols into my holster, Bathurst; it would be awfully awkward if you came across the beast."
>
> "I never carry firearms," the young man said shortly; and then more lightly, "I am a peaceful man by profession, as you are, Mr Hunter, and I leave firearms to those whose profession it is to use them. . . . I always carry this heavy hunting-whip, which I find

---

96. Carlyle, *On Heroes*, 47.
97. Jong, *Sappho's Leap*, 144.

useful sometimes, when the village dogs rush out and pretend they are going to attack me;"[98]

Henty's Bathurst resembles the historical figure of the administrator John Nicholson (1821–57) who worked in India between 1839 and 1857 and carried only a hunting-whip on his journeys. He is described by Kathryn Tidrick[99] in much the same terms as Mr Hunter describes Bathurst, "full of energy, and, they say, the very best linguist in Oude."[100] The conversation continues, establishing Bathurst's oddness, and ends with a short commentary which clarifies the difference between the Arnoldian boy hero, the product of the public school, and the Henty hero,

> "He will take a very high place in the service before he is done."
> "I am not so sure of that," the other said. "He is a man with opinions of his own. . . . He has been in hot water with the Chief Commissioner more than once. When I was over at Lucknow last, I was chatting with two or three men, and his name happened to crop up, and one of them said, 'Bathurst is a sort of knight-errant, an official Don Quixote. Perhaps the best officer in the province in some respects, but hopelessly impracticable.'"
> "Yes, that I can quite understand, Garnet. That sort of man is never popular with the higher official, whose likings go to the man who neither does too much nor too little, who does his work without questioning, and never thinks of making suggestions, and is a mere official machine. Men of Bathurst's type, who go to the bottom of things, protest against what they consider unfair decisions, and send in memorandums showing that their superiors are hopelessly ignorant and idiotically wrong, are always cordially disliked."[101]

The delineation of Bathurst as a man who is prepared not only to act on his own initiative, but to record unfairness with a view to rectifying it, portrays a more complex character than the man who acts from a limited set of criteria inculcated into him. The outspokenness never stretches to questioning the governing presence of the English in India, an indication of how deeply Henty is embedded in the dominant imperial political intent of his time. The exchange quoted above is an example of the ability of literature within any given period to remain

98. Henty, *Rujub*, 7.
99. Tidrick, *Empire*, 18.
100. Henty, *Rujub*, 7
101. Ibid., 8.

imprisoned by historical context and yet to step outside of it into a broader ethical context at the same time. Whilst travelling to the village, Bathurst does come across the tiger, "standing with a foot upon a prostrate figure. . . . Bathurst sprang off [his horse] and rushed at the tiger, and brought down the heavy lash of his whip with all his force across its head."[102] And so Bathurst meets Rujub and his daughter, an incident which elicits an internal reflection from Bathurst to appraise the reader of the reason for his apparent oddness and reserve, "That is a new character for me to come out in," he said bitterly; "I do not know myself—I, of all men. But there was no bravery in it; it never occurred to me to be afraid; . . . there was no noise, and it is noise that frightens me; if the brute had roared I should assuredly have run. . . . It is an awful curse that . . . I tremble and shake like a girl at the sound of firearms."[103]

Later in the story, the arrival of an army officer tells the story of Bathurst's departure from the army in detrimental terms indicating cowardice and failure as a soldier, due to his inability to function in the midst of gunfire. The character Dr Wade attempts to explain the situation to the female character Isobel, newly arrived in India to live with her uncle and who cannot accept that a man who crumbles in battle can show courage in any other circumstance. The doctor's discourse on the nature of courage is an assessment of the human condition when he says, "Courage, my dear, is not a universal endowment—it is a physical as much as a moral virtue. Some people are physically brave and morally cowards; others are exactly the reverse."[104] Henty provides an example of the physically brave in the character of Captain Forster, the officer who rumors Bathurst's failure. He is presented as the exact opposite of Bathurst. Their acquaintance began at school where the differences were immediately obvious and accompanied by mutual loathing. Forster acts as a foil to Bathurst's character and demonstrates that recklessness in the guise of courage is superficial when compared to the moral courage displayed by Bathurst.

The protagonist of MacDonald's short story *The Broken Swords* (1854) finds himself in a similar situation to Bathurst, although his misgiving in battle is due to his perceptions of the "enemy" as brother and of the horrors of war, which render him unable to enter battle with

102. Ibid., 11.
103. Ibid., 14.
104. Henty, *Rujub*, 129.

the single-minded attitude of fighting to win. MacDonald's commentary on courage is delivered by the story's narrator, who reflects upon the psychological make-up of the youth, reflected in his physical demeanor before battle in contrast to "a great, broad-shouldered lieutenant," "Many men who have courage, are dependent upon on ignorance and a low state of the moral feeling for that courage; and a further progress towards the development of the higher nature would, for a time at least, entirely overthrow it. Nor could such loss of courage be rightly designated by the name of cowardice."[105] Both authors place an emphasis on moral courage rather than on purely physical courage, but the rehabilitation of both protagonists, portrayed as flawed heroes, is by their overcoming their paralysis in the face of battle. Bathurst's disgrace is compounded in his own estimation when he escapes from a boat under fire, leaving Isobel behind. Although he vindicates himself in the eyes of others by extreme courage in rescuing Isobel, he is not able to come to terms with his perceived failure of courage until he realizes that he is no longer reacting to noise, due to an opportune blow on the head. He subsequently distinguishes himself in battle, recovers his self-respect, and marries Isobel. MacDonald's hero, who is never named and is known only by the identifiers of brother, in relation to his two sisters, nephew to his uncle and as ensign to the officer in charge of him, rejoins his old regiment, fights in a war he perceives to be just, and dies vindicating his honour. In explanation of the war in question, MacDonald notes, "The English armies were employed in expelling the enemy from an invaded and helpless country. Whatever might be the political motives which had induced the Government to this measure, the young man now felt able to go and fight, individually and for his part, in the cause of liberty. He was free to possess his own motives for joining in the execution of the schemes of those who commanded his commanders."[106] MacDonald's concern is with the moral issues of the individual, not with the political motives of the Government, as he clearly states. Writing in 1854, before the escalation of Britain's colonial wars, MacDonald accepts imperialist activity as part of the contemporary scene, only drawing upon it as circumstantial detail subordinate to his purpose. The case of the Coleman's trade with exotic parts of the empire *in At the Back of the North Wind* (1871) is another example of such circumstantial detail. Both Bathurst

105. MacDonald, *Broken Swords*, 267–68.
106. Ibid., 287.

The Construct of the Hero 1850-1900

and the youth in *The Broken Swords* (1854) illustrate the statement that "Real adventure cannot happen to superheroes; by nature they would be insensitive to it."[107] Henty's discussion of the distinction between moral and physical courage in *Rujub the Juggler* is closer to MacDonald's emphasis on moral and spiritual courage, an essential characteristic of the hero according to Carlyle, than to the stereotypical figure of the Henty, and by implication, the Victorian, active hero.

The concept of the flawed hero links not only with the possibility of identification with the hero, thus easing the process of emulation, but also with the Victorian eulogistic acceptance of the hero in defeat. Tennyson's poem *The Charge of the Light Brigade* (1855) turned the disastrous charge of the Light Brigade at the battle of Balaclava during the Crimean War into a legend, despite the catalogue of incompetence and misunderstanding that led to the soldiers' annihilation. Ignoring the surrounding circumstances, the charge was hailed as an act of collective heroism. The emphasis on sacrifice, both on this occasion and in the life and death of General Gordon, incorporates the active hero and the spiritually/morally aware hero. In the fictional examples of Ralph Bathurst and the youth in MacDonald's *The Broken Swords*, the willingness to sacrifice life for someone else demonstrates the moral aspect that is integral to the construct of the Victorian hero, an aspect that is taken further in the construct of the female hero.

The Gendered Hero

"The best thing that can be said about a girl is that she has all the virtues of a boy."[108] When Robert Huttenback made this observation he was commenting on Dick Holland's statement in *The Tiger of Mysore* (1896) that he had thought of Annie, the girl he rescued from a tiger attack, "as the dear plucky little girl of the old days." Dick makes the statement after he has proposed to her, having realized that she has now grown up and that he loves her. Had Annie not shown "pluck" on their journey of escape no doubt the outcome would have been different. Annie assures him that she "is in no way changed,"[109] and the matter is settled. It goes without saying that Annie is now anglicized, socialized and feminized in

---

107. Southall, *Real Adventure*, 101.
108. Huttenback, *G. A. Henty*, 70.
109. Henty, *Tiger of Mysore*, 377.

the mold of the Victorian young lady, at least outwardly. Annie's appearance as an exemplary Victorian lady after her early experience of kidnapping and her upbringing in Tippoo Saib's harem, which is, according to the Western norm, unconventional, is "at once true and unreal."[110] Her risky escape and dangerous journey in India serve as a story that functions "to shape our perceptions of reality."[111] Henty "shapes our perceptions" of the reality of the female hero by constructing a character in which the conventional Victorian female passivity conflicts with the active reality whilst still endorsing the normative perception of femininity.

Henty's positive construction of the active girl is portrayed in *The Young Franc-Tireurs* (1872) by the use of oppositional negative characteristics. The character and appearance of Milly Barclay, the sister of the two male hero figures, is described in a series of contrasts to her French cousins. The Barclay children have an English father and a French mother, a significant factor in their differing levels of activity and initiative. As Milly's aunt and cousins approach the house, her aunt remonstrates with Milly's mother, "My dear Melanie," Madame Duburg began, when her daughters had walked away in a quiet, prim manner, hand in hand, "I was really quite shocked as we came along. There was Milly laughing and calling out as loudly as the boys themselves, handing up baskets and lifting others down, with her hair all in confusion, and looking—excuse my saying so—more like a peasant girl than a young lady." Milly herself, "greatly preferred being with the boys, and always felt uncomfortable with Julie and Justine, who, although little older than herself, were already as prim, decorous, and properly behaved as if they had been women of thirty years old."[112] I will not examine whether the implicit assumption that "women of thirty years old" will be "prim and decorous" is correct or not. I include the quotation in order to indicate that Milly's cousins are set up from the outset as insipid and uninteresting in contrast to the active Milly.

The positive portrayal of tomboyish activity and interests continues in the most distinctive of Henty's female heroes, Nita, the main protagonist of *A Soldier's Daughter* (1906). The story opens with a discussion between Nita and her father as to the necessity of sending Nita back to

---

110. Barthes, *Myth Today*, 40.
111. Hourihan, *Deconstructing the Hero*, 12.
112. Henty, *Young Franc-Tireurs*, 17, 16.

England from the North-West frontier of India so she may be "taught to behave as a young lady," since her "accomplishments are not strictly feminine in their character." Reviewing her accomplishments, her father reminds her, "You are as good a shot as there is in the regiment both with rifle and revolver, you can fence very fairly, you have a very good idea of cricket, but you know nothing of music." Nita's protestation, "I wish I had been a boy instead of a girl," meets with the response, "I rather wish so too, Nita."[113]

Figure 2: "I wish I had been a boy instead of a girl"

After further discussion they agree that Nita should attend a school in England "where girls play games—hockey, football, and cricket, and have gymnastics."[114] Henty's emphasis on the benefits of boxing have also been noted and is again stressed in this instance as Nita brings to her father's attention her proficiency in boxing as evidence that she

113. Note the relative positions of Nita and her father in this illustration, the father standing over Nita, conveying to the reader the extent of male dominance within her discourse.

114. Henty, *Soldier's Daughter*, 8, 9.

would be able to "hold her own" at school. Her father, Major Ackworth, strongly discourages her from using her skill as a method of defence in the context of a girl's school, stating that, "Women fight with words, not with fists,"[115] a statement which widens the increasing gender divide in acceptable behavior. Hourihan comments on the role played by sport in the construction and development of masculinity within Western culture, stating, "Sport is one of the major means by which values and attitudes are shaped."[116] Henty constructs Nita Ackworth as able to compete in masculine spheres of activity, shooting, games playing, and boxing, in order to introduce her as the hero of the story. Without male accomplishments, she cannot be cast in the role of the hero. Hourihan notes, "heroism is gendered," and continues with a comment that the hero story reinforces the limited sphere of female activity.[117] When Nita has her adventure she is, essentially, masculine. The story continues after the conversation with a timescale as to when Nita will be sent to an English school. At this point the second significant character in the adventure is introduced, Charlie Carter, a young lieutenant. Carter is to be left in charge of the fort until the Major, Nita's father, returns from an expedition. He expects to be away for a fortnight after which time, on his return, Carter will go on leave and accompany Nita to Bombay where she will take a passage for England. As the major leaves the fort, he shouts back to Nita, "Take care of yourself, . . . I expect to hear, when I come back, that you have been doing junior subaltern's work to Lieutenant Carter." Nita takes him at his word. "As soon as the force were beyond the gate she went up to the lieutenant. 'You heard, sir,' she said, saluting in military fashion, 'that my father has deputed me to act as your sub.?' The young man looked at her in surprise. 'I understood the major was joking, Miss Ackworth.' 'Partly in jest, partly in earnest, sir,' she said calmly." Carter protests, "I do not think there is the most remote chance of your services being called into requisition." To which Nita replies, "'I don't know,' she said; 'somehow or other I have a sort of uneasy conviction that there is trouble brewing.'"[118]

This comment, early in the story, is pivotal to the subsequent action. Carter is instantly alert, questioning her as to her reason for suspicion.

115. Ibid., 13.
116. Hourihan, *Deconstructing the Hero*, 14.
117. Ibid., 68.
118. Henty, *Soldier's Daughter*, 13, 14.

Although Nita has no concrete evidence, she has made her surmise based on minor incidents which put together, point to a potentially dangerous situation. Carter accepts her interpretation of events and begins preparations to defend the fort. Nita's "uneasy conviction of trouble brewing" is one instance of Henty's reliance on female intuition to further a story. Preparations for defending the fort include the decision that in the event of an attack, Nita will put on Carter's spare uniform so that she will not be recognized as female. The planned disguise includes the cutting of her hair. In so doing, she conforms to the type of the literary tomboy and appears to fulfil the role of the "hero in drag."[119] However, referring back to her character at the beginning of the story, before her adventure, she does not put on the role of the hero with the men's clothes; she acts in keeping with her initial character depiction in terms of leadership and action.

The attack, of course, does come and Nita is transformed into her male persona in which she takes a key role in the defence, is one of the few survivors of the raid who are taken as prisoners into the mountains, is imprisoned in the house of a village chief and set to work as a servant. In her male role, Nita behaves exactly as the male Henty hero. She never shows any fear, remains calm and observant, "set to work to pick up the language,"[120] and watches for an opportunity to escape. Not only does she escape herself, with enough food and a pony to make a prolonged journey possible, but she also manages to rescue Carter, having ascertained the whereabouts of the village to which he has been taken. On the journey back to the frontier, Nita predominantly takes the lead when a difficult situation, such as an attack, presents itself, enabling their return to what is left of the fort, where the remains of the company, including Nita's father on his return, have set up camp. During the journey Carter reflects on the strangeness of the situation, in a passage acknowledging the unconventionality of their position as travelling companions compared to the accepted standards of their English societal norms of chaperoning women in the company of men, "It has certainly been very strange, a young man and a girl thus wandering about together, but somehow it has scarcely felt strange to me. . . . [I]n spite of the hardships and dangers we have had to go through, our companionship has been a very pleasant one."

119. Paul, *Enigma Variations*, 199.
120. Henty, *Soldier's Daughter*, 61.

During the journey, Nita is still just young enough to be considered a tomboy, and her disguise as a youth enables the relationship to remain on the level of "chums," a term used later in the story. Not only does Nita have to "become male" in order to be the hero, but also Henty as author has to deflect any accusation of impropriety in the story. Nita reinforces her position in response to Carter's observation by another comment, "Oh, dear!" Nita sighed; "how disgusting it will be to have to put on girl's clothes again, and settle down into being stiff and proper!"[121] Norman Vance, commenting on the dearth of Victorian female heroes in the popular imagination, writes, "It was still felt that women should normally be private and almost anonymous."[122] In *A Soldier's Daughter*, Nita's "anonymity" is a "kind of ultimate dissolution of the self" that, Levine notes, "becomes a positive heroism"[123] in itself. In Barbara Waxman's discussion of heroism in the work of Matthew Arnold (1822–88) and George Eliot (1819–80), she argues that, "Any heroic role that takes a woman out of her conventional role seems bound to create more tension and suffering for a woman than a similar heroic summons would create for a man."[124]

Whereas the "tension and suffering" involved in Nita's role as hero is minimal compared to that of the characters discussed by Waxman, the emphasis on the sacrifice of her identity in order to become the heroic figure with a leadership role demonstrates Levine's comment on "the ideal of sacrifice *defining* identity"[125] (emphasis in text). The tension Nita experiences is represented at the end of the story when she and Charlie reach the camp, "The sun was just setting as they arrived at the edge of the camp. Evident surprise was caused among the soldiers at the appearance of two officers in khaki. Their uniforms were in ribbons, and so dirty and travel-stained that it was difficult to make out that they were officers." Their arrival "just as the sun was setting" imbues the scene with symbolic significance for Nita who immediately assumes a secondary position to Carter by merging into the background, conveying a sense of closure on her particular role as leader on their journey: "No one noticed Nita, who, seized with a new shyness, followed Carter, who could move but slowly as the soldiers pressed forward to salute him." This pas-

121. Henty, *Soldier's Daughter*, 104.
122. Vance, *Heroic Myth*, 169.
123. Levine, *Not like My Lancelot*, 68.
124. Waxman, *Ethnic Heroism*, 119.
125. Levine, *Not like My Lancelot*, 69.

sage is full of words indicating Nita's subsumption to the accepted role of the female in Victorian society as secondary to Carter, and his primary role as male. He takes the lead in Nita's reintroduction to her father, the Major. The description of the reunion of daughter and father reinforces the deferential role played by Nita as she is reintroduced into the cultural norm. Carter takes the initiative, "'I will enter your tent, if you will allow me, major. I have something of importance to tell you.' The major entered, followed by Carter, with Nita three or four paces behind him."[126]

Nita's reversion to the female role is represented by her reversion to female clothes when she is back in society on the completion of her adventure. The constricted life of Nita's female persona is represented by her reaction to her clothes as she says, "I feel horribly uncomfortable in these clothes. Of course I shall get used to them in time, but at present they seem to cling about me in a most disagreeable way."[127]

In her discussion on the significance of clothes in the characterisation of characters, Nikolajeva notes that, "The protagonist of *The True Confessions of Charlotte Doyle* (1991) finds herself in a situation in which cross-dressing is the only possible survival strategy."[128] This position is commensurate with Nita's need to survive although Nita accepts the need to dress in men's clothes more readily than does Charlotte. When Nita returns to her female form of dress, she accepts the cultural limitations of her female identity as inevitable and continues on the path laid out for her before her adventure, that is, to go to school in England and return to India, where she renews her friendship with Charlie Carter and eventually marries him. Charlotte chooses to reject the conventions of the nineteenth century construct of femininity after her return to her family, and runs away again to resume her male persona.[129] Nita's two irreconcilable roles demonstrate the position of woman as "other,"[130] in this instance, in a world of masculine action. Henty's representation of active women means that she remains a subversive figure in spite of her outward conformity in terms of dress. Her character as active hero has been depicted before the adventure which she performs in male clothing but she remains the strong, unstereotypical female after her resumption into societal norms. Her position again models the contradictions

126. Henty, *Soldier's Daughter*, 106, 107.
127. Ibid., 111.
128. Nikolajeva, *Rhetoric of Character*, 275.
129. Avi, *True Confessions*.
130. For a discussion on woman as other, see Irigaray, *Je, Tu, Nous*.

prevalent in the nineteenth-century society into which she is written. Victoria Flanagan (1999) and Mia Österlund (2000) have examined the prevalence of female to male and male to female cross-dressing in children's literature from the position of gender performativity and the transgression of social norms. I have not examined Nita's position as the "hero in drag" employing the theories of Flanagan and Österland here because the sexual nuances are more openly recognized in the twenty-first-century context. This extensive area of investigation is outside of my focus, which is the construct of the hero in terms of character.

Jane Williams, the distinctive female hero of Henty's short story *The Plague Ship* (1889), remains in her conventional role, but demonstrates a level of courage beyond any of the men on the ship in which she is a passenger. The story is based upon the encounter of the ship, *The Two Brothers*, with another vessel, after riding a fierce storm en route to the Cape. The second ship appears almost deserted but is found to have fever sufferers on board. Few of the crew remain alive but to rescue them would mean putting the entire crew and passengers of *The Two Brothers* at risk. The story continues, "The men had shown themselves brave enough in their fight with the Malays, but standing as they were by the bulwark, watching the strange ship, there wasn't one but shrank back when he heard that hail; and well they might, for when the Indian fever gets on board a ship there is no saying what may come of it." Fear brings the crew of the *The Two Brothers* close to mutiny as they rebel against the decision to rescue the remaining crew of the doomed ship, but Jane Williams, with her parents and any crew member who is willing, board the ship where she and her parents nurse the few surviving seamen whilst the ship, "ran four days before the gale, and when it died out got sail on again, and made our way safely to the Cape." [131] During the journey, Jane catches the fever and dies, an outcome which indicates that her heroism is entirely based on her willingness to sacrifice her own life to do what she believes to be right. Since Jane demonstrates the heroic attributes discussed in this chapter, together with decision making initiative and leadership, she may be viewed as hero despite her conformity to the female sacrificial role. Although enough other members of the crew had volunteered to go on board to sail the ship, one of the reasons given for their potential sacrifice was that, "there was not one of them who did

---

131. Henty, *Plague Ship*, 45, 61.

not at heart feel ashamed at being beaten in courage by a girl."[132] Henty's comments on the bravery of women appear throughout his fiction, but an observation he made on the quality of women's courage indicates his view as follows, "I think they are every bit as brave [as men]. . . . They are silly about little things; they are frightened at mice, they are mortally afraid of burglars . . . but I think it is only that they are more nervous than men, for when it comes to real danger, they are just as brave. . . . I know that in Paris, when the bombardment was going on, they used to stand at their doors and knit and talk to each other across the street when the shells were coming down thickly."[133]

Conversely, the "heroism" of the Amazonian warriors in *By Sheer Pluck* (1884) does not fit the paradigm of sacrificial female heroism, neither are they viewed as deserving of the chivalric behavior accorded to Western women. The warrior women of Dahomey, by their full acceptance of their position as the primary soldiers, are regarded as beyond the reach of special treatment even though they "fight with extraordinary bravery and ferocity." The reason given, is that, "When women leave their proper sphere and put themselves forward to do man's work they must expect man's treatment."[134] Henty's females may be spirited, brave and athletic, but they all eventually remain in "their proper sphere" determined by their gender, which is, "a set of qualities that are defined—or socially constructed—in a particular society or culture" and "part of learning to live in a family and a society."[135] Henty both supports and subverts the Victorian female construct, encouraging the masculine qualities of initiative and action whilst denying the expression of these qualities in the encultured masculine sphere of public life. In so doing he instances another apparent contradiction within Victorian society, and by polarizing action and sacrifice as gendered, affirms "the paradox at the core of the heroic ideal."[136]

Contrary to the ambiguously oppositional gender roles represented in Henty's writing, MacDonald's books, "press towards a vision of mutuality in which divisions of masculine and feminine . . . are no more."[137] MacDonald's position differs from that of Henty since Henty

132. Ibid., 52.
133. Forbes, *Camps and Quarters*, 29.
134. Henty, *By Sheer Pluck*, 211, 212.
135. Allen, *Literature, Gender*, 117.
136. Levine, *Not Like My Lancelot*, 57.
137. McGillis, *Phantastes and Lilith*, 32.

is working within recognized geographical and cultural boundaries, whereas MacDonald creates and constructs his own boundaries which enable him to move beyond accepted constraints. Whilst revealing the necessity of "mutuality," MacDonald turns the accepted notions of masculine bravery upside down in his tale *The Day Boy and the Night Girl* (1883). When the boy Photogen first experiences darkness, "The courage he had had . . . left him, and he could scarcely stand." The girl Nycteris finds him and, never having seen a male human being, assumes he is another girl. When he protests at being called a girl, she states, "No, of course! You can't be a girl: girls are not afraid–without reason. I understand now: it is because you are not a girl that you are so frightened."[138] Although the situation is resolved when the sun comes up and Nycteris is in turn afraid, MacDonald's point has been made. The naïve statement made by Nycteris unwittingly demolishes the masculine monopoly on courage by announcing the unexpected situation that it is in fact, girls who are primarily unafraid.

Whilst Henty's female heroes are portrayed as equally courageous as men in situations requiring initiative and action when they are in a male role (with the exception of Jane Williams and a number of incidents in other stories where women appear in a courageous supporting role), MacDonald's female heroes are more integrated than those constructed by Henty. MacDonald's female heroes initiate action, exhibit leadership qualities and moral strength whilst retaining their essential femininity. His male heroes, such as Curdie before his spiritual awakening, are portrayed as lacking a capacity for leadership until they display traits of character critically perceived as feminine, such as spiritual awareness, intuition, tenderness and a desire to evolve spiritually rather than to degenerate.

In addition to the influence of sources for the heroic ideal already noted, that is, the classical, active, adventure and fairy tale, MacDonald, rooted in Christianity and Romanticism, subverts the stereotypical masculine hero. Hourihan writes, "Romanticism represents the most significant rebellion in Western culture against the programme of the hero, against the exaltation of rationalism in the service of patriarchal dominance."[139] In singling out Romanticism, Hourihan underestimates the influence of radical Christianity in the construct of the nineteenth-

---

138. MacDonald, *The Day Boy*, 107, 118.
139. Hourihan, *Deconstructing the Hero*, 188.

century hero figure. Whilst active, "muscular" aggression fits the political imperialist intent and Darwinian social construct of survival of the fittest and upwardly mobile, the growth of the heroic ideal of service as social concern was developing within both the High Church Ritualist movement and within the evangelical Low Church and non-conformist movements. MacDonald aligned himself with the Christian Socialism of F. D. Maurice, and the heroes in both his children's and adults' work (in so far as the works can be categorized as such) live out the ideals both of service to their neighbor in the context of society, and the priority of the imaginative and the spiritual aspects of life.

The implications of MacDonald's construct of the hero have already been noted in discussing the character of Curdie and Ranald Bannerman as male heroes. The implications of this construct for his female heroes are also significant. They demonstrate integration rather than polarization, which allows them to retain their essential femininity. Princess Irene displays all the characteristics of the active hero in her undertaking of a journey to rescue Curdie from the mine, although she does not know that is her mission at the outset. Whilst Irene remains in the feminine role of obedience, she also transcends the submissive nature of the role by acting on her spiritual perception, which is stronger than Curdie's. Lee Edwards explains that "heroism involves both doing and knowing," therefore, "Action . . . exists not for its own sake but as a . . . symbolic expression of underlying psychic structures."[140] It is the ability to act on such structures that makes female heroism possible without recourse to a male sphere of action. The essential difference between the character of the active hero discussed above and Irene's action lies in her unselfconscious obedience to the tug of her great grandmother's thread. She does not consider her own bravery, or her own self-interest, but acts in trust. Irene demonstrates the construct of heroism that has regained faith and acts in faith. When Curdie and Irene act together as hero in *The Princess and Curdie* (1883) they display the same characteristics of courage (although not of action in the final battle), whilst both are aware of the guiding presence of Irene's great-grandmother (the spiritual) before they are aware of her physical presence. MacDonald's paradigm of service is fulfilled in the action of the great-grandmother after the final battle for the kingdom. Her presence in the palace has been one of housemaid. After Curdie's recognition of her, "She went from the room,

140. Edwards, *Towards a Christian Poetics*, 39.

and in a moment returned in royal purple.... Then the king yielded her his royal chair. But she made them all sit down, and with her own hands placed at the table seats for Derba and the page. Then in ruby crown and royal purple she served them all."[141] By this action she demonstrates the Christian position of the leader as servant (Luke 22:26). The great grandmother's authority, her influence over the outcome of the battle and her supernatural abilities place her beyond the role of hero herself, but within the ranks of the "strong, autonomous beings," discussed by Hourihan as powerful female figures, "relatively ignored by popular image-makers."[142] Her position as enabler to the hero, although never as hero herself, raises questions posed by Bal as "the problem of the hero." In Bal's narratological discussion of "who is the hero," she writes, "Nineteenth-century heroes were characters who could survive in a hard and ruthless society, or who attempted to do so but failed."[143] Bal's definition of hero is equated in this instance with the actantial subject.

MacDonald's male heroes with feminine characteristics, Clare Skymer and Diamond, are both characters who survive their "hard and ruthless society" whilst impacting their immediate contacts with a spirituality that elicits either love or hate depending on the recipient, imbuing them with Christ-like qualities which set them apart from both their peers and the construct of the active, public sphere of heroism. Throughout their stories, these character's immediate actions remain in the domestic or feminine sphere, subverting the active male hero. At the end of his story, the implication is that Clare Skymer enters the masculine realm, although the reader is told little of his active life, whilst the introductory chapter indicates that his inner character remains aligned to the spiritual and imaginative realm whatever actions he performs in the course of military duty.

MacDonald's story *The Golden Key* (1867) includes dual protagonists, Mossy and Tangle. Critics argue Mossy's advantage over Tangle in the ease of his journey as compared to hers. For example, "Why," Wolff asks, "has [Mossy] this advantage over Tangle, except that he is a man?"[144] Cynthia Marshall perceives the apparent inequality as potentially symbolic and interprets the story as a parabolic narrative based

---

141. MacDonald, *Princess and Curdie*, 316.
142. Hourihan, *Deconstructing the Hero*, 167.
143. Bal, *Narratology*, 131.
144. Wolff, *Golden Key*, 144–45.

upon the biblical parable of the hired labourers which culminates in the statement, "the first shall be last; and the last shall be first" (Matt 20:16). Marshall discusses the story as parable with the emphasis on the goal rather than the journey.[145] However, as Marshall continues in her discussion, Tangle's pathway could also be interpreted as given to the character with the greater strength and vision, while the experience Tangle gains makes her the wiser of the two. Kirstin Jeffrey interprets Tangle's longer and more painful journey as dependent upon her point of departure compared to that of Mossy, and concludes, "The point of departure, then, not gender, decides the pattern."[146] Nevertheless, the position of Tangle in overcoming difficulties and reaching her goal through the experience of suffering, places her in the position of hero with some of the characteristics of the hero-victim. Bal draws a distinction between the active, successful hero and the hero-victim which is not clear-cut in MacDonald's work; she notes, "the hero-victim will be confronted by opponents [or difficulties] but will not vanquish them."[147] Both MacDonald's female heroes, such as Irene, Tangle and, in his adult novel *Paul Faber* (1879), Juliet, and his male heroes such as Clare and Diamond, include characteristics of both the active hero and the hero as victim. It is perhaps worth noting that the contemporary, twenty-first-century popular hero, Carlyle's, "any kind of Hero,"[148] also incorporates both these elements, in for example, the child carer or the achiever with a disability who is honoured as a hero. At the same time, he or she is still held in oppositional balance to the celebrated active hero.

The Fairy Tale Hero

There is one category of hero not usually associated with the work of Henty, that of the fairy tale hero. In traditional tales, the fairy tale hero is often found in the persona of the youngest or only son, a character described by Max Lüthi as, "one of the true folk tale heroes,"[149] and viewed as one of the disadvantaged. He is often an orphan or at least has lost his father and his inheritance. Although the focus of this book does not include an examination of the differences between folk and fairy

145. Marshall, *Reading the Golden Key*, 23.
146. Jeffrey, *Progressive Key*, 75.
147. Bal, *Narratology*, 132.
148. Carlyle, *On Heroes*, 69.
149. Lüthi, *European Folktale*, 65.

tale, the character is universal. The youngest or only son operates in the fairy tale world in which, as Maria Tatar states, "compassion counts."[150] He is characterized by unselfishness and a desire to help in response to immediate need and is not motivated by the expectation of a reward, although his actions usually result in good fortune. Examples from Henty can be found in *With Kitchener in the Soudan* (1903), *By Sheer Pluck* (1884) and *Captain Bayley's Heir* (1889). In the first example, Gregory Hilliard, an orphan, leaps over the side of a ship to rescue a drowning woman who turns out to be the wife of his greatest enemy. Consequent events lead him to discover his true identity and aristocratic inheritance. In the second example, Frank Hargate, also an orphan, shares what little he has with a friend who has lost everything in a fire, the first of many sacrificial acts, and ultimately he receives an unexpected inheritance. The progress of Frank Norris, the hero of *Captain Bayley's Heir* (1889), demonstrates the integral characteristics of the traditional fairy tale hero whilst retaining the persona of the "Henty boy," as is explicated by the examination of his story above in chapter 3. Although the Henty hero rarely falls into the category of the ridiculed and despised in the same way that the fairy tale hero in both traditional and literary tales does, he demonstrates enough elements of the fairy tale hero in his circumstances and behavior for this category to be included in his construct.

The heroes of MacDonald's fairy tales noted above, Richard (*Cross Purposes*, 1862) Curdie and Irene (*The 'Princess' books*, 1872 and 1883) and Mossy and Tangle (*The Golden Key*, 1867) are essential to his critique of society. Curdie and Irene are engaged in a battle against the self-interested materialism of Gwyntystorm and Richard is instrumental in foregrounding the seemingly insurmountable barriers of social class. Both stories illustrate the role of the fairy tale hero as, "rectifying principle."[151] The failure of Richard to cross the social divide despite his demonstration of heroic qualities in fairyland indicates a failure of the initial subversion of cultural norms by the retention of the status quo and is an example of, "pessimism ... about the possibilities of subversion, viewing resistance as ultimately always contained."[152] MacDonald's hero Gilbert Galbraith, from the novel *Sir Gibbie* (1879) provides a connection between the fairy tale hero and the gentleman, with connotations of

150. Tatar, *Off With Their Heads*, 79.
151. Rohrich, *Folktales and Reality*, 209.
152. Rice and Waugh, *Modern Literary Theory*, 254.

the chivalry and devotion of the medieval warrior saint, resulting in the combination of a parochial "Miles Christianus," Victorian waif, and the fairy tale hero who finds his fortune. He maintains the "tone of positive hopefulness"[153] which is found in the fairy tale hero and which takes him beyond the immediacy of a hope for personal wealth and comfort, although these are invariably the reward of the Henty hero and an outcome that Sir Gibbie also experiences, to a hope for the restoration of the whole community. The characteristics of the fairy tale hero do not displace the characteristics found in the earlier categories; rather they are present in addition to those previously examined.

From these six categories, of the classical, active, adventure, flawed, gendered and fairy tale hero, the composite character displays the following major characteristics. From the classical hero, courage and honour are the most prominent characteristics. The character of the active hero builds on the classical to incorporate initiative, courage, coolness in the face of danger, intelligence (but not cleverness), patriotism (but not nationalism), sincerity and integrity. The adventure hero adds the ability to seize opportunities fortuitously encountered to the characteristics of the classical and the active hero. He also displays maturation in his development of character but without significant change. Finally, the fairy tale hero demonstrates compassion, self-sacrifice and disinterested action as his defining characteristics. All the above characteristics have been discussed in the contexts of the flawed hero and the gendered hero, which two categories demonstrate facets of the hero figure linking him to "everyman" and to the female protagonist.

The figure of the ideal hero constructed out of the political and cultural milieu in the second half of the nineteenth century embraced both the real and the imagined. He grew out of a need for stability in a period of unprecedented change at home and an unprecedented expansion of English influence abroad. His ideal character held implications in both spheres, the domestic and the exotic, and the ideological freight he carried formed how he viewed "the other" in both of these contexts. The links between the domestic and the exotic and representations of "the other" are discussed in the next chapter.

---

153. Haughton, *Tales*, 153.

6

The Ideology of the Hero and the Representation of the "Other"

The Importance of Being English

THE HERO FIGURE IS constructed as a subject and located in the dominant ideological discourses into which he is written by his position as a representative of those discourses. It is this subjectification and location that I investigate in this chapter.

Elias states, "one of the peculiarities of the traditional image of man is that people often think and speak of individuals and societies as if these were two phenomena existing separately."[1] In discussing the impossibility of this separation, Elias tracks the development of the notion of the individual as a free, independent, and "closed personality" in European societies. The implications for the hero's subjectivity can be formulated from Kenneth Gergen's observation, "As it is variously reasoned, it is not the self-contained individual who precedes culture, but the culture that establishes the basic character of psychological functioning."[2] Accordingly, the Victorian hero's subjectivity is inextricably linked to the desires of Victorian society for an ideal hero figure and to the values of that society which constructs such a figure. Englishness, as part of his persona, is also part of the societal construct of the ideal hero. Henty discovered this when his story *The Young Carthaginian* (1887) did not sell as well as expected, an outcome Henty attributed to the inclusion of a non-English hero, a point noted above. Current literature on the notion

---

1. Elias, *Homo Clausus*, 284.
2. Gergen, *Social Construction*, 38.

of the self in terms of personal identity differentiates the core self from the social self. Rina Onorato and John Turner write, "Self-schema theory maintains that the core self comprises our self-schemas," whereas, "self-categorization theory draws a distinction between the personal and the social." They also maintain that the notion of the core self "is not an outdated view."[3] In terms of the Victorian hero's subjectivity, the influence of context, together with his self-schema, merge to construct his ideal character. In his relation to the "other," the hero's desire to propagate the ideal character results in his attempt to turn the "other" into "himself" (or "us"), that is, the English.

When Disraeli stated, "Genius, when young, is divine," he established youth and spirituality as a thread that runs through his political novel *Coningsby* (1844). He elevates the "commonplace" of everyday life to a spiritual plane when he takes the connection into the realms of soteriology in his observation, "It is a holy thing to see a state saved by its youth."[4] This metaphysical language seems far removed from both the nineteenth-century political turmoil in which Disraeli operated and the gritty action of Henty's stories, but in voicing the ideal and the possibility of an ideal, it joins the worlds of Henty and MacDonald and begins to dissolve their opposition as perceived by critics. The popular perception of Henty as the stereotypical representative of the Victorian era is foregrounded in the work of critics from Hugh Walpole (1926) to Margery Hourihan (1997). As I have demonstrated throughout this book, this perception is too simplistic and does not take into account either the breadth of viewpoint represented in Henty evidenced in his work or the complexities of the historical period 1850–1900 indicated in chapter 2 (Historical Context). The subjectivity of the hero articulated in the writing of Henty and investigated in chapter 5 (The Construct of the Hero), inextricably links the ideal youth with the growth, development and support for the British Empire. Henty's ideal youth is partially constructed educationally, by the English public school system, interwoven with the legacy of the symbolically "good" child constructed from Romantic concepts rooted in the imaginative and the spiritual. His idealization in the arena in which he operates, which is predominantly a faraway, exotic location within or outside of the British Empire, is reflected in the idealization of place found in the representation of

3. Onorato and Turner, *Fluidity*, 257, 259.
4. Disraeli, *Coningsby*, 98, 298.

England as a geographical location. His ideal mode of action therefore attempts not only to recreate England geographically, abroad, but to recreate "the English" by enculturation. The physical dominance by land acquisition becomes emotional dominance by cultural imposition and spiritual dominance by the assumption of religious and moral superiority. The faraway lands of the empire, and Africa in particular, as representative of the inner, psychological landscape, is described by Claudia Gualtieri as, "a reflection of the traveller's identity in the mirror of 'the other.'"[5] Nikolas Rose notes the, "elements of self-mastery ... entailed in many regimes of subjectification," result in, "the conjunction to control or civilize an inner nature."[6] In this context the subduing of "the dark continent" within is achieved by socialization and conformity to the Western traveller's cultural norms. The two controlling motives of socialization and conformity to Western norms can relate to both the subconscious mind and the domestic, internal, political situation of change and turmoil found in the transition from an agrarian to an urban social milieu. MacDonald's "other" world of the goblin kingdom can be interpreted as representing both or either of these locations and is illustrative of, "an identity between individual and social quests ... latent in romance."[7] Frye's comment on the position of identity in romance places identity in the same position as that of fantasy (discussed in chapter 3), that is, in the space between the real and the imagined.

Henty's prefaces reinforce his message and encourage reader recognition and hero emulation. One of the borders between history and fiction in Henty's work is found in the hero figure. The hero's education as an English public schoolboy is realized in the persona of the ideal colonial administrator. This persona was the imagined product of the delivery of the curriculum and character education devised by Thomas Arnold to reform and refine the character of the English upper and middle class schoolboy. The result was a body of men (a social identity) who understood exactly the principles upon which they were expected to act. Their mutual understanding developed into a recognizable "type," identifiable with historical figures. Some of their characteristics are found in the fictional figure of the Henty hero. The reality of the subverse position, that position which "subverts" the ideal

---

5. Gualtieri, *The Discourse of the Exotic*, 274.
6. Rose, *Identity*, 317–18.
7. Frye, *Secular Scripture*, 58.

inculcated by education and accepted as the epitome of civilization, is fulfilled in the possibility of the administrator "going native," thereby undermining his designated role. I noted in chapter 5, how Henty subverts his stereotype in the character of Bathurst (*Rujub the Juggler* 1892), and MacDonald constructs heroes with the same characteristics as those found in Henty's work in the character of Curdie and of Turkey (*Ranald Bannerman's Boyhood* 1871). MacDonald's work recognizes that the concept of selfhood delineated in the ideal youth, who is a Victorian social ideal as well as a personal ideal, is not achievable without external, supernatural (or spiritual), intervention. For example, the work that Curdie has to perform in "saving the kingdom" is only possible after a spiritual experience which provides him with the necessary strength (physical and spiritual) and resources. Henty is not so explicit in his integration of spirituality although his heroes frequently demonstrate Christian faith, usually after surviving a life-threatening situation. Examples include Godfrey's prayer in *Condemned as a Nihilist* (231) and Frank Hargrave's in *By Sheer Pluck* (59). In terms of identification, MacDonald's heroes, both male and female, invite emulation as they present an aspirational character. In Henty's work, his prefaces explicitly point to the benefits of aspiring to behave like the boy hero in his story. Henty's explicit comment on how George Andrews in *Sturdy and Strong*, "had opportunities and took advantage of them," aligns him with the adventure hero theorized by Bakhtin whilst simultaneously identifying him potentially with any boy reader. Both Henty and MacDonald lead their heroes through a series of adventures which enable them to discover more about their own identity, both personal and social, although the discovery may happen in the space of romance found in between the two.[8] Curdie reaches a crisis when he has to choose to change his path and take the pigeon he has killed to the Grandmother figure in the attic of the Castle, or continue on his route to becoming "a commonplace man."[9] Gregory Hilliard is faced with moral choices throughout his journey to find evidence of his lost father. His search culminates in the discovery of his true identity and reconciliation with his father's family (*With Kitchener in the Soudan: A Story of Atbara and Omdurman*). Henty's heroes frequently go through a number of identity changes in the form of disguise, whilst his female heroes change

8. Frye, *Secular Scripture*, 58.
9. MacDonald, *Princess and Curdie*, 22.

identity and become "male" in order to have their adventure. When the adventure has reached a successful conclusion, usually in the form of homecoming or reunion with friends who take on the role of protector, the female hero reverts to her female role. Her alter ego as independent male is always depicted by cross-dressing, demonstrated by Nita in *A Soldier's Daughter* (1906), discussed in chapter 5, Clotilde in *The Young Carthaginian* (1887) and Annie in *The Tiger of Mysore* (1896).

Frye's discussion of identity[10] includes the need to escape from a single identity, as seen in the disguise motif, in order to preserve one's real identity when threatened with danger, and the need to recover one's identity. MacDonald's Princess Irene (*The Princess and the Goblin*) recovers her identity as the king's daughter as she discovers more about her forbears (her great-great-grandmother) and as she travels with the king, after being "lost" in the half castle/half house halfway up a mountain, a motif that is evocative of a half-grown child, discovering who she is and her place in life. In this instance, her identity has not exactly been lost, rather it has not yet been found. Henty's characters recover their identity after disguise, not only having switched gender, but often having switched race and apparent political allegiance. This position is demonstrated when Dick Holland is appointed as an officer in the retinue of Tippoo Saib.

In Frye's discussion of themes in romance, his comment on the recovery of identity as a "theme of ascent"[11] brings to the reader's attention escape from a false identity in the discovery of one's core identity. In both Henty and MacDonald, escaping from a perceived identity is preceded by allusions to a different origin. For example, Henty's character Willie Gale is left outside a workhouse on a stormy night. The porter's wife, who hears his cry and sends her husband to investigate, "never wavered in the opinion she had first formed, that the dead tramp was not Billy's mother; but as no one else agreed with her she kept her thoughts to herself." Throughout the story, the "lost child" motif recurs. The porter's wife informs the workhouse guardians of her belief, "I believe he is a gentleman's child, sir. Look at his white skin; see how upright he is . . . he is altogether different from the run of them."[12] Willie Gale is born with a distinctive "blood mark" on his shoulder and it is by means of this

---

10. Ibid., 29, 106.
11. Frye, *Secular Scripture*, 129.
12. Henty, *For Name and Fame*, 31, 32.

mark that he is conclusively identified by his father, an army officer, as a young man. Willie Gale illustrates this extreme form of identity recovery, as does Clare Skymer in his discovery of his father in MacDonald's *A Rough Shaking*. Frye denotes it in terms of a, "growing freedom, and the breaking of enchantment,"[13] language which places these stories not only within the genre of romance but also moves them into the realm of fairy tale.

The hero's growing sense of self in both Henty's and MacDonald's stories involves ideological choices, and the consistent forward movement toward maturation in terms of values and lifestyle. These choices are both personal and social. They also reflect the hero's growing awareness of "the other," those from whom he is different and has chosen to remain different, referred to by Onorato as, "us" versus "them" categorizations.[14] In Henty's stories, the hero's patriotism, which is part of his identity, politicizes him. He is perceived by his contemporaries, by his compatriots and by those of other races who befriend him, as the ideal in character and leadership. MacDonald's representation of the other is less overtly political or social. As a Scot, he is an outsider in England and his critique of his milieu is that of both an observer and of one whose faith and political leanings, seen in his support of Maurice's Christian Socialism, give him insight into that view of society which questions the dominant discourse even whilst working within it and colluding with aspects of it. This questioning is the Marxist notion of "the paradox of art" which Hayden White glosses as, "the fact that artwork 'reflects' the conditions of the time and place of its production and is therefore to be regarded as purely 'timebound' as to its content, while it will manifestly transcend those conditions and speak meaningfully to the problems and concerns of other ages, times and places."[15] Whilst the act of questioning does not necessarily mean that any art will always "speak meaningfully to the problems and concerns of other ages, times and places," in the instances where art is perceived by its audience to do so, it remains, in Marxist theory, a paradox. MacDonald's spirituality casts him in a prophetic role in his critique of the materialism, consumerism, commercialism and the self-seeking he encounters. His stories and novels, for example, *The Princess and Curdie*, provide

13. Frye, *Secular Scripture*, 129.
14. Onorato and Turner, *Fluidity*, 259.
15. White, *Content of the Form*, 156.

evidence of this critique and place him, according to this theory, in a position to speak to other ages. In *The Princess and the Goblin* MacDonald takes this critical position further by extending the representation of "the other" to include the recognition that the other is also "us." This extension added a complication in the pursuit of nineteenth-century imperialism that resulted in the perennial Hegelian argument of justification for empire from the point of both difference and similarity. In the next section, I include investigation of constructs and representations of the "other" in the work of Henty and MacDonald, as a method of, "interrogating notions of hegemony,"[16] in order to elucidate the complexity of the hero figure and his location within nineteenth-century thought. Nineteenth-century imperialist culture requires a synergy between the hero in reality and in the imagination, which transforms their single realities into a regenerated third entity which is the ideal.

The definition of "otherness" as, "the quality or state of existence of being other or different from established norms or social groups,"[17] assumes a centre of normality from which otherness can be perceived. John Stephens discusses "the illusion that ... the present time ... constitutes a normative position,"[18] from the reader's perspective. The starting point for the following discussion is that, in the work of Henty and MacDonald, the nineteenth-century English domestic middle/upper class cultural position is the established norm, despite MacDonald's position as a cultural outsider (a Scot) by birth. This established position therefore brings to the fore the distinction made between the hero's sense of self and his perception of the "other," since this perception reflects the normative position. The discussion then progresses through an investigation of the "other" within that norm, which is, the possibility of "us" turning into the "other," and concludes with the "other" as "us" in the Lacanian sense of, "that which is not really other but is a reflection and projection of the ego."[19]

In Victorian England, the perception of "otherness" through both similarity and difference created a duality characteristic of the period, as the "other," in both the exotic or the domestic context, became an object to be viewed from a position of either perceived brotherhood or

16. Webb, *Discussion*.
17. Wolfreys, Robbins, and Womack, *Key Concepts*, 74.
18. Stephens, *Language and Ideology*, 205.
19. Wolfreys, Robbins, and Womack, *Key Concepts*, 74.

as victim to be rescued from "difference." Geoffrey Galt Harpham notes that the "centre of ethics [is] its concern for 'the other.'"[20] In Victorian England, this concern emanated from an Anglo-centric position and although its apparent focus was on the external "other," I argue that it was also an internal fear situated both in the domestic domain and within the individual. Whether the approach to the colonized "other" was through similarity or difference, it produced the same outcome in terms of action. From the point of view of the colonized, this action would be mirrored as acted upon, in their position as subject peoples.

MacDonald, writing from observations during his stay in Algeria North Africa in the winter of 1856–57, demonstrated an empathy with the colonized which reflected his position as an outsider in English society since he was Scottish, when he wrote, "One cannot help wondering, when he sees the little, jerky, self-asserting, tight-laced Frenchman beside the stately, dignified, reserved, loose-robed Arab, how the former could ever assume and retain authority over the latter."[21] In this quotation MacDonald's comments encapsulate two concepts that come together to form the predominant outlook of the English public toward the people and lands of the British Empire, for, as Gayatri Spivak states, "it should not be possible to read nineteenth-century British literature without remembering that imperialism ... was a crucial part of the representation of England to the English."[22] Although MacDonald was writing about the French occupation of Algeria, the two concepts form a basis for the justification of the British Empire. The first concept, that is, the similarity of other races to "us," the European, rests in the argument of justification for empire from the position of similarity, as Georges-Louis Leclerc, Comte de Buffon, wrote, c. 1748, "Upon the whole, every circumstance concurs in proving that mankind are not composed of species essentially different from each other; that, on the contrary there was originally but one species."[23] From a literary point of view, the concept relates to Frye's positive hermeneutic, that is, an interpretative position with the emphasis on continuity and similarity with the "other." In the quotation above, MacDonald as the outsider is empathetically drawn to the Arab, the occupied, demonstrating his

20. Harpham, *Shadows of Ethics*, 26.
21. MacDonald, *Invalid's Winter*, 146.
22. Spivak, *Thre Women's Texts*, 146.
23. Buffon, in, Eze, *Race and Enlightenment*, 27.

affirmation of a common humanity.[24] The belief that "we" (the civilized) could help "them" (the uncivilized) to attain order and civilization is situated on the premise that what is accepted within the dominant discourse as good for "us" is also good for humanity. Whether the accepted cultural norms and societal structures of Victorian England were "civilized" or not is outside of this discussion, although both Henty and MacDonald critiqued aspects of the society in which they lived. In Kenneth Womack's writing on ethical criticism, he observes that Levinas' moral philosophy "highlights notions of responsibility,"[25] that is, makes clearer a recognition that a perception of sameness brings responsibility. Levinas notes that, "the human . . . begins . . . (with) a preoccupation with the other, even to the point of sacrifice . . . ; a responsibility for the other."[26] The implication of "a preoccupation with the other" is that it would lead to a different outworking of the perception of sameness from that of "the white man's burden" with its connotations of superiority as in a parent-child relationship. The "other" is seen as similar but inferior because not yet "like us." Levinas' view sees the "other" as similar but culturally different with a difference that can only be understood by us as "other" to the "other" if our inherited western assumptions about civilization are interrogated and reassessed.

The second concept, that of difference, rests in the need to bring what the colonizers regard as their own superior civilization to establish order and enlightenment to the other as "different." Stephen Prickett notes that the concept of civilization carries a meaning of "an ideal order of human society involving the arts, learning, and manners" and was used in France in the mid-eighteenth century with "connotations justifying colonial expansion and European linguistic hegemony."[27] Evidence for this assertion is again found in the writing of Georges-Louis Leclerc, Comte de Buffon (1707–88), quoted in Eze, who wrote, "Nothing can reflect greater honour in religion than the civilizing of these nations of barbarians, and laying the foundations of empire without employing any other arms but those of virtue and humanity."[28] Although this concept

24. MacDonald's antipathy towards the French in this passage reflects the English rather than the Scottish position. The Scots as a nation had sympathetic and positive relations with the French.
25. Womack, *Ethical Criticism*, 107.
26. Levinas, *Entre Nous*, xii.
27. Prickett, *Narrative*, 121.
28. Buffon, in, Eze, *Race and Enlightenment*, 20.

may have originated in France with a belief in "the evident superiority of la civilisation française,"[29] Edward Said observes that French imperialism "rarely had the same sense of imperial mission as that found in Britain."[30] The notion of superiority stemmed from a perception of difference, a need to squeeze the culture and lives of the "other" into an English (or French) mold. By so doing, the changes brought about would, so the argument went, improve both the social and moral lives of the unenlightened nations, that is, those nations whose people were outside the European cultural norm. The background to this argument in England is situated in the rise of the evangelical movement with its twin objects of religious conversion and social improvement. In Victorian England, the argument for civilizing the unenlightened viewed the development of nations/races in terms of individual development and growth, from babyhood to adulthood. Consequently, not only were the colonized people regarded as children, incapable of ruling themselves but their nations as a whole were believed to be in an earlier stage of development than that of the English. It followed that as the analogy of the child was applied to a nation or race, then education and discipline were appropriate ways to approach relationship with them. The eighteenth-century imperialists had a different approach. Although they were more overtly and single-mindedly interested in commercial and trade advantage, they generally accepted diversity and viewed local cultural traditions with an element of respect.[31] The adventure stories of the early nineteenth century often went beyond passive acceptance of diversity. Many were influenced by the Rousseauean concept of the noble savage, that is, the purity of life lived in closer harmony with the natural world and driven by a desire for freedom from the encumbrances of Western European "civilization." An example of this type of story can be found in E. J. Trelawney's *Adventures of a Younger Son* (1831). Trelawney wrote, "The light is not less bright because unobscured by, what is falsely called, civilization, on these wild children of the desert."[32] Despite the apparent acceptance of the negative elements of Western European civilization, and praise of the native freedom that the hero finds in exotic locations, it is notable that the indigenous people are still represented as children, an

29. Prickett, *Narrative*, 121.
30. Said, *Culture*, and Imperialism. 74.
31. Hugh Ridley discusses this position in Ridley, *Images*, 1–30.
32. Trelawney, *Adventures*, 46.

implicit endorsement of the developing attitude of white superiority that became entrenched within the second half of the nineteenth century and noted by Eze. David Lorenzo points out that activist policies use both similarities and differences for justifying imperialistic activity, the former in terms of the probable success and consequent benefit of such intervention to the people who experience intervention,[33] and the latter in terms of the need for intervention as a "rescuing" gesture. Hourihan comments on, "the relative nature of terms such as . . . 'civilized' and 'savage' as contingent upon the implied existence of *innately* superior and inferior people."[34]

In early twentieth-century boys' magazines, the morally degenerated "other" became more specifically identified with other races. The resultant enmification helped to create the hostile conditions from which the Great War (1914–18) erupted. It is notable that Henty's writing does not enmify the "other" because he is "other," but represents him partly according to the prevailing view of the time and partly according to his actions. The next section investigates Henty's representation of race, the occupied and the colonized.

Henty, Imperialistic Representation, and Heroic Characteristics

Existing criticism[35] of Henty written before 1990 represents him as almost exclusively racist in his portrayal of nationals other than the English. Although this critique reinforces bell hooks' assertion that, "colonial imperialist paradigms . . . represent blackness one-dimensionally in ways that reinforce and sustain white supremacy,"[36] it does not take into account representations of otherness that do not conform to the stereotype. In the above quotation from hooks I have taken "blackness" as synecdochical for any race other than the English. This critical representation includes Henty's portrayal of other European nationals as well as those of African, Asian, Chinese, or Russian origin. I mentioned earlier, (chapter 2, Historical Context), that Henty's reading of the available scientific texts informed him of the contemporary classification of races in a hierarchy of superiority with the white Anglo-Saxon male at

---

33. Lorenzo, *Portrayal*, 35–37.
34. Hourihan, *Deconstructing the Hero*, 144.
35. See for example Schmidt, *Writer as Teacher*.
36. hooks, *Postmodern Blackness*, 366.

the top. Henty's generalization of the characteristics of other European races such as that found in *The Young Franc-Tireurs* (1872) is often contradicted by individual characters from those races. For example, "The French boy does not play; at least he does not play roughly. . . . [H]e considers any exertion which would disarrange his hair or his shirt-collar as barbarous and absurd. . . . This is the general type of French schoolboy. Of course there are many exceptions." Henty continues by citing exceptions, with the proviso that they are exceptions partly because of the influence of their English cousins, "Their [the English boys] example has had some effect; their cousins . . . are almost as fond of cricket and other games . . . as they are themselves."[37] In his review of Arnold's *Held Fast for England* (1980), C. P. Snow points out that what Arnold missed in substantiating his sub-title, *Imperialist boy's writer*, was that,

> In many ways Henty's books show a kind of racial tolerance that wasn't in unison with majority singing. He believed in the Empire, certainly: he had an acute feeling for hierarchy, and had his class partiality much more highly developed than his racial one. It was perfectly proper in the Henty world for gentlemanly, if impoverished, young English adventurers to love and marry girls of any race and colour provided that the girls were high enough born. That would have seemed heresy in the circles Henty lived with, and for whose children he wrote.[38]

Eric Stokes concurs with this assessment when he writes, "Henty's ethnic stereotypes are . . . much less simple and fixed than Guy Arnold at first suggests. Having set them up Henty deliberately punctures the partition walls between them."[39]

Although Henty undoubtedly portrays other races in a way a contemporary reader now finds unacceptable in some instances, he counterbalances this description in other texts and frequently subverts his own stereotype, noted above in the character of Sam (*The Young Buglers*, 1880) who, through his initiative and bravery, emerges as the true hero of the story. An example of such a contradiction can also be found in the way his character Mr. Goodenough describes the character of the West African in *By Sheer Pluck* (1884), "They are just like children . . . they are absolutely without originality, absolutely without inventive

37. Henty, *Young Franc-Tireurs*, 9.
38. Snow, *True Grit*, 15.
39. Stokes, *From Mexico*, 406.

power . . ."⁴⁰ Not only does this quotation perpetuate the construction of the native" as "child," but it includes an unwritten assumption that the measure of imagination (originality, inventive power) is based upon Western European cultural norms. The contradiction lies in comparison with Henty's portrayal of Sam in *The Young Buglers* as imaginative, full of initiative and heroic. A similar Eurocentric argument is found in Hegel's theories which state that non- European peoples have no history, "history is in fact out of the question," on the premise that non-Europeans are "less aware of themselves as conscious historical beings."[41]

Henty also demonstrates the use of speech structures to convey "otherness."[42] His portrayal of the old chief in *By Sheer Pluck* (1884) who greets Mr. Goodenough and Frank with "Me berry glad to see you"[43] demonstrates this tendency. The use of pidgin English in these contexts emphasizes the superiority of the white man by the implication that the African cannot speak "proper" English, despite the fact that the story and behavior of the character cited exceeds that of other characters in "gentlemanliness" and courage. A discursive passage found in *A Soldier's Daughter* (1906), focalized through the officer Charlie Carter, includes the description of the outstanding fighting prowess of the African regiment, "There are no finer fighters in the world than the Sikhs. . . . They are all magnificent, but are equalled in Africa by the Hausas and other tribes."[44] Comparable passages exist with reference to other races, the Turks for example. Henty occasionally delivers a disparaging comment on a character in such a matter of fact way that he appears unconscious of how belittling it is, as in this comment from *Condemned as a Nihilist*, "Petrovytch was an excellent agent as far as he went. The business he did was sound, and he was careful and conscientious; but he lacked push and energy, had no initiative, and would do nothing on his own responsibility."[45] Henty applies this judgement to the character of the Russians available to work in the Bullen family firm generally, and in the process uses it as point of detrimental comparison to the "push, energy,

---

40. Henty, *By Sheer Pluck*, 118.
41. Eze, *Race and Enlightenment*, 126, 109.
42. This concept is discussed by Stephens, *Language and Ideology*, 220.
43. Henty, *By Sheer Pluck*, 168.
44. Henty, *Soldier's Daughter*, 24.
45. Henty, *Condemned as a Nihilist*, 15.

The Ideology of the Hero and the Representation of the "Other"

initiative and willingness to take responsibility" of his young English hero Godfrey who travels to St Petersburg to begin his career.

My final example on the subject of Henty and race representation comes from two disparate portrayals of Jewish people. Both are found in stories set in a pre-nineteenth-century historical context. The first is from *A Jacobite Exile* (1894). The character of Ben Soloman Muller, a Polish Jew, is represented as the archetypal evil Jew, in line with the Victorian portrayal of the evil Svengali. He is unscrupulous, has a total disregard for the value of human life and cares only about adding to his money. From the moment he is introduced into the story, when he is "one . . . of whom he (the hero) felt doubtful," he is portrayed as a man who exerts his influence by terror. He has "agents all over the country," which would make it difficult "to get beyond (his) clutches" he attacks the hero Charlie "with an angry snarl," he is described even by brigands as, "an artful fox," and carries a "long knife" (shown in the illustration as curved) with which he attacks Charlie.[46]

Figure 3: Charlie encounters Ben Soloman in the wood

46. Henty, *Jacobite Exile*, 177, 193, 195, 201, 195.

In contrast to Ben Soloman Muller are the characters Solomon Ben Manasseh and John, the hero of the story *For the Temple* (1887). Solomon Ben Manasseh is described as, "a man of considerable influence in Galilee. He was a tall stern-looking old man, with bushy black eyebrows, deep-set eyes, and a long beard of black hair streaked with grey."[47] He is portrayed as wise, kind and reliable. John himself displays all the characteristics of the Henty hero examined in chapter 5. He is so exemplary a hero, that his modelling of the moral code underpinning the English public school system, that is, the Hebrew Old Testament, ensures the reader's knowledge of its origin despite its British enculturation. John is an example of Henty writing the nineteenth century into the first century. He illustrates White's proposition that historical narratives are informed by "the moral authority of the narrator."[48] The historical context for the story is AD 70 when the land was under Roman occupation, whilst the geographical context is Galilee to Jerusalem. It could be argued that the representation of John as Jew is embedded in the context of the Hebrew race in Palestine, whereas Ben Soloman Muller represents the perceived degeneration of some of the Jewish community in Europe at a much later date,[49] but this suggestion is speculative rather than corroborated by Henty's writing.

Henty also demonstrates an awareness of the difficulties caused by racial prejudice to those of non-English origin living in England. A passage from *With the Allies to Pekin* (1904) represents Ah Lo reflecting on Rex's suggestion that he should marry. (Ah Lo accompanies Rex to England chiefly in order to "keep up" Rex's knowledge and use of the Chinese language through conversation). Apart from the risk of not getting "the right woman," Ah Lo concludes, "Suppose I had married before I came over here, . . . I could not have brought her over here; the people would have pointed at her in the street, the boys would have called after her, and she would have been miserable."[50] This statement demonstrates awareness that "this is how people are," without any

---

47. Henty, *For the Temple*, 7.
48. White, *Value of Narrativity*, 271.
49. This character is depicted in Disraeli's *Coningsby*, which may or may not have been read by Henty, but was a standard prop in the popular drama of the nineteenth century in the character of Svengali. As such, the character of Ben Soloman may have been a deliberate depiction of a well-known villain/comic character.
50. Henty, *With the Allies*, 28–29.

further comment, but a passage in *The Tiger of Mysore* (1901) takes this awareness further. Dick Holland and his mother set out for India with the intention of searching for his lost father. Mrs. Holland cautions Dick, as follows, "Say nothing about my having been born in India, or that my father was a native rajah. Some of these officials—and still more, their wives—are very prejudiced, and consider themselves to be quite different beings to the natives of the country."[51] Margaret Holland's precaution derives from previous experience and illustrates a particular instance of the "other" as "the factor that enables the subject to build up a self-image."[52] Her brief description of the attitude of "some of these officials—and still more, their wives," in itself provides a gloss on the question put by Isobel in *Rujub the Juggler* (1892) as to why the English should be hated in India. Henty's inclusion of mixed marriages and his treatment of the exemplars cited above, demonstrates a more liberal outlook than his stereotypical persona has allowed. Henty's work, critiqued almost exclusively as that of "the most imperialistic of all imperialists"[53] also contains passages of insight into the position of the occupied, the colonized, the marginalized and the oppressed. This assertion can be demonstrated from the following stories: *For the Temple* (1887), *Rujub the Juggler* (1892), *The Tiger of Mysore* (1901), *A Jacobite Exile* (1894), and *Condemned as a Nihilist* (1893). In all of these stories there are quite unexpectedly discursive passages relating to the position of the occupied, the colonized, the marginalized and the oppressed which are rarely mentioned in the critique of Henty which continues the view of Henty as a stereotypically insensitive propagator of the imperial myth. He was a propagator of imperialism, and often followed the perceived scientific evidence of his time in terms of racial classification, fitness of the English as rulers, and the gospel of "the white man's burden" in a general sense, but within his stories are subversive passages that undermine this persona. This subversion can be illustrated by the following examples. The first example is primarily from a story in which the hero is living under oppressive occupation which propels him into resistance.

---

51. Henty, *Tiger of Mysore*, 21.
52. Cavallaro, *Critical and Cultural Theory*, 120.
53. Downey, *Book of Anecdote*, 115–16.

The Occupied

In *For the Temple* (1887), John, the son of a Jewish farmer and the hero of the story, belongs to the Jewish race currently living in a land occupied by the Romans. The subtitle of the book is "*a tale of the fall of Jerusalem.*" The date is therefore c. 70 AD. As an historical novel, this story displays two basic flaws. The first is that John shows all the attributes of Henty's boy heroes as discussed in chapter 5 (The Construct of the Hero), and is therefore an English boy with a public school background in the persona of a Jewish farmer's son. The second is the tendency of the narrator to step out of historic time in order to comment on a particular situation or action from a point of view contemporary to the writer. An example of this narratorial intrusion is the comment, "for the modern feeling that it is right to kill even the bitterest enemy only in fair fight was wholly unknown in those days, when men . . . would cut the throat of a sleeping foe with no more compunction than if they were slaughtering a fowl."[54] This passage is an example of Henty's concern to instruct his young readers in moral and honourable behavior as well as encouraging bravery and resourcefulness. His story *The Young Carthaginian* (1887) includes similar passages. In *For the Temple* (1887), John's chosen method of harassing the Roman soldiers after the destruction of the town of Jotapata and Gamala is guerrilla warfare. John recognizes the impossibility of fighting the Romans in conventional battle conditions early in his service to Josephus and determines to, "collect a band, and take to the mountains, and harass them [the Romans] whenever we may find the opportunity." The rationale was to, "do the Romans as much harm as possible."[55] John begins by harassing the troop sent to cut wood for the Roman camp and in this way builds up the confidence of his band before making plans to set fire to the Roman camp, an action which is successfully carried out. The kind of tactics adopted by John and his band would be regarded in a twenty-first-century context as terrorism. The actions are defended as gestures, "for our country and for the Temple," from men who, "must be ready to give their lives when need be." Later in the story, John is captured by the Romans as a result of a direct encounter with Titus, the son of the Governor Vespasian. John's account of his humane treatment at the hands of Titus leads to a reflec-

---

54. Henty, *For the Temple*, 139.
55. Ibid., 111, 22.

tion on behavior in warfare generally. Simon, John's father, demonstrates an awareness of the point of view of "the enemy" when he observes,

> It is rarely that pity enters into the heart of a Roman . . . and yet it is hardly for us to complain, for when we crossed over the Jordan and conquered Canaan we put all to the sword and spared none. It may be that in the future, if wars do not altogether cease in the world, they will be waged in another spirit; but so far, from the commencement of the world until now, it has ever been the same, war has brought desolation and destruction upon the vanquished.[56]

In voicing such reflections through his characters, Henty steps out of the historical time in which his story is set, as he does in *A Soldier's Daughter*, demonstrating an awareness of the consequences of war not usually associated with his writing. Another interpretation of this passage could be that Henty is writing an oblique message to his readers to indicate that war "waged in another spirit" applies to "England's many little wars,"[57] although, taken with the comments on war cited above and his own experience this interpretation does not seem likely.

Comparable, yet converse, situations can be cited in *A Soldier's Daughter* (1906) and in *For Name and Fame* (1886) which feature uprisings in Northern India and in Afghanistan, where the "'natives" carry out just the sort of hill country based skirmishes described in *For the Temple*. The difference is that it is the British who are in the position of the Romans, the heroes of both stories are English and the assumption is that for the sake of the empire, the uprisings should be "dealt with." It is beyond the remit of this work to examine such comparisons within Henty's work from a political aspect. For the current purposes it is sufficient to say that the hero figure is interchangeable, his or her personal attitudes and actions map to the same set of values, regardless of affiliation. Both occupation and colonization inevitably feature as situational in stories of empire, with India as a major location for British imperial activity. Henty's representation of the point of view of the colonized is largely drawn from a story of the Indian uprising of 1857.

---

56. Henty, *For the Temple*, 187, 188, 212–13.
57. Henty, *On the Irrawaddy*, vii.

The Colonized

> "But why should he hate us, Doctor?"

This question is asked by Isobel Hannay soon after her arrival in India. Her bewilderment is because, she reasons, "he is none the worse off now than he was before we annexed the country," and the question is asked of Dr. Wade after he has pointed out that, "The one would pick your pockets of every penny you had got, . . . the other would cut your throat with just as little compunction. . . . [A]nd three out of four of those men you see walking about there, would not only cut the throat of a European to obtain what money he had about him, but would do so without that incentive, upon the simple ground that he hated us."[58] Isobel's lack of experience has led her to accept the received wisdom that the "natives" are better off under British rule and the British are the right people to govern as they are improving the lot of benighted peoples. This view is illustrated by the statement, "No worse government has ever existed than that of Burma when, with the boast that she intended to drive the British out of India, she began the war, . . . the occupation of the country by the British has been an even greater blessing to the population than has that of India."[59] This quotation is from Henty's preface to *On the Irrawady* and indicates that this was his belief, in keeping with the dominant discourse in England in the mid- to late-nineteenth century. Nevertheless, Henty also demonstrates a more complex understanding of the political situations into which he writes his stories. In *Rujub the Juggler* (1892), a story written in the context of, from a Victorian viewpoint, the Indian mutiny, he continues the conversation between Isobel and Dr. Wade with an explanation as to why "he should hate us," "Well yes, that class of man is worse off. In the old days every noble in Zemindar kept up a little army for the purpose of fighting his neighbours, just as our Barons used to do in the happy olden times people talk of. We put down private fighting, and the consequence is these men's occupations are gone."[60]

Dr. Wade breaks off the explanation to point out the Rajah amongst the crowd and the discussion turns to his friendliness to the English, which the Doctor finds unnatural, given that, as he observes, "We

---

58. Henty, *Rujub*, 67.
59. Henty, *On the Irrawaddy*, viii.
60. Henty, *Rujub*, 67–68.

undoubtedly, according to native notions, robbed him of one of the finest positions in India."[61] Both of these explanations and observations on the behavior of, on the one hand, the poor man and, on the other, the rich in Indian society indicate an understanding of the impact of British intervention in Indian affairs and another example of the Victorian mind's ability to live with what appears to the modern and post-modern mind as a contradiction, since the beneficial effect of British annexation is not in question for Henty.

Whilst holding the view that it is right and proper for the British to govern India, Henty is able to put forward a coherent argument for the impact, political problems and hostility encountered. In his explanation of the reasons the poor man has to hate Europeans, Henty focalizes the view through Dr. Wade that the colonized people are at a less developed stage of political evolution than are the English, when he adds, "just as our Barons used to do." The implication is that the stage of development was, to quote Iain Wright citing Barthes, "progressive in relation to its past, but barbarous in relation to our present."[62] In voicing this argument Henty's character Dr. Wade not only retains the assumption that "we" are therefore at a more advanced stage of civilization but also implies the process of maturation commensurate with the development of a child is applicable to national development, and in so doing, reinforces the construct of "the natives" as children. The same argument is found in *With the Allies to Pekin* (1904) where the Darwinian concept of the nation as evolving is applied to China. Methods of punishment and reasons for capital punishment are compared to Elizabethan England, when, "any persons found begging were executed, or, as a mild punishment for a first offence, had their hands or ears cut off."[63]

In this story of the relief of the Legations, Henty includes a sympathetic advocate for the Chinese point of view in the character of Rex's father and a comment on the unreasonable reaction to two deaths on the part of the European powers (in this case German) which fuelled the uprising. Henty also subverts his characters' and his own assertions of superiority on the occasions he inserts a brief discussion about war. For example, in *A Soldier's Daughter* (1906) Nita Ackworth reflects on her feelings should she be involved in defending the fort if attacked whilst

61. Ibid., 68.
62. Wright, *Hermeneutical Ethics*, 86.
63. Henty, *With the Allies*, 99.

the main body of soldiers is away on an expedition. Nita is identified as the hero early in the story. She has "pluck," courage, and initiative, and displays "all the virtues of a boy."[64] She is in conversation with Charlie Carter, the officer in charge in her father's absence, when she reflects, "It is a funny thing, isn't it, that men should be so fond of fighting?" Charlie responds, "It is; . . . all savage races love fighting and certainly our own people do. . . . I'm afraid this instinct brings us very near the savage. I think no other nation possesses it to anything like the same extent as the British race." "I expect," Nita said, "it is because we have that feeling that we always win our battles." The same discussion includes accolades to the fighting ability of other races, the Sikhs, the Punjaubis, the Ghoorkhas and the Hausas (spelling of names as in the text). Henty's perception of the European situation, focalized through Charlie, demonstrates a prescience of future events when he writes, "If there were a great war, hundreds and thousands of men would volunteer at once. . . . I thoroughly believe that the Volunteers would turn out as one man if we had a very serious war, say with France or Germany." "That would be a very serious war," Nita said.[65]

A Soldier's Daughter was published posthumously in 1906 as a "long short-story"[66] in a volume with two further stories. Henty died in 1902 therefore even if it was amongst his last pieces of work it was written approximately thirteen years before the outbreak of World War I, demonstrating Henty's intuitive apprehension of the direction in which both the English and the European political situation was moving. A discussion on the European political situation continues for another three pages, an inclusion which demonstrates Henty's political awareness and willingness to insert analysis into his stories, and to voice the serious personal impact of war as well as the possibility of honor to be gained. The accusation of his unmitigated glorification of war is balanced by less quoted passages highlighting the barbarity and terrible consequences of war. The preface to *The Tiger of Mysore* (1896) begins with the unexpected sentence, "While some of our (the English) wars in India are open to the charge that they were undertaken on slight provocation, and were forced on by us in order that we might have an excuse for annexation, our struggle with Tippoo Saib was, on the other hand,

---

64. Huttenback, *G. A. Henty*, 70.
65. Henty, *Soldier's Daughter*, 23–24, 22, 25.
66. Pruen and Berlyne, *Henty Companion*. 6.

The Ideology of the Hero and the Representation of the "Other"

marked by long endurance of wrong, and a toleration of abominable cruelties perpetrated upon Englishmen and our native allies."[67] Henty then briefly describes the background to the war with Tippoo Saib (the Tiger of Mysore). Henty's criticism of the way the "struggle" was conducted continues even whilst he justifies the need for it. This story includes passages in which Dick (the hero) discusses with his uncle the Rajah the politics of the regions under his uncle's supervision and those regions through which he, Dick, may have to pass in order to discover his father's whereabouts. During the course of the story the complexity of the political situation, both historically and contemporarily, unfolds. On occasion this discussion includes the involvement of the French, their treatment of the native population and the additional complications of the "quarrels and jealousies" of the Mahratti chiefs.[68] A picture emerges of utter confusion, fuelled by the attempts of European countries to subdue each other by their support of different native rulers. Henty's reading of the historical situation is corroborated by John Keay in his study *India: a History* (2000). Henty describes, "the direct impact on internal human groupings"[69] effected by annexation, including a passage voiced by a Hindoo soldier, an officer, who comments on the changes effected in the Rajah's region, "Now there is no longer a need for an army; there is no one to fight. Some of the young men grumble but the old ones rejoice at the change. . . . Now that the Rajah has no longer to keep up an army, he is not obliged to squeeze the cultivators; therefore they pay but a light rent for their lands."[70] This description, included in Henty's text in order to foreground the benefits of English rule, adds to the complications of the debate and can be set alongside a short passage in *With Kitchener in the Soudan* (1903) where the Mahmud's men are debating the fate of the captured Gregory. One of the emirs contends, "Were it for ourselves only, we would say let him live. . . . But our people complain. They say his folk, with whom we have no quarrel, come here and aid the Egyptians against us."[71] The implicit question is "why are they here?," but this question is never asked since Henty is writing out of "the complexes of ideas which the author assumed to be the natural property of his audience,"

67. Henty, *Tiger of Mysore*, preface.
68. Ibid., 362.
69. Preiswierk, *The Slant of the Pen*, 3.
70. Henty, *Tiger of Mysore*, 55.
71. Henty, *With Kitchener*, 191.

as Milman Parry, quoted in Jerome McGann, explains."[72] One of these "ideas" was that the British rule was unquestionably beneficial, justified by both the similarity and the difference arguments cited above.

In the story *Condemned as a Nihilist* (1893), the hero, Godfrey Bullen, asserts, "I hate revolutionists and assassins." He listens to a rationale for the growth of nihilism starting with the statement that, "the pioneers of this movement were earnest and thoughtful men, with noble dreams for the regeneration of Russia."[73] Whilst not condoning the anarchist method, the speaker, Ivan Petrovytch, with whom Godfrey lodges, explains the growth of the movement and concludes, "Their propaganda was at first a peaceful one. It is cruelty that has driven them to use the only weapon at their disposal, assassination."[74] Understanding the motivation for extreme political actions, also demonstrated in *For the Temple* and *Rujub the Juggler*, is inserted into these narratives and gives an unexpected slant on the expected simplistically imperialistic argument. The accepted view that "Henty distilled for his young readers the approved doctrines and dogmas of his age"[75] is modified by Michael Edwardes who notes that the continuing interest in Henty is partially due to his inclusion of detail that "turns out, not only to be historically satisfying, but courageous, unpleasant, above all-critical."[76] Edwardes refers not only to issues of race and politics but also to Henty's commentary on political decisions of the English Government and on his criticism of the behavior of some of the accepted "heroes" of empire.

Henty frequently subverts his overt imperialistic message by the inclusion of instances of superior behavior in other races. That Henty was an Imperialist does not mean he was in agreement with every action taken in the name of imperial expansion. Although Henty does not approach the level of empathy towards occupied people found in MacDonald's essay *An Invalid's Winter in Algeria* (1864), he demonstrates a broader understanding and critique of political perspective in British colonial affairs and in European politics than his critics[77] recognize in their writing. Eric Stokes' comment that "Henty's ethnic

72. McGann, *Introduction*, 8.
73. Henty, *Condemned as a Nihilist*, 12, 63.
74. Ibid., 66.
75. Richards, *Imperialism*, 73.
76. Edwardes, *True to the Old Flag*, 459.
77. For example, Arnold, *Held Fast for England*; Hastings, *When Boys*.

stereotypes are ... much less simple and fixed than Guy Arnold ... suggests," is followed by Stokes' suggestion that the reason for Arnold's position may be, "a sense of guilt that gets in the way of objective appreciation, because of the apparent acceptance ... of the unacceptable faces of 'capitalist imperialism.'"[78] Written in 1980 at a time when, as Stokes intimates, Britain's colonial activity was regarded more as an embarrassment than an historical study, assessment was less acceptable than it was in 2003 when Niall Ferguson's work *Empire*, in which the impact of empire is discussed, was published. As with other, more eminent figures such as Ruskin, Henty's work demonstrates what is perceived in the twenty-first century as the contradictory and inconsistent views found in the nineteenth-century milieu. He takes a Victorian imperialistic stance and a belief in the benefits of British rule whilst providing a commentary to answer the question, "Why should he [a native of Oude] hate us?" Spivak observes, "imperialism ... was a crucial part of the representation of England to the English."[79] This collective representation in the domestic sphere transferred to the exotic spaces of the empire on an individual level through the ideal character of the Henty hero. This ideal constructed the hero both to himself and to the wider world, as leader, thus determining the hero's view of the "other," and also establishing him as a leader at home, in the domestic sphere, on his return to England, often to become a Member of Parliament.

MacDonald and Imperialistic Representation

MacDonald is not typically critiqued from an imperialistic perspective,[80] although his stories do contain allusions to the imperial historical context out of which he wrote. For example, on Diamond's first journey with her, North Wind's task is to sink a ship. The discussion between Diamond and North Wind centres on how the apparent cruelty and distress entailed in such an act fits in with the wider scheme of understanding on a spiritual level, but the ship is later revealed as Mr Coleman's "last venture," which had, "gone out ... with the hope of turning its cargo to the best advantage."[81] Although the failure of the enterprise might imply

78. Stokes, *From Mexico*, 406.

79. Spivak, *Three Womwn's Texts*, 146.

80. The only directly imperialistic critique of MacDonald I am aware of is Elmer Schenkel's essay on *Lilith* in Schenkel, *Lilith*.

81. MacDonald, *At the Back*, 247.

some criticism of imperial trade in the form of retributive justice for commercial exploitation, the loss of the ship is addressed in terms of the effect on the Coleman family, financially, emotionally, intellectually and spiritually, and as an illustration of North Wind's other-worldly approach to this-worldly events. The overseas trade with the colonies entailed in its loss is accepted as part of the historical setting out of which MacDonald wrote the story. MacDonald's inclusion of such detail is evidence of interpellation, the unrecognized acceptance of ideological assumptions theorized by Althusser.[82] In this instance I suggest that MacDonald demonstrates the acceptance of empire as so much part of life that it is not recognized as ideology. A similar example can be found in *A Rough Shaking* where the context of Clare's presence in Italy is his father's captaincy of a gunboat, a symbol of English imperial control and power. MacDonald makes no comment on this detail, it is incidental to his story, but it may be permissible to speculate that as the first ironclad gunboat was stationed in Italy (and visited by Henty in his capacity of correspondent in 1865), this milestone of Victorian engineering was part of the furniture of the Victorian mind by 1891 when MacDonald wrote *A Rough Shaking*. His inclusion of the gunboat is therefore part of a context of "beliefs, politics and customs" that are shared and understood"[83] and is evidence of Levine's assertion that a critic of economic, social and religious positions in his own society, as MacDonald was, could also be unaware of his own complicity in aspects of the society he critiqued.[84] In his essay *An Invalid's Winter in Algeria* (1864) MacDonald notes the prominent military presence of the French in French Algeria and describes the, "mortifying hand of the conquerors," not only over the inhabitants but also over the environment. MacDonald never refers to the Arabs as "natives," and notes their personal dignity as superior to any European when he writes, "There is something in the bearing and manners of the Arab significant, whether truly or not, of a personal dignity far beyond that common to the German, or French, or English." He emphasizes the commonality that "knew that England and Africa were of the same earth."[85] In this essay he demonstrates an empathy with the occupied people that is not unexpected. As mentioned above, as a

82. Althusser, *On Ideology*, 308–10.
83. Stephens, *Language and Ideology*, 10.
84. Levine, *Victorian Studies*, 133.
85. MacDonald, *An Invalid's Winter*, 143, 146, 144.

Scot and an outsider in English society, MacDonald would be in a better position to identify with the "other" in an occupied land, and in this essay he represents the occupied people as "the person on the other side of the barrier . . . as a human being worthy of sympathy."[86] In his novel *What's Mine's Mine* (1886), MacDonald writes, "how many, who seemed respectable people at home, become vulgar, self-indulgent, ruffianly, cruel even, in the wilder parts of the colonies! . . . No perfection of mere civilization kills the savage in a man."[87] The concern of MacDonald for a person's inner life is clearly paramount. The first half of the quotation, "how many, who seemed respectable people at home, become vulgar, self-indulgent, ruffianly, cruel even, in the wilder parts of the colonies!" indicates his interest in the possibility of degeneration as well as of progression. This concept of degeneration will be explored more fully below but his comment demonstrates an awareness of the effect a position of power, the need to ensure order and a potentially hostile environment, all of which a colonial official would encounter, could have upon a person. It encapsulates all the underlying fears about the Englishman "going native," since the cultural assumption was that "going native" meant a reversion to "savagery."

The second half of the quotation, "No perfection of mere civilization kills the savage in a man," brings the same concept back into the domestic sphere, raising the question of the "savages" at home and linking the colorized subject to the position of the urban poor in England. The comment goes beyond this analogy to the internal savagery potentially present in everyman, even the Victorian hero figure, and correlating colonial space and internal, psychological landscape. In drawing on images from an imperialistic framework of thought, MacDonald taps into his contemporary context, using familiar concepts. His purpose, treated in depth by John Pridmore,[88] was to elicit a response in his readers that would cause them to question their own internal, spiritual, state. Commensurate with his radical Christian outlook, MacDonald used a term such as "race" not in the scientific sense of the classification of human "races," but in terms of mankind or family, the human "race," and generally in the context of redemption. Typical examples can be found in the novels *Adela Cathcart* (1864) and *Robert Falconer* (1868).

---

86. Nussbaum, *Exactly and Responsibly*, 354.
87. MacDonald, *What's Mine's*, 362.
88. Pridmore, *Transfiguring Fantasy*.

MacDonald does however use racial connotations and demonstrates his familiarity with the scientific and theological texts on the subject of human origins in the following passage, "His foolish arguments against infidelity, drawn from Paley's *Natural Theology*, and tracts about the inspiration of the Bible, touched the sore-hearted unbelief of the man no nearer than the clangour of negro kettles affects the eclipse of the sun."[89] Similarly, "I was once present at the worship of some being who is supposed by negroes to love drums and cymbals, and all clangorous noises"[90] reveals a use of the stereotypical image of the "negro" as synonymous with noise and primitivism. The apparent contradiction of these passages with the assertion that, "Nothing will do for Jew or Gentile, Frenchman or Englishman, Negro or Circassian, town boy or country boy, but the kingdom of heaven which is within him, and must come to the outside of him,"[91] in its eclecticism and egalitarianism is another instance of the belief in a common humanity and condition, overlaid by a contextual, "system of representations."[92] MacDonald's novel *Sir Gibbie* (1879) includes the character of Sambo, "a negro sailor."[93] Despite the stereotypical name, the standard epithet given to black characters and found in Henty in the characters of Sam *The Young Buglers* (1880), and Sam in *By Sheer Pluck* (1884), Sambo's behavior is represented as far superior to that of the other sailors who frequent the lodging house where he meets Gibbie. MacDonald describes him as "not easily provoked," as he "bore even with those who treated him with far worse than the ordinary superciliousness of white to black" so emphasizing this treatment as offensive. Sambo is treated as "other" by the sailors and eventually murdered. The ostensible reason for his murder is that he stood up to, and humiliated, his tormentors. The implied reason is that this humiliation was unacceptable because he was "other." His acceptance by, and befriending of, Gibbie emphasizes Sambo's position as "such a good man,"[94] and the note that his murderers were discovered, tried, and executed,"[95] establishes his equal entitlement to justice.

89. MacDonald, *Robert Falconer*, 340.
90. MacDonald, *David Elginbrod*, 327.
91. MacDonald, *Robert Falconer*, 110.
92. Barker, *Making Sense*, 54.
93. MacDonald, *Sir Gibbie*, 44.
94. Ibid., 45, 46.
95. Ibid., 47.

Martha Nussbaum, in her defence of ethical criticism, notes that an encouragement to empathetically understand the other is a function that literary works may fulfil, when she writes about "the role of the imagination in promoting compassion,"[96] and Harpham states, "I see this intimate and dynamic engagement with otherness as "the key to the kingdom of ethics,"[97] a statement which strongly reinforces Nussbaum's observation. MacDonald's work encourages such empathy whilst still holding images of otherness in line with contemporary stereotypes. He occasionally uses the image of the Arab to convey otherness in the form of the exotic, as in *Wilfrid Cumbermede*,[98] but his emphasis is on the commonality of the human race. MacDonald's belief that in constructing the hero figure he is representing the possibility of what a person could become in terms of the ideal does not preclude his representing the possibility of degeneration, the movement away from the ideal, which is discussed in the next section.

"Us" Turning into the "Other"

The perceived need for education and discipline as appropriate ways to approach relationship with the "other" was applied not only in the colonial context but also to Victorian domestic policy. The perception of the dominant authorities within society, that is, the ruling classes, was that the growing underclass of urban poor within nineteenth century cities was equally in need of socialization and education. The position of the poor in this context has been discussed at length in an article by Jules Zanger.[99] Both the colonized and the poor were viewed as "child," and therefore in need of socialization in order to teach conformity to the norms of society. In MacDonald's *Princess* books, the position of the goblins can be read as a reflection of the Victorian preoccupation with the position of the "other" and therefore another instance of the social commentary embedded in MacDonald's writing.

The possibility of "us" turning into the "other" is both collective and individual. Collectively the concept centres on a regressive Darwinian model, the fear of degeneration, or downward evolution. The fear of a

---

96. Nussbaum, *Exactly and Responsibly*, 350.
97. Harpham, *Shadows of Ethics*, x.
98. MaDonald, *Wilfrid Cumbermede*, 33, 423, 54.
99. Zanger, *Goblins, Morlocks, and Weasels: Classic Fantasy and the Industrial Revolution*.

growing underclass in which the ideal English youth, with heroic potential, may be swallowed up was ever present to the Victorians. Disraeli's novel *Sybil: or the Two Nations* (1845) refers to the rich and the poor and foregrounds the need to address the discrepancy between them before it is too late, too late being the realization of another anxiety, the fear that a repeat of the French revolution would come to England. I noted above Henty's preface to *St George for England* (1885), where he writes, "The courage of our forefathers has created the greatest Empire in the world[;] . . . if this Empire is ever lost, it will be by the cowardice of their descendants,"[100] implicitly voicing the awareness that the present courage of the English was in danger of degenerating into cowardice. The passage referring to the decline of Carthage in *The Young Carthaginian* concludes "the result is inevitable—wasted powers, gross mismanagement, final ruin."[101]

Later in the story, the same statement is made about Rome, "as Rome increases in wealth and luxury she will suffer from the like evils that are destroying Carthage."[102] This thinly disguised gloss on Victorian England and the potential for similar loss of empire lends a sense of urgency to his prefaces in which he urges his boy readers to emulate the hero. The passage above, written in 1887, precedes Max Nordau's study *Degeneration* (1892) by five years and is indicative of a wider European perception of the dangers of degeneration. Nordau also advocates emigration as a solution to unemployment, envisaging the displacement of "lower races" by emigrants, with the implication of colonization and dominance. His contrast between fictional characters whom he regards as degenerates and "men who rise early . . . who have clear heads, solid stomachs and hard muscles,"[103] correlates with the characteristic of physical strength promoted by muscular Christianity discussed in chapter 5 of this book.

MacDonald goes further in his warning about the corrupting influence of "wealth and luxury" in the second of his longer fairy tales, *The Princess and Curdie* (1883). Critiqued as a prophecy of doom by, for example, Robert Lee Wolff,[104] this story depicts the corruption of the

100. Henty, *St George*, preface.
101. Henty, *Young Carthaginian*, 38.
102. Ibid., 263.
103. Nordau, *Degeneration*, 541.
104. Wolff, *Golden Key*, 176–79.

palace officials who are slowly poisoning the king with a view to seizing power, the unscrupulous behavior of the citizens for whom wealth creation and personal advantage has become paramount, and the ultimate destruction of the city of Gwyntystorm as greed for gold and jewels have literally under-mined the city's foundations causing it to collapse in on itself, "One day at noon, when life was at its highest, the whole city fell with a roaring crash. . . . All around spreads a wilderness of wild deer, and the very name of Gwyntystorm has ceased from the lips of men."[105]

The message is the same from both Henty and MacDonald: moral degeneration leads to destruction of society. Their view aligns with that of the English author William Cobbett, writing in the earlier part of the nineteenth century, in his denunciation of "the corruption of the commercial system,"[106] and Thomas Carlyle who wrote on the decline of society in his *Latter-Day Pamphlets* as, "Days of endless calamity, disruption, dislocation, confusion worse confounded."[107] Throughout MacDonald's story, the emphasis for action is on individual character. The most important aid that Curdie can have in his mission, he receives from the old Princess, Irene's great-great-grandmother, that is, the ability to tell by their hands what people are becoming. As the hero, Curdie himself must be prepared for his mission by undergoing a trial to purify his own hands and thus enable him to read the hands of others. Those with human hands are to be trusted, others' hands feel like the animal they are turning into and so demonstrate in physical reality their spiritual and moral state. The Princess explains, "Since it is always what they *do*, whether in their minds or their bodies, that makes men go down to be less than men, that is, beasts, the change always comes first in their hands—and first in the inside hands, to which the outside ones are but as gloves. They do not know it of course; for a beast does not know that he is a beast, and the nearer a man gets to being a beast the less he knows it."[108] Gregory notes, "every choice reflects the self we are or the self we are becoming."[109] This image of literal individual degeneration and the subsequent depiction of the unravelling of a corrupt society

105. MacDonald, *Princess and Curdie*, 320.
106. Reitzel, *Autobiography of William Cobbett*, 92.
107. Carlyle, *Latter Day Pamphlets*, 421.
108. MacDonald, *Princess and Curdie*, 98.
109. Gregory, *Ethical Criticism*, 209.

is MacDonald's strongest critique of Victorian society. His adult novels contain characters that display moral degeneration, greed, and materialism but do not have the same impact as the animal-handed officials of this parabolic story. However, *The Princess and the Goblin* (1872) includes an underclass that can be read as both "us" turning into the "other" and the other being part of "us." The goblins in *The Princess and the Goblin* had, so legend recounted, "at one time lived above ground, and were very like other people. But for some reason or other ... the king laid what they thought too severe taxes upon them, or had required observances they did not like, or had begun to treat them with more severity, in some way or other, and impose stricter laws; and the consequence was that they had all disappeared from the face of the country."[110] What is not certain in this passage is whether the demands of the king were legitimate or not, leaving interpretation open to either they were or they were not, or some were and some were not. Leaving this question unanswered exonerates the goblins from taking all the responsibility for their degeneration, and invites an application of their situation to "reality." In providing this invitation, MacDonald is fulfilling the role of the artist who, "cutting through the blur of habit ... strives to come to terms with reality in a world that shrinks from reality."[111] and to communicate that reality. One reading of this reality is to equate the goblins with both the urban poor in the domestic context, as Zanger has done, and with the "native" as colonial subject. In both instances, responsibility for their degeneration lies only partially with themselves, thus placing part of the responsibility on the king, the political master. Reading this text in terms of imperialist expansion and the marginalization of the colonial subject serves to embed MacDonald in his historical context by uniting the analogy of the urban poor with the colonized subject as under classes that must be subdued, and the construction of both as children, who must be "subdued" by means of education in order to socialize them into conformity with the dominant culture. In this instance, "according to the legend ... instead of going to some other country they had all taken refuge in the subterranean caverns ... and ... seldom showed themselves.... Those who had caught sight of any of them said that they had greatly altered in the course of generations; and no wonder, seeing they

---

110. MacDonald, *Princess and Goblin*, 11.
111. Nussbaum, *Exactly and Responsibly*, 344.

The Ideology of the Hero and the Representation of the "Other"

lived away from the sun, in cold and wet and dark places."[112] The "alteration" is also internal "as they grew in cunning, they grew in mischief, and their great delight was in every way to annoy people who lived in the open-air-story above them."[113] Thus the degeneration is both physical and moral and the reason lies partly in the driving out of the country and partly because "they so heartily cherished a grudge," and choose to be cunning, mischievous and tormenting. MacDonald explains that the goblins have become as they are partly through choosing to degenerate from the human, or at least, through choosing not to resist degeneration, but that their marginalization as a result of dominating human activity pushed them underground where the downward regression continued unseen.

In MacDonald's story, the goblins become more hostile, hatch a plot to carry off Princess Irene and to flood the mine, drowning the miners. The plot is discovered by Curdie, the miner boy, who at this point in his development is, "of the upper world where the wind blew."[114] As often happens in MacDonald's stories[115] the perpetrators of evil suffer the consequences of their own actions. In this instance the plot to drown the miners backfires and the water drowns the goblins. At this point the correlation between the poor and the colonized breaks down as they are being read here as embodiments of the fear of degeneration and not as direct allegories. As they have degenerated physically and morally, they provide the antithesis to the hero, Curdie, and to the Victorian ideal of the hero examined in chapter 5 of this work. They illustrate the result of what happens not only to a degenerative society but also to individuals in the process of degeneration. An example of the influence of external and internal factors on individual progression or regression can be found in MacDonald's novel *Robert Falcon*er. MacDonald narrates Robert's visit to an unemployed silk weaver and writes he was, "one ... in whose countenance, after generations of want and debasement, the delicate lines and noble cast of his ancient race were yet emergent."[116] In this case, the degenerative movement is directly linked

112. MacDonald, *Princess and Goblin*, 11–13.

113. Ibid., 13.

114. MacDonald, *Princess and Curdie*, 22.

115 Other examples are *The Light Princess* (1864) and *The Princess and Curdie* (1883).

116. MacDonald, *Robert Falconer*, 339.

to personal poverty and the connection between the "debasement" and the "ancient race" is retained, thus merging the "other" with "us," which leads to an investigation of the other as part of "us," that is, internal.

The "Other" as "Us"

> "Neither the savage, nor the self-sufficient sage, is rightly human. It matters nothing whether we regard the one or the other as degenerate or as undeveloped—neither I say is human."[117]

The psychological aspects of MacDonald's goblins have received much critical attention. From G. K. Chesterton, through Robert Lee Wolff to Rolland Hein[118] the goblins are critiqued as personal. Therefore I will confine my examination here to the focus on the goblins as subject peoples, but from the point of departure of the relationship between potential colonial landscape, the "blank" space on the map and psychological landscape, the unexplored regions of the unconscious, representative of, "the mythic connection between the land and the psyche."[119] Thomas Howard observes "The poet's [or writer's] appeal, unlike the scientist's or the explorer's, can never rest on his bringing exciting new facts to light." It is, "primarily something imaginative,"[120] it discovers fresh images and sets them out freshly. Stephen Greenblatt and Giles Gunn describe literature, "as an imagined territory,"[121] and it is this "imagined space" that MacDonald, in tandem with his contemporary Victorian travellers in exotic landscapes, explores the unknown regions of the mind. MacDonald's goblins live underground and can only come up into the house, where civilization reigns, through the cellar, the underground part of the house. Although they had once been, "very like other people," their degeneration had turned them into "the other." Just as the urban poor, colonial subject and the child were regarded as both like and unlike, similar and different from "us" in terms of their humanity. In terms of the cultural norm, "we" ourselves can only become part

---

117. MacDonald, *Unspoken Sermons*, 315.

118. Chesterton, *Introduction*, 11; Wolff, *Golden Key*, 166; Hein, *George MacDonald*, 233.

119. McGillis, *Nimble Reader*, 58.

120. Howard, *Charles Williams*, 7.

121. Greenblatt and Gunn, *Redrawing Boundaries*, 6.

The Ideology of the Hero and the Representation of the "Other"

of the norm by being educated into that norm. In the mid-nineteenth century education became a mechanism for control and socialization which, through the public school system in particular, internalized a set of ideas which were spread across the empire through the administrative system. Cultural imperialism included art, science, and English literature, the imaginative product of England as a system of interpellation.[122] William Blake, quoted by Said, writes: "The foundation of Empire is art and science and not vice versa."[123] In this way the education system that dominated in the domestic context, civilizing the "other" as child and turning him into "us," became a method by which to attempt to turn the colonial subject into "us."

In his discussion of otherness, Delany, states, "Discourse tells us what is central and what is peripheral."[124] In the Victorian context this is a complex concept when taken beside Rainer Emig's comment that in Victorian thought "the centre is more marginal than it itself likes to believe."[125] If we accept this argument, then the converse must also be valid, that is, that the marginal is more central than the centre would like to believe. This reversal brings the marginalized "goblins" into the centre, into "us," not only in the domestic political situation mentioned above in terms of the urban poor, but in individual terms, as part of "us." The underlying political fear during the second half of the nineteenth century was that the growing numbers of degenerating urban poor would overwhelm the ruling classes, that is, the margins would be brought into the centre, causing social breakdown as the hierarchical pattern of society went into reversal. Given the interaction between the margins and the centre, as discussed by Emig, the margins are integral to the centre and therefore needed. The imperialistic centre, in order to retain control, needs the marginalized "other" in the form of the colonial subject, the urban poor and the child, as the individual needs to explore his own psychological landscape in an effort to integrate the unconscious mind into the "open-air-story above."[126] The marginalized are needed as the socialized subject to serve and become part of the centre, therefore they are, as MacDonald's goblins are, both "us" and the

122. Bhabha, *Of Mimicry*, 382.
123. Said, *Culture and Imperialism*, 13.
124. Delany, *Shorter Views*, 11.
125. Emig, *Eccentricity*, 379.
126. MacDonald, *Princess and Goblin*, 13.

"other." I argue that the work of Henty and MacDonald meet in both the marginalized and the centre. The place of departure for the Henty hero is colonial space, just as the place of departure for the MacDonald hero is psychological space and, as Jean Webb notes, "Both the physical and the imagined landscapes are those which satisfy the cultural imagination."[127] They are both drawn into the centre as the margins are either defeated or integrated. Henty wrote apparently realistic stories out of an historical time that Disraeli termed "like a fairy tale," with a fairy tale narrative structure and a fairy tale ending. MacDonald wrote fairy tales addressing realistic issues of the same historical time which did not all have the happy ending expected of a fairy tale.

---

127. Webb, *Conceptualising Childhood*, 365.

7

My Hero

The Complete Identity

The Victorian preoccupation with the hero and the heroic, requires the hero to be both "other'" and "everyman." As "other," he transcends the experience of the everyday, or, in MacDonald's terms, "the commonplace," although MacDonald's use of this term includes the implication of dull unawareness and a lack of desire for the spiritual aspect of life.[1] As "everyman" the hero embraces the heroic aspirations of "the dullest daydrudge,"[2] and so opens the way for any person to become a hero no matter what his or her perceived status in society.

Carlyle's exposition of the hero as everyman opens the fairy tale path by means of which, in metaphorical terms, the swineherd can become a king. The key to the difference between "the commonplace man" whose growth, "is a continuous dying" and the aspiring hero whose growth is "a continuous resurrection,"[3] is his attitude. Henty, in more prosaic terms, asserts, "if similar qualities and similar determination are yours, you need not despair of similar success in life,"[4] hoping to encourage the reader, primarily the domestic, English boy, to emulate the hero. As the "other," the hero takes the reader into another world, an exotic landscape, either geographical or psychological.

---

1. See MacDonald, *Princess and Curdie*, 21–23.
2. Carlyle, *On Heroes*, 70.
3. MacDonald, *Princess and Curdie*, 22.
4. Henty, *Sturdy and Strong*, iv.

As everyman, "us," the hero enters the reader's inner landscape and by emulation, as the hero becomes "us," we become the hero. The way is open for "everyman," potentially, to become the ideal hero.

The landscape of adventure in Henty's work is located predominantly in the geographically exotic which is brought into the domestic sphere through trade, propaganda and informational dissemination at all levels of society, from children's alphabet books to music hall songs. The heroes of empire, exemplified by historical characters such as John Nicholson and General Gordon, entered the realms of romance by their conformity to the notion of the ideal, constructed by their culture. They constitute a merging of the historical and the fictional which becomes apparent in an examination of Henty's settler stories[5] and is exemplified in the life of Samuel White Baker, who was himself likened by his biographer Michael Brander, to a "Henty hero."[6]

The emphasis of the heroic character constructed by MacDonald lies predominantly in his spiritual strength, a facet of the ideal heroic character also found in the cultural construct of the ideal hero, and one emphasized in the historical character of General Gordon in particular.[7] MacDonald's heroes enter adulthood through a symbolic initiation after which they accept responsibilities within society. This acceptance is the same outcome as that of the Henty hero who may become the country gentleman, the professional or the local Member of Parliament. This figure becomes part of the "centre" to which he brings his experience gained on the margins, often the exotic geographical margins of the empire, which he draws with him into the established centre. The acceptance of responsibility in terms of estate is spelled out in MacDonald's first adult fantasy *Phantastes* (1858), although Anodos retains his dominant spiritual dimension which marks him as an outsider within the cultural norm of everyday life, as MacDonald himself was in England. Anodos' unconscious, "almost, looking about for the mystic mark of red,"[8] distances him from his immediate society and ensures that he will never become "commonplace" as he searches for ultimate fulfilment in

---

5. See Johnson, *Recreating England* for such an examination.
6. Brander, *Perfect Victorian*, 16.
7. For evidence of Gordon's spirituality see Waller, *Gordon*.
8. MacDonald, *Phantastes*, 318.

the good which he believes is coming to him. His "kingdom," therefore, is never fully "of this world."[9]

I have demonstrated the complementary characteristics of the nineteenth-century hero figure in the work of G. A. Henty and George MacDonald. The quotation, "The boy stood in the doorway, staring at his reflex self in the mirror"[10] is taken from the penultimate chapter of MacDonald's *A Rough Shaking* (1891) and illustrates the nature of the hero figure in the work of Henty and MacDonald. The image represented in the mirror, although different from the person standing before the mirror, is nevertheless the same person. The images combined create the single idealized figure constructed through the reading of Henty and MacDonald throughout this book. The Henty hero progresses along a linear route to maturity, developing physically and morally but remaining essentially unchanged by his experiences. Although his main characteristics are those of the active and adventure hero in Henty's emphasis on physical development and action, he also manifests characteristics which include those associated with the fairy tale hero.

In the investigation of genre and mode in the work of Henty and MacDonald in chapter 3, I have established that Henty's narrative includes elements found in non-mimetic, mythical forms and the stories of Henty's heroes reach a predictable conclusion. MacDonald's heroes, both male and female, continue to develop through experiences which transform them and their circumstances. They manifest chiefly the characteristics of the fairy tale hero in their emphasis on spiritual development which leads to compassionate actions and decisions but also indicate the presence of physical strength found in the active hero. MacDonald's narratives demonstrate the characteristics of a poetic, cyclical form associated with myth. Those stories critiqued here as realistic narratives are embedded in realism as a framework, but present non-mimetic characteristics.

I have considered and discussed the hypothesis that Henty's writing reveals complexities beyond the stereotypically linear, masculine and imperialistic assessment of existing criticism and that MacDonald's work contains more evidence of imperialist interpellation than critical opinion

---

9. Cf the biblical reference John 18:36, where Jesus, the antithesis of worldly self-interest, states that the priorities of his kingdom do not rest on values deemed important in "the world." MacDonald's radical Christian faith pervades all of his work.

10. MacDonald, *Rough Shaking*, 375.

notes. Both writers critique nineteenth-century society at differing levels and with different emphases, each presenting an image of the hero that is complementary to the other. This complementarity becomes visible in the contexts of the authors' historical period, the construct of the child, the construct of the hero and in the ideology present in the narrative structure of their writing. The representation of the "other" in the work of Henty and MacDonald reflects the connection between the colonized "other," the urban poor as "other" and the unconscious mind as "other," a connection which is present in the Victorian desire to civilize the "other." This construct of the ideal hero is therefore presented also as the desired ideal subject.

The ideal hero is the point at which the real and the imagined merge, a symbol of the Victorian desire for both imperialistic supremacy and an ethical spirituality which exemplifies the antithetical ideological values co-existing in the turmoil of a rapidly changing society. The ideological values embedded in Henty's work uncover a greater complexity than existing criticism allows, exposing the position which views Henty's values as predominantly imperialistic and commercial as too simplistic. MacDonald's work, the complexity of which is not questioned in the critical arena, is shown to include interpellation into the dominant discourse as well as countercultural and anti-materialistic messages. By reconsidering the perceived opposition of the texts it is possible not only to understand them more fully, but also to understand their contribution to the construct of the society in which their authors lived. The hero figure in Henty and MacDonald has been established as a common ideal with different emphases. Put together, these emphases construct a single ideal figure through the imagined world of story. The necessity of the imagined to the construct of the ideal hero is encapsulated in the following observation by Karen Blixen, "By the time ... you have no more stories, you will have no more heroes,"[11] an observation which illuminates the interdependence between the real and the imagined and vice versa.

If, as McGann notes, "Focus upon history constituted in what we call "the past" only achieves its critical fulfilment when that study of the past reveals its significance in and for the present and the future,"[12] then the study of the hero figure presented in this book leads to further

11. Blixen, *Cardinal's First Tale*, 24. In Dinesen, *Last Tales*, 3–26.
12. McGann, *Historical Studies*, 18.

avenues of investigation into the contemporary construction of Western heroism in literature for young people. Such investigation will feed into the contemporary political and commercial estimation of the superiority of Western cultural products, in spite of moves to counter this position. The construct of a contemporary hero figure reinforces constructions of national character, masking the multi-ethnic characteristics which become subsumed into the Western norms which emphasize individual rather than collective action. Consequently those from other cultures, where collectivity is valued above individualism, become dislocated from the society in which they live.

In his discussion on the impact of ideology upon the publishing industry, McGillis notes that, "Books that are unsettling or socially subversive are unlikely to do well"[13] therefore, one way to produce books that people will buy is to "promote the values and cultural conceptions of the ruling group."[14] The reprinting programmes in the United States for both authors are promoted with the rationale that the project is worthwhile because of the values these stories convey to the reader.[15] Henty's work is being reprinted mainly for the home schooling market in the U.S. with the additional marketing point that it teaches children history. No mention is made of the predominantly Anglo-centric positioning of historical information conveyed in the stories as evidence of Henty's embedding in his own contemporary milieu. In terms of Henty's imperialism, Peter Hollindale's argument that it is better to discuss works "which do not entirely accord with current moral priorities,"[16] than to ban them, is applicable. Pat Pinsent's discussion of the need to expose children to material not currently regarded as politically correct as part of their critical education, corroborates this position.[17]

Many of the characteristics of the hero found in the work of Henty and MacDonald have transferred into the twenty first century hero and heroine of many children's stories, which is an example of White's comment in his discussion of the paradox of art, that is, that art, "reflects the conditions of the time and place and is therefore to be regarded as time

13. McGillis, *Nimble Reader*, 111.
14. Ibid., 112.
15. See www.robinsonbooks.com and www.johannesen.com.
16. Hollindale, *Ideology*, 6.
17. Pinsent, *Children's Literature*, 9.

bound as to its content, whilst ... speaking meaningfully to problems and concerns of other ages."[18]

George MacDonald's works have been reprinted in the U.S. within the last twenty years and are frequently appropriated by a wide variety of interest groups all of whom see his work in their own image, testimony in itself to the multivalent nature of his writing. Reprinting continues on the premises of support for his critique of the predominant values of a materialistic society, be it nineteenth or twenty-first centuries, and recognition of a perceived need for a greater emphasis on the spiritual. MacDonald's embedding in the politically imperialistic nineteenth-century context is rarely mentioned in critical appraisals of his work. That the concerns driving the reprinting programmes reflect the same concerns that made Henty and MacDonald popular authors in their own time is an instance of Leon Garfield's statement that, "history becomes a mirror in which we see ourselves."[19]

The desire for the ideal English hero constructs and is constructed by the nineteenth-century English context, and the view of the "'other'" as exotic in the imperial context reflects the inner, "exotic," spaces of the unconscious. This compulsion to control both the outer and the inner exotic "other" is addressed by the attempt to "civilize" both of these spaces, through education and socialization. The hero is constructed to be emulated and so perpetuate the representation of the desired outcome in the idealized male hero, who is, potentially, Everyman. The construct of the hero figure in the work of Henty and MacDonald reflects the desire of the Victorians for the ideal physical and spiritual hero as a single entity. The Victorian construction of an ideal viewed as attainable, is an attempt "to look at the reality of heaven from the earth,"[20] which results in a complete identity, embodying the physical and spiritual. This is the image demonstrated as present in the work of the two authors examined in this book. The resultant image draws the imagined into the real by a process of integration, making a "complete identity."

18. White, *Content*, 156.
19. Garfield, *Historical Fiction*, 738.
20. Edwards, *Towards a Christian Poetics*, 224.

Bibliography

Allen, Richard. "Literature, Gender, Feminist Criticism." In *A Handbook to Literary Research*, edited by Simon Eliot and W. R. Owens, 114–27. London: Routledge in Association with The Open University, 1998.
Althusser, Louis. "On Ideology." In *Critical Theory: A Reader*, edited by Douglas Tallack, 304–13. London: Harvester Wheatsheaf, 1995.
Altick, Richard. *The English Common Reader: A Social History of the Mass Reading Public 1800–1900*. Chicago: The University of Chicago Press, 1957.
Andersen, Hans. *Hans Andersen: His Classic Fairy Tales*. Translated by Erik Haugaard. London: Book Club Associates, 1977.
Aries, Phillipe. *Centuries of Childhood*. Translated by Robert Baldrick. London: Cape, 1962.
Arnold, Guy. *Held Fast for England: G. A. Henty Imperialist Boy's Writer*. London: Hamilton, 1980.
Arthur, James. *Education with Character*. London: RoutledgeFalmer, 2003.
Ashcroft, Bill. "Primitive and Wingless: The Colonial Subject as Child." In *Dickens and the Children of Empire*, edited by W. Jacabson, 184–202. Basingstoke, UK: Macmillan, 2000.
Avery, Gillian. *Childhood's Pattern: A Study of the Heroes and Heroines of Children's Fiction 1770–1950*. London: Hodder and Stoughton, 1975.
———. "George MacDonald and the Victorian Fairytale." In *The Gold Thread: Essays on George MacDonald*, edited by William Raeper, 126–39. Edinburgh: Edinburgh University Press, 1990.
Avi. *The True Confessions of Charlotte Doyle*. London: Orchard, 1991.
Bakhtin, Michael M. *The Dialogic Imagination: Four Essays*. Edited by Michael Holquist. Austin, TX: University of Texas Press, 1981.
Bal, Mieke. *Narratology: Introduction to the Theory of Narrative*. 2nd ed. Toronto: University of Toronto Press, 1997.
Barker, Chris. *Making Sense of Cultural Studies: Central Problems and Critical Debates*. London: Sage, 2002.
Barr, James. "A Great Writer of Christmas Books: An Interview with Mr. G. A. Henty, Who Has Taken Part in Many Wars, and Written More Than Eighty Romances." *The Golden Penny*, 1898.
Barthes, Roland. "Myth Today." In *Critical Theory: A Reader*, edited by Douglas Tallack, 27–42. London: Harvester Wheatsheaf, 1995.
———. *S/Z*. Translated by Richard Miller. London: Cape, 1975.
Barzini, Luigi. *The Impossible Europeans*. London: Penguin, 1983.

Battin, Melba N. "Duality Beyond Time: George MacDonald's 'The Wise Woman, or the Lost Princess: A Double Story.'" In *For the Childlike: George MacDonald's Fantasies for Children*, edited by Roderick McGillis, 207-18. Metuchen, NJ: The Children's Literature Association, 1992.

Beattie, James. "A Response to Hume." Excerpt from *An Essay on the Nature and Immutability of Truth, in Opposition to Sophistry and Skepticism*. 1770. In *Race and the Enlightenment: A Reader*, edited by Emmanuel Chukwudi Eze, 34-37. Oxford: Blackwell, 1997.

Berman, Jessica. "No Consensus on Ethics: New Work in Ethical Criticism." *Modern Fiction Studies* 46.4 (2000) 941-48.

Berry, Laura C. *The Child, the State, and the Victorian Novel*. Charlottesville, VA: University Press of Virginia, 1999.

Bhabha, Homi. "'Of Mimicry and Man: The Ambivalence of Colonial Discourse.' October 28, Spring (1983), 125-33." In *Modern Literary Theory*, edited by Philip Rice and Patricia Waugh, 380-87. London: Arnold, 2001.

Blanch, Stuart. "My Personal Debt to George MacDonald." Lecture Given to the George MacDonald Society, November 1982, Church House, London.

Boas, George. *The Cult of Childhood*. London: The Warburg Institute University of London, 1966.

Booth, Wayne. "Are Narrative Choices Subject to Ethical Criticism?" In *Reading Narrative: Form, Ethics, Ideology*, edited by James Phelan, 57-78. Columbus, OH: Ohio State University Press, 1989.

Brander, Michael. *The Perfect Victorian Hero: Samuel White Baker*. Edinburgh: Mainstream, 1982.

Brannigan, John. *New Historicism and Cultural Materialism*. London: Macmillan, 1998.

Bristow, Joseph. *Empire Boys: Adventures in a Man's World*. London: Harper Collins, 1991.

Bronte, Charlotte. *Jane Eyre*. 1908. Reprint. London: Dent & Sons, 1969.

Broome, F. Hal. "The Scientific Basis of MacDonald's Dream Frame." In *The Gold Thread: Essays on George MacDonald*, edited by William Raeper, 87-108. Edinburgh: Edinburgh University Press, 1990.

Brown, A. B. E. "A Search for a Secret (1867)." In *Hugh Pruen's Henty Companion: Resumes of All the Books of G. A. Henty with Valuable Cross-References*, edited by Gordon Berlyne, 5. Kelshall: The Henty Society, 1997.

Brown, Basil. "Henty and the Historians." *The Henty Society Bulletin* 12.89 (1999) 6-9.

Brown, Lesley, ed. *The New Shorter Oxford English Dictionary on Historical Principles*. 5th ed. Vol. 1. Oxford: Clarendon, 1993.

Buckle, George Earle. *The Life of Benjamin Disraeli Earl of Beaconsfield: Volume IV. 1855-1868*. London: Murray, 1916.

Burgh, Hugo de, ed. *Investigative Journalism: Context and Practice*. London: Routledge, 2000.

Burns, Norman T., and Christopher Reagan, eds. *Concepts of the Hero in the Middle Ages and Renaissance*. London: Hodder and Stoughton, 1976.

Butts, Dennis. "The Adventure Story." In *Stories and Society*, edited by Denis Butts, 65-83. London: Macmillan, 1992.

———. "Henty and the Folk Tale: By Sheer Pluck, for Example." *The Henty Society Bulletin* IV.28 (1984) 10-16.

———, ed. *Stories and Society*. London: Macmillan, 1992.

———. "True to Whose Flag?: Studies in G. A. Henty (1832–1902) in the 1990s." Draft copy of talk given at Winchester Henty Gathering 1991.
Byatt, A. S. *On Histories and Stories: Selected Essays*. London: Vintage, 2001.
Campbell, Joseph. *The Hero with a Thousand Faces*. London: Fontana, 1993.
Cargill-Thompson, John. *The Boys Dumas: G. A. Henty: Aspects of Victorian Publishing*. Cheadle: Carcanet, 1975.
Carlyle, Thomas. "Characteristics." In *A Carlyle Reader: Selections from the Writings of Thomas Carlyle*, edited by G. B. Tennyson, 67–103. Cambridge: Cambridge University Press, 1984.
———. "Latter Day Pamphlets" In *A Carlyle Reader: Selections from the Writings of Thomas Carlyle*, edited by G. B. Tennyson, 420–59. Cambridge: Cambridge University Press, 1984.
———. *On Heroes, Hero-Worship and the Heroic in History Edited with an Introduction by Carl Niemeyer*. Lincoln, NE: University of Nebraska Press, 1966.
———. "Past and Present." In *A Carlyle Reader: Selections from the Writings of Thomas Carlyle*, edited by G. B. Tennyson, 408–17. Cambridge: Cambridge University Press, 1984.
———. "Signs of the Times." In *A Carlyle Reader: Selections from the Writings of Thomas Carlyle*, edited by G. B. Tennyson, 31–54. Cambridge: Cambridge University Press, 1984.
Carpenter, Humphrey, and Mari Pritchard. *The Oxford Companion to Children's Literature*. Oxford: Oxford University Press, 1984.
Carron, Juliet. "The Role of the Child as a Route to Spiritual Reality in Literature 1860–1930: A Jungian Approach." PhD, University of Reading, 1998.
Cavallaro, Dani. *Critical and Cultural Theory: Thematic Variations*. London: Athlone, 2001.
Chesterton, G. K. "Introduction." In *George MacDonald and His Wife*, by Greville MacDonald, 9–15. London: Allen and Unwin, 1924.
Chitty, Susan. *The Beast and the Monk: A Life of Charles Kingsley*. London: Hodder and Stoughton, 1974.
Cohan, Steven, and Linda M. Shires. *Telling Stories: A Theoretical Analysis of Narrative Fiction*. London: Routledge, 1988.
Cohoon, Linda B. "Necessary Badness: Reconstructing Post-Bellum Boyhood Citizenships in 'Our Young Folks' and 'The Story of a Bad Boy.'" *Children's Literature Quarterly* 29.1/2 (2004) 5–31.
Coleridge, Samuel Taylor. *The Collected Works of Samuel Taylor Coleridge: Biographia Literaria or Biographical Sketches of My Literary Life and Opinions*. Edited by James Engell and W. Jackson Bate. 1817. Reprint. London: Routledge & Kegan Paul, 1983.
Delany, Samuel R. *Shorter Views: Queer Thoughts and the Politics of the Paraliterary*. Hanover, NH: Wesleyan University Press, 1999.
Darton, F. J. Harvey. *Children's Books in England: Five Centuries of Social Life*. 3rd ed. Cambridge: Cambridge University Press, 1982.
Davin, Bernard. "A School for Heroes." *The Times*, December 3, 1932, 11–12.
Dentith, Simon. *Society and Cultural Forms in Nineteenth Century England*. Edited by Jeremy Black. Social History in Perspective. Basingstoke, UK: Macmillan, 1998.
Dettmar, Ute. "19th Century Children's Literature and Concepts of Childhood between Conservative Revolution and Carnival." Lecture delivered at Norchilnet Seminar Copenhagen Nov 20, 2004.

Dinesen, Isak (Karen Blixen). "The Cardinal's First Tale." In *Last Tales*, 3–26. London: Penguin, 2001.
Disraeli, Benjamin. *Coningsby: Or, the New Generation*. 1911. Reprint. London: Dent & Sons, 1967.
Downey, Edmund. *A Book of Anecdote Illustrating Literary Life on London: With Sixteen Portrait Sketches*. London: Hurst and Blackett, 1905.
Duin, Julia. "Victorian Children's Books Gain Latter-Day Following." *Washington Times*, May 6, 1998.
Edwardes, Michael. "True to the Old Flag." *The Twentieth Century* CLV.927 (1954) 457–67.
Edwards, Lee R. "The Labours of Psyche: Toward as Theory of Female Heroism." *Critical Enquiry* 6 (1979) 33–49.
Edwards, Michael. *Towards a Christian Poetics*. London: Macmillan, 1984.
Elias, Norbert. "Homo Clausus and the Civilizing Process." In *Identity: A Reader*, edited by Paul du Gay, Jessica Evans and Peter Redman, 284–96. London: Sage in association with the Open University, 2000.
Elliot, Hugh S. R., ed. *The Letters of John Stuart Mill: With a Note on Mill's Private Life, by Mary Taylor. Vol. II*. London: Longmans, Green and Co., 1910.
Elliott, Dorice Williams. *The Angel out of the House: Philanthropy and Gender in Nineteenth-Century England*. Charlottesville, VA: University of Virginia Press, 2002.
Emig, Rainer. "Eccentricity Begins at Home: Carlyle's Centrality in Victorian Thought." *Textual Practice* 17.2 (2003) 379–90.
Eze, Emmanuel Chukwudi, ed. *Race and the Enlightenment: A Reader*. Oxford: Blackwell, 1997.
Faber, Richard. *The Vision and the Need: Late Victorian Imperialist Aims*. London: Faber & Faber, 1966.
"A Favourite of Our Boys: Mr. G. A. Henty." *The Gem: a Magazine for the Home and the Train*, December 16, 1899, 209.
Fenn, G. Manville. *George Alfred Henty*. London: Blackie & Son, 1911.
Ferguson, John, ed. *War and the Creative Arts: An Anthology*. London: Macmillan in association with the Open University Press, 1972.
Ferguson, Niall. *Empire: How Britain Made the Modern World*. London: Penguin, 2003.
Fisher, Margery. *The Bright Face of Danger: An Exploration of the Adventure Story*. London: Hodder and Stoughton, 1986.
Fitzgerald, Penelope. *The Blue Flower*. London: HarperCollins, 1995.
Forbes, Archibald, George Henty, and Charles Williams. *Camps and Quarters*. Facsimile edition [n.d.]. Military Sketches and Stories. New York: Ward Lock & Co., 1889.
Ford, Harvey S. "G. A. Henty." *The Saturday Review of Literature*, March 2, 1940, 645–49.
Frye, Northrop. *Anatomy of Criticism: Four Essays*. Princeton, NJ: Princeton University Press, 1957.
———. *The Secular Scripture: A Study of the Structure of Romance*. Cambridge: Harvard University Press, 1976.
Furst, Lilian R., ed. *Realism*. Harlow, UK: Longman, 1992.
Garfield, Leon. "Historical Fiction for Our Global Times." *The Horn Book Magazine* Nov/Dec 1988, 736–42.
Genette, Gerard. *Narrative Discourse*. Translated by Jane E. Lewin. Oxford: Blackwell, 1980.

"George MacDonald and Hero Worshippers." *Wingfold* 53 (2006) 25. Reprinted from the *Aberdeen Evening Express*, Nov 4, 1889.
Gergen, Kenneth J. *Social Construction in Context*. London: Sage, 2001.
Gilligan, Carol. *In a Different Voice*. Cambridge: Harvard University Press, 1982.
Gittins, Diana. "The Historical Construction of Childhood." In *An Introduction to Childhood Studies*, edited by Mary Jane Kehily, 26–38. Maidenhead, UK: Open University Press, 2004.
Golden, Joanne M. *The Narrative Symbol in Childhood Literature: Exploration in the Construction of Text*. Berlin: Mouton, 1990.
Greenblatt, Stephen. "Resonance and Wonder." In *Modern Literary Theory*, edited by Philip and Patricia Waugh Rice, 305–24. London: Arnold, 2001.
Greenblatt, Stephen, and Giles Gunn, eds. *Redrawing the Boundaries: The Transformation of English and American Literary Studies*. New York: MLA of America, 1992.
Gregory, Marshall. "Ethical Criticism: What It Is and Why It Matters." *Style* 32.2 (1998) 194–220.
Griffiths, Dennis. *Plant Here "The Standard."* London: Macmillan, 1996.
Gualtieri, Claudia. "The Discourse of the Exotic in British Colonial Travel Writing in West Africa." PhD diss., Leeds University, 1999.
Gunther, Adrian. "'Little Daylight': An Old Tale Transfigured." *Children's Literature in Education* 26.2 (1995) 107–17.
Haines, Simon, "Defining the Self: The Language of Ethics and the Language of Literature." *The Critical Review: Renegotiating Ethics: Essays Towards a New Ethical Criticism* 33 (1993) 15–28.
Hall, Donald E. *Muscular Christianity*. Cambridge: Cambridge University Press, 1994.
Harpham, Geoffrey Galt. *Shadows of Ethics: Criticism and the Just Society*. Durham, NC: Duke University Press, 1999.
Harrison, Frederic. *Autobiographic Memoirs,* vol. 1. London: Macmillan, 1911.
Hastings, Max. "When Boys Were Boys." *The Spectator*, March 29, 2003, 23.
Haughton, Rosemary. *Tales from Eternity: The World of Fairy and the Spiritual Search*. London: Allen and Unwin, 1973.
Hayward, Dierdre. "George MacDonald and Three German Thinkers." PhD diss., University of Dundee, 2000.
———. "The Mystical Sophia: More on the Great Grandmother in the Princess Books." *North Wind: Journal of the George MacDonald Society* 13 (1994) 29–33.
Hein, Rolland. *George MacDonald: Victorian Mythmaker*. Nashville, TN: Star Song, 1993.
———. *The Harmony Within: The Spiritual Vision of George MacDonald*. Grand Rapids, MI: Christian University Press, 1982.
Henty, G. A. *By Sheer Pluck*. Glasgow: Blackie & Son, n.d.
———. *Captain Bayley's Heir*. London: Blackie, 1889.
———. *Condemned as a Nihilist*. London: Blackie & Son Limited, 1893.
———. *Facing Death*. London: Blackie, 1882.
———. *For Name and Fame: Or to Cabul with Roberts*. London: Blackie & Son, n.d.
———. *For the Temple: Or a Tale of the Fall of Jerusalem*. Mill Hall, PA: Preston Speed, 1995.
———. *A Jacobite Exile*. London: Blackie & Son, 1909.
———. "On the Irrawaddy." In *The G. A. Henty Omnibus Book: On the Irrawaddy; By Sheer Pluck; Captain Bayley's Heir*. London: Blackie & Son, n.d.

———. *The Plague Ship*. London: Sheldon, n.d.
———. *Rujub the Juggler*. London: Chatto & Windus, 1895.
———. *A Soldier's Daughter and Other Stories*. London: Blackie & Son, 1906.
———. *St. George for England*. London: Blackie & Son, 1885.
———. *Sturdy and Strong: Or How George Andrews Made His Way*. London: Blackie & Son, n.d.
———. *Through the Sikh War: A Tale of the Conquest of the Punjab*. London: Blackie & Son, 1894.
———. *The Tiger of Mysore: A Story of the War with Tippoo Saib*. London: Blackie & Son, 1896.
———. "True Heroism: A Talk with the Boys." *The Home Messenger* XII (1903) 54–56.
———. *True to the Old Flag: A Tale of the American Civil War of Independence*. New ed. London: Blackie & Son, 1912.
———. *With Buller in Natal: Or, a Born Leader*. London: Blackie & Son, n.d.
———. *With Kitchener in the Soudan: A Story of Atbara and Omdurman*. London: Blackie & Son, 1903.
———. *With the Allies to Pekin: Story of the Relief of the Legations*. London: Blackie & Son, 1904.
———. "Writing for Boys." *Answers*, Dec 13, 1902, 105.
———. *Young Buglers*. n.d. Reprint. London: Oxford University Press, 1919.
———. *The Young Carthaginian: A Story of the Times of Hannibal*. London: Blackie & Son, n.d.
———. *The Young Colonists: A Story of the Zulu and Boer Wars*. New ed. London: Blackie & Son, 1897.
———. *The Young Franc-Tireurs*. London: Oxford University Press, n.d.
Hignell, Andrew. *Rain Stops Play: Cricketing Climates*. Edited by J. A. Mangan. Sport in the Global Society No. 27. London: Cass, 2002.
Higonnet, Anne. *Pictures of Innocence: The History and Crisis of Ideal Childhood*. London: Thames and Hudson, 1998.
Hollindale, P. *Ideology and the Children's Book*. Stroud, UK: Thimble, 1988.
hooks, bell. "'Postmodern Blackness,' in Yearning: *Race, Gender and Cultural Politics* (1991), 23–31." In *Modern Literary Theory*, edited by Philip Rice and Patricia Waugh, 362–68. London: Arnold, 2001.
Houghton, Walter E. *The Victorian Frame of Mind*. London: New Haven, 1957.
Hourihan, Margery. *Deconstructing the Hero: Literary Theory and Children's Literature*. London: Routledge, 1997.
Howard, Thomas. "Charles Williams, the 'Other' Inkling." In *Inklings Forever. Volume V: A Collection of Essays Presented at the Fifth Frances White Ewbank Colloquium on C. S. Lewis and Friends*, edited by Rick Hill, 7–11. Upland, IN: Taylor University, 2006.
Howe, Suzanne. *Novels of Empire*. New York: Columbia University Press, 1949.
Hughes, Thomas. *Tom Brown's Schooldays*. The World's Classics. Oxford: Oxford University Press, 1989.
Huttenback, Robert A. "G. A. Henty and the Imperial Stereotype." *Huntington Library Quarterly* 29.1 (1965) 63–75.
Hyndman, Henry Mayers. *Clemenceau: The Man and His Time*. London: Richards, 1919.
———. *The Record of an Adventurous Life*. London: Macmillan, 1911.

"Hyndman, Henry Mayers," Microsoft Encarta Online Encyclopedia." 1997-2008 Microsoft Corporation.
Irigaray, Luce. *Je, Tu, Nous: Toward a Culture of Difference*. Translated by Alison Martin. London: Routledge, 1993.
James, Laurence. *The Rise and Fall of the British Empire*. London: Little, Brown and Co., 1994.
Jameson, Fredric. *The Political Unconscious: Narrative as a Socially Symbolic Act*. Ithaca, NY: Cornell University Press, 1981.
Jeffrey, Kirstin. "The Progressive Key: A Study of Bunyan's Influence in MacDonald's 'The Golden Key.'" *North Wind: Journal of the George MacDonald Society* 16 (1997) 69-75.
Johannesen, Andy. "Johannesen Printing and Publishing." www.johannesen.com.
Johnson, Rachel. "Recreating England." Worcester Papers edited by Andreas Muller. Worcester, UK: University of Worcester, 2008.
Jong, Erica. *Sappho's Leap*. London: Arcadia, 2004.
Jordan, Gerald H. S. "Popular Literature and Imperial Sentiment: Changing Attitudes, 1870-1890." *Canadian Historical Association Annual Report* (1967) 149-55.
Jordan, Pamela. "Clergy in Crisis: Three Victorian Portrayals of Anglican Clergymen Forced to Redefine Their Faith." PhD diss., Ball State University, IN, 1997.
Kegler, Adelheid. "Below in the Depths: MacDonald's Symbolic Landscape." *North Wind. A Journal of the George MacDonald Studies* 24 (2005) 29-40.
———. "The Sleep of the Soul: Night's Pore in Torments: The Blending of Swedenborgian Structures of Thought in *Lilith*." *North Wind: Journal of the George MacDonald Society* 14 (1995) 22-35.
Kincaid, James. *Child-Loving: The Erotic Child and Victorian Culture*. New York: Routledge, 1992.
King, Ann. "G. A. Henty in West Africa 1873-1874: Some Notes on the Yarn and Essay." *The Henty Society Literary Supplement*. Special Literary Supplement 14 (2007) 3-4.
King, Don. "The Childlike in George MacDonald and C. S. Lewis." *Mythlore* 46 (1986) 17-22.
Kingsley, Charles. *The Water-Babies: A Fairy Tale for a Land Baby*. London: Dent, 1908.
———. *Westward Ho!: Or the Voyages and Adventures of Sir Amyas Leigh*. London: King & Co., n.d.
Knight, George. "When I Was a Boy: An Afternoon Talk with G. A. Henty." *The Captain: A Magazine for Boys and "Old Boys,"* April to September 1899, 3.
Knoepflmacher, U. C. *Ventures into Childhood: Victorians, Fairy Tales, and Femininity*. Chicago: Chicago University Press, 1998.
Leighton, Robert. "George Alfred Henty: A Reminiscence." *Boys of Our Empire*, Dec 13, 1902, 224.
Levinas, Emmanuel. *Entre Nous: On Thinking-of-the-Other*. Translated by Michael B. Smith and Barbara Harshav. New York: Columbia University Press, 1998.
Levine, George. "'Not Like My Lancelot': The Disappearing Victorian Hero." In *Perspectives on Nineteenth-Century Heroism: Essays from the 1981 Conference of the Southeastern Nineteenth Century Studies Association*, edited by Sarah M. Leonard and David C. Putzell, 47-72. Madrid: Jose Porrua Turanzas, 1982.
———. "Victorian Studies." In *Redrawing the Boundaries: The Transformation of English and American Literary Studies*, edited by Stephen and Giles Gunn Greenblatt, 130-53. New York: Modern Language Association of America, 1992.

Lewes, George Henry. *The Life of Goethe*. London: Dent & Sons, 1908.
Lewis, C. S. *George MacDonald: An Anthology*. London: Bles, 1946.
———. *Surprised by Joy*. London: Collins, 1959.
Lewis, Naomi. "Children's Books: George MacDonald." *New Statesman*, Nov 10, 1961.
Lochhead, Marion. *The Renaissance of Wonder in Children's Literature*. Edinburgh: Canongate, 1977.
Lorenzo, David J. "The Portrayal of Similarities in the Justification of Empire: G. A. Henty and Late 19th-Century British Imperial Literature." *The McNeese Review* (1999) 14–42.
Lukacs, Georg. *The Historical Novel*. Translated by Hannah and Stanley Mitchell. London: Merlin, 1962.
Lurie, Alison. *The Language of Clothes*. London: Heinemann, 1981.
Luthi, Max. *The European Folktale: Form and Nature*. Translated by John D. Niles. Philadelphia: Institute for the Study of Human Issues, 1982.
MacDonald, George. *At the Back of the North Wind*. Whitethorn: Johannesen, 1992.
———. "The Broken Swords." In *The Portent and Other Stories*, 261–92. Whitethorn, CA: Johannesen, 1994.
———. "Cross Purposes." *The Light Princess and Other Fairy Tales*. Published as individual title in 1862. First published as collection in 1893. Whitethorn, CA: Johannesen, 1993.
———. *David Elginbrod*. Whitethorn, CA: Johannesen, 1995.
———. *A Dish of Orts: Chiefly Papers on the Imagination and on Shakespeare*. London: Dalton, 1908.
———. "The Fantastic Imagination." In *A Dish of Orts: Chiefly Papers on the Imagination and on Shakespeare*, 313–22. London: Dalton, 1908.
———. "The Giant's Heart." In *The Light Princess and Other Fairy Tales*, 67–96. Whitethorn, CA: Johannesen, 1993.
———. "The Golden Key." In *The Light Princess and Other Fairy Tales*, 172–215. Whitethorn, CA: Johannesen, 1993.
———. *Gutta Percha Willie: The Working Genius*. London: King, 1873.
———. "The History of Photogen and Nycteris: A Day and Night Marchen." In *Stephen Archer and Other Tales*, 79–147. Whitethorn, CA: Johannesen, 1994.
———. *The Hope of the Gospel*. Whitethorn, CA: Johannesen, 1995.
———. "An Invalid's Winter in Algeria." In *George MacDonald: A Bibliographical Study*, edited by Raphael B. Shaberman, 140–53. Winchester, UK: St. Paul's Bibliographies, 1990.
———. "Little Daylight." In *The Light Princess and Other Fairy Tales*. Whitethorn, CA: Johannesen, 1993.
———. *Paul Faber: Surgeon*. Whitethorn, CA: Johannesen, 1992.
———. *Phantastes*. Whitethorn, CA: Johannesen, 1994.
———. *The Poetical Works of George MacDonald in Two Volumes*. Whitethorn, CA: Johannesen, 1996.
———. *The Princess and Curdie*. Whitethorn, CA: Johannesen, 1993.
———. *The Princess and the Goblin*. Whitethorn, CA: Johannesen, 1993.
———. *Ranald Bannerman's Boyhood*. London: Strahan and Co., 1871.
———. *Robert Falconer*. Whitethorn, CA: Johannesen, 1995.
———. *A Rough Shaking*. Whitethorn, CA: Johannesen, 1991.
———. *The Seaboard Parish*. 1st ed. London: Daldy, Isbister & Co., 1877.

———. *Sir Gibbie*. Whitethorn, CA: Johannesen, 1991.
———. *Thomas Wingfold, Curate*. Whitethorn, CA: Johannesen, 1996.
———. *Unspoken Sermons Series I, II, III in One Volume*. Whitethorn, CA: Johannesen, 1997.
———. *What's Mine's Mine*. Whitethorn, CA: Johannesen, 1991.
———. *Wilfred Cumbermede*. Whitethorn, CA: Johannesen, 1997.
———. *The Wise Woman: A Parable and Gutta Percha Willie: The Working Genius*. Whitethorn, CA: Johannesen, 1993.
———. "Wordsworth's Poetry." In *A Dish of Orts: Chiefly Papers on the Imagination and on Shakespeare*, 245–63. London: Dalton, 1908.
MacDonald, Greville. *The Child's Inheritance: Its Scientific and Imaginative Meaning*. London: Smith, Elder & Co., 1910.
———. *The Fairy Tale in Education*. London: The Froebel Society, n.d.
———. *George MacDonald and His Wife*. London: Allen and Unwin, 1924.
———. *Reminiscences of a Specialist*. London: Allen and Unwin, 1932.
MacDonald, Ronald. *From a Northern Window*. Edited by Michael Phillips. New Edition. Vol. 1. Masterline Series. Eureka, CA: Sunrise, 1989.
MacIntyre, Alasdair. *After Virtue: A Study in Moral Theology*. 2nd ed. Notre Dame, IN: University of Notre Dame Press, 1984.
Maier, Sarah E. "Romanticising and Fantasising: The Construction of the Child in the Children's Fiction of George MacDonald." In *From Kievan Prayers to Avantgarde: Papers in Comparative Literature*, edited by Fast-Piotr and Osadnik-Waclaw-Osadnik, 109–26. Warsaw: Wydawnictwo Energeia, 1999.
Manlove, Colin. "MacDonald's Shorter Fairy Tales: Journeys into the Mind." *VII: An Anglo-American Literary Review* 22 (2005) 11–28.
Manlove, Colin. *Modern Fantasy: Five Studies*. Cambridge: Cambridge University Press, 1975.
Marshall, Cynthia. "Psychoanalyzing the Prepsychoanalytic Subject." *PMLA: Publications of the Modern Language Association of America* 117.5 (2002) 1207–16.
———. "Reading 'the Golden Key': Narrative Strategies of Parable." *Children's Literature Quarterly* 1 (1989) 22–25.
McGann, Jerome J., ed. *Historical Studies and Literary Criticism*. Madison, WI: University of Wisconsin Press, 1985.
———. "Introduction: A Point of Reference." In *Historical Studies and Literary Criticism*, edited by Jerome J. McGann, 3–24. Madison, WI: University of Wisconsin Press, 1985.
———. "'The Text, the Poem, and the Problem of Historical Method,' in *The Beauty of Inflections*, Pp. 111–32." In *Modern Literary Theory*, edited by Philip Rice and Patricia Waugh, 289–305. London: Arnold, 1985.
McGillis, Roderick. "Childhood and Growth: George MacDonald and William Wordsworth." In *Romanticism and Children's Literature in Nineteenth-Century England*, edited by James Holt McGavran, 150–67. Athens, GA: University of Georgia Press, 1991.
———, ed. *For the Childlike: George MacDonald's Fantasies for Children*. Metuchen, NJ: The Children's Literature Association, 1992.
———. "George MacDonald's Princess Books: High Seriousness." In *Touchstones: Reflections on the Best in Children's Literature*, edited by Perry Nodelman, 142–62. West Lafayette, IN: Children's Literature Association, 1985.

———. "Language and Secret Knowledge in 'At the Back of the North Wind.'" In *For the Childlike: George MacDonald's Fantasies for Children*, edited by Roderick McGillis, 145–59. Metuchen, NJ : The Children's Literature Association, 1992.

———. *The Nimble Reader: Literary Theory and Children's Literature*. New York: Twayne, 1996.

———. "*Phantastes* and *Lilith:* Femininity and Freedom." In *The Gold Thread: Essays on George MacDonald*, edited by William Raeper, 31–55. Edinburgh: Edinburgh University Press, 1990.

Miller, Dean A. *The Epic Hero*. Baltimore, MD: Johns Hopkins University Press, 2000.

Montrose, Louis. "New Historicisms." In *Redrawing the Boundaries: The Transformation of English and American Literary Studies*, edited by Stephen Greenblatt and Giles Gunn, 392–418. New York: MLA, 1992.

Moore, Caroline. "The Questions Dated, the Answers Fresh." *The Spectator*, May 14, 2005, 61.

"Mr George MacDonald on Shelley." *Wingfold: Celebrating the Works of George MacDonald* 56 Fall Special Edition (2006) 35–37.

Newbolt, Henry. *Poems: New and Old*. London: Murray, 1915.

Newbolt, Peter. *G. A. Henty 1832–1902: A Bibliographical Study of His British Editions with Short Accounts of His Publishers, Illustrators and Designers and Notes on Production Methods for His Books*. 2nd edition with addenda and corrigenda by Peter Newbolt and Stuart Wilson. Philadelphia: Polyglot, 2005.

Nikolajeva, Maria. *From Mythic to Linear*. Lanham, MD: Scarecrow, 2000.

———. "The Identification Fallacy: Perspective and Subjectivity in Children's Literature." In *Telling Children's Stories: Narrative Theory and Children's Literature*, edited by Mike Cadden, 187–208. Lincoln, NE: University of Nebraska Press, 2011.

———. *The Rhetoric of Character in Children's Literature*. Lanham, MD: Scarecrow, 2002.

Nordau, Max. *Degeneration*. Translated from the 2nd edition of the German Work. Introduction by George L. Mosse. Lincoln, NE: University of Nebraska Press, 1968.

Novalis, and Arthur Versluis. *Pollen and Fragments: Selected Poetry and Prose of Novalis Translated from the German with an Introductory Essay by Arthur Versluis*. Grand Rapids: Phanes, 1989.

Nussbaum, Martha C. "Exactly and Responsibly: A Defence of Ethical Criticism." *Philosophy and Literature* 22.2 (1998) 343–65.

Onorato, Rina S., and John C. Turner. "Fluidity in the Self-Concept: The Shift from Personal to Social Identity." *European Journal of Social Psychology* 34 (2004) 257–78.

Osterland, Mia. "Girls in Disguise: Gender Transgression in Swedish Young Adult Fiction in the 1980s." In *Text, Culture and National Identity in Children's Literature*, edited by Jean Webb, 175–85. Helsinki: Nordinfo, 2000.

Ousby, Ian. "Carlyle, Thackeray and Victorian Heroism." *The Yearbook of English Studies* 12 (1982) 152–68.

Pakenham, Thomas. *The Scramble for Africa 1876–1912*. London: Weidenfeld and Nicolson, 1991.

Paul, Lissa. "Enigma Variations: What Feminist Theory Knows about Children's Literature." *Signal* 54 (1987) 186–202.

———. "From Sex Role Stereotyping to Subjectivity: Feminist Criticism." In *Understanding Children's Literature: Key Essays from the International Companion*

Encyclopedia of Children's Literature, edited by Peter Hunt, 112-23. London: Routledge, 1999.

———. *Reading Otherways*. Stroud, UK: Thimble, 1998.

Peers, Douglas M. "Sir Garnet Wolseley: Victorian Hero. Review." *War in History* 9.3 (2002) 362-64.

Pennington, John. "Alice at the Back of the North Wind, or the Metafictions of Lewis Carroll and George MacDonald." *Extrapolation* 33.1 (1992) 59-72.

———. "Muscular Spirituality in George MacDonald's Curdie Books." In *Muscular Christianity*, edited by Donald E Hall. Cambridge: Cambridge University Press, 1994.

Petzold, Dieter. "Maturation and Education in George MacDonald's Fairy Tales." *North Wind: Journal of the George MacDonald Society* 12 (1993) 10-24.

Pinsent, Pat. *Children's Literature and the Politics of Equality*. London: Fulton, 1997.

———. "Paradise Restored: The Significance of Coincidence in Some Children's Books." *Children's Literature in Education* 20.2 (1989) 103-10.

Porter, Bernard. *The Lion's Share: A Short History of British Imperialism 1850-1983*. 2nd ed. London: Longman, 1984.

Potter, William. *The Boy's Guide to the Historical Adventures of G. A. Henty*. Bulverde, TX: The Vision Forum, 2000.

Pratchett, Terry. *Witches Abroad*. London: Corgi, 1992.

Preiswierk, R., ed. *The Slant of the Pen: Racism in Children's Books*. Geneva: World Council of Churches, 1981.

Prickett, Stephen. "Narrative, Theology, and Irony: A Twentieth-Century Paradigm Shift." *Christianity and Literature* 50.1 (2000) 111-23.

———. "The Two Worlds of George MacDonald." *North Wind: Journal of the George MacDonald Society* 2 (1983) 14-23.

Pridmore, John. "Nature and Fantasy." *North Wind: Journal of the George MacDonald Society* 19 (2000) 2-8.

———. "Transfiguring Fantasy: Spiritual Development in the Work of George MacDonald." PhD diss., University of London, 2000.

Propp, Vladimir. *Morphology of the Folktale*. 2nd ed. Austin, TX: University of Texas Press, 1968.

Pruen, Hugh. *Hugh Pruen's Henty Companion*. Compiled by Gordon Berlyne. Royston, UK: The Henty Society, 1997.

Rabinowitz, Rebecca. "Messy Freedoms: Queer Theory and Children's Literature." In *New Voices in Children's Literature Criticism*, edited by Sebastian Chapleau, 19-28. Lichfield, UK: Pied Piper, 2004.

Raeper, William. *George MacDonald*. Oxford: Lion, 1987.

———, ed. *The Gold Thread: Essays on George MacDonald*. Edinburgh: Edinburgh University Press, 1990.

Reis, Richard H. *George MacDonald's Fiction: A Twentieth Century View*. Rev. ed. Eureka, CA: Sunrise, 1989.

Reitzel, William, ed. *The Autobiography of William Cobbett: The Progress of a Plough-Boy to a Seat in Parliament*. London: Faber and Faber, 1967.

Rice, Philip, and Patricia Waugh, eds. *Modern Literary Theory*. 4th ed. London: Arnold, 2001.

Richards, Jeffrey. *Imperialism and Juvenile Fiction*. Manchester: Manchester University Press, 1989.

Ridley, Hugh. *Images of Imperial Rule*. London: Croom Helm, 1983.
Robb, David S. *George MacDonald*. Edited by David Daiches. Scottish Writers. Edinburgh: Scottish Academic Press, 1987.
———. "Realism and Fantasy in the Fiction of George MacDonald." In *History of Scottish Literature*, edited by Douglas Gifford, 275–90. Aberdeen: Aberdeen University Press, 1988.
"Robert Burns Lecture by George MacDonald." *Wingfold: Celebrating the Works of George MacDonald* 45 (2004) 21–24.
Rodari, Gianni. *The Grammar of Fantasy*. New York: Teachers and Writers Cooperative, 1996.
Rodrick, Anne Baltz. "The Importance of Being an Earnest Improver: Class, Caste, and Self-Help in Mid-Victorian England." *Victorian Literature and Culture* (2001) 39–50.
Rohrich, Lutz. *Folktales and Reality*. Translated by Peter Tokofsky. Bloomington, IN: Indiana University Press, 1991.
Rose, Nikolas. "Identity, Genealogy, History." In *Identity: A Reader*, edited by Paul du Gay, Jessica Evans and Peter Redman, 311–24. London: Sage in association with The Open University, 2000.
Rosenberg, John D., ed. *The Genius of John Ruskin: Selections from His Writings*. London: Routledge & Kegan Paul, 1979.
Russell, D. A. "Plutarch and the Antique Hero." *The Yearbook of English Studies* 12 (1982) 24–24.
Ryken, Leland. "The Bible and Literary Study." In *The Discerning Reader: Christian Perspectives on Literature and Theory*, edited by David Barratt, Roger Pooley, and Leland Ryken, 121–53. Leicester, UK: InterVarsity, 1995.
Sadler, Glen Edward. *The Gifts of the Child Christ: Fairytales and Stories for the Childlike*. 2 vols. London: Mowbray, 1973.
Said, Edward W. *Culture and Imperialism*. London: Chatto and Windus, 1993.
Saintsbury, Elizabeth. *George MacDonald: A Short Life*. Edinburgh: Canongate, 1987.
Schenkel, Elmer. "Journeys into Darkness: Joseph Conrad's 'Heart of Darkness' and George MacDonald's 'Lilith.'" In *A Noble Unrest: Contemporary Essays on the Work of George MacDonald*, edited by Jean Webb, 104–21. Newcastle, UK: Cambridge Scholars, 2007.
Schmidt, Nancy J. "The Writer as Teacher: A Comparison of the African Adventures Stories of G. A. Henty, Rene Guillot, and Barbara Kimenye." *African Studies Review* 19.2 (1976) 69–80.
Schmitt, Doug. *Preface to the Boy's Guide to the Historical Adventures of G. A. Henty by William Potter*. Bulverde, TX: The Vision Forum, 2000.
Seamon, Roger G. "Narrative Practice and the Theoretical Distinction between History and Fiction." *Genre* 16 (1983) 197–218.
Shaberman, Raphael B. *George MacDonald: A Bibliographical Study*. Winchester, UK: St. Paul's Bibliographies, 1990.
Sidney, Sir Philip. *A Defence of Poesie and Poems*. London: Cassell & Company, 1889.
Skyggebjerg, Anna Karlskov. "The History of the Historical Novel in Danish Children's Literature." Paper delivered at the Fifth Norchilnet Postgraduate Workshop, Åland, Sept 21–25, 2005.
Smiles, Samuel. *Self-Help: With Illustrations of Character and Conduct*. London: Murray, 1862.

Bibliography

Snow, C. P. "True Grit: Review of 'Held Fast for England: G. A. Henty, Imperialist Boys' Writer.'" *Financial Times*, April 26, 1980, 15.
Southall, Ivan. "Real Adventure Belongs to Us: May Hill Arbuthnot Lecture. 10 May 1974." In *Top of the News*, 83–101. Chicago: American Library Association, 1974.
Spivak, Gayatri C. "Three Women's Text and a Critique of Imperialism." In *Postcolonial Criticism*, edited by B. J. Moor-Gilbert and Gareth Maley Stanton, 145–65. London: Longman, 1997.
Stephens, John. *Language and Ideology in Children's Literature*. New York: Longmans, 1992.
Stephens, John, and Robyn McCallum. *Retelling Stories, Framing Culture: Traditional Story and Metanarratives in Children's Literature*. New York: Garland, 1998.
Steward, James. "An Interview with New Child Curator." Online: http://www.bampfa. berkeley.edu/exhibits/newchild/ncinterview.html.
Stokes, Eric. "From Mexico to Mysore." Book Review. *Times Literary Supplement*, April 11, 1980, 406.
Sutherland, Robert D. "Hidden Persuaders: Political Ideologies in Literature for Children." *Children's Literature in Education* 16.3 (1985) 143–57.
Tampierova, Helena. "Some Aspects of the Fairy Tale." In *Children's Literature in English at the Turn of the Millennium: Selected Papers and Workshops from the First and Second International Biennial Conferences in Children's Literature in English, University of Hradec Kralove 27-29 January 1999 and 24-26 January 2001*, edited by Bohuslav Manek, Ralph D Slayton, and Pavla Machova, 97–102. Hradec Kralove, Czech Republic: The British Council Gaudeamus, 2002.
Tatar, Maria. *Off with Their Heads! Fairy Tales and the Culture of Childhood*. Princeton: Princeton University Press, 1992.
Tennyson, G. B., ed. *A Carlyle Reader: Selections from the Writings of Thomas Carlyle*. Cambridge: Cambridge University Press, 1984.
Thacker, Deborah Cogan, and Jean Webb. *Introducing Children's Literature—from Romanticism to Postmodernism*. London: Routledge, 2002.
Tidrick, Kathryn. *Empire and the British Character*. London: I. B. Tauris, 1992.
Todorov, Tzvetan. *The Fantastic: A Structural Approach to a Literary Genre*. Translated by Richard Howard. Ithaca, NY: Cornell University Press, 1975.
Trelawney, E. J. *Adventures of a Younger Son*. Oxford: Oxford University Press, 1974.
Triggs, Kathy. *George MacDonald: The Seeking Heart*. Basingstoke, UK: Pickering & Inglis, 1984.
———. *The Stars and the Stillness: A Portrait of George MacDonald*. Cambridge: Lutterworth, 1986.
Vance, Norman. "Heroic Myth and Women in Victorian Literature." *The Yearbook of English Studies* 12 (1982) 169–85.
Vloeberghs, Katrien. "Constructions of Childhood and Giorgio Agamben's 'Infantia.'" In *New Voices in Children's Literature Criticism*, edited by Sebastian Chapleau, 71–78. Lichfield, UK: Pied Piper, 2004.
Wagner, Gillian. *Children of the Empire*. London: Weidenfeld and Nicolson, 1982.
Walhout, Clarence, and Leland Ryken, eds. *Contemporary Literary Theory: A Christian Appraisal*. Grand Rapids: Eerdmans, 1991.
Waller, John H. *Gordon of Khartoum: The Saga of a Victorian Hero*. New York: Atheneum, 1988.
Walpole, Hugh. *Reading: Being One of a Series of Essays Edited by J. B. Priestley and Entitled: These Diversions*. Edited by J. B. Priestley. London: Jarrolds, 1926.

Walvin, James. *A Child's World: A Social History of English Childhood 1800-1914.* London: Penguin, 1982.

———. *Victorian Values.* London: Penguin, 1987.

Waxman, Barbara. "Ethnic Heroism: Matthew Arnold's and George Eliot's Gypsies." In *Perspectives on Nineteenth-Century Heroism: Essays from the 1981 Conference of Southeastern Nineteenth Century Studies Association,* edited by Sarah M. Leonard and David C. Putzell, 115-26. Madrid: Jose Porrua Turanzas, 1982.

Webb, Jean. "Conceptualising Childhood: Robert Louis Stevenson's 'a Child's Garden of Verses.'" *Cambridge Journal of Education* 32.3 (2002) 359-65.

———, ed. *A Noble Unrest: Contemporary Essays on the Work of George MacDonald.* Newcastle, UK: Cambridge Scholars, 2007.

Welch, Claude. "Confidence and Questions: The 19th Century." In *Christian Thought: A Brief History,* edited by Adrian Hastings, Alistair Mason and Hugh Pyper, 138-52. Oxford: Oxford University Press, 2002.

Wesley, Mary. *The Camomile Lawn.* London: Macmillan, 1984.

White, Hayden. *The Content of the Form: Narrative Discourse and Historical Representation.* Baltimore, MD: The Johns Hopkins University Press, 1987.

———. "From 'The Value of Narrativity in the Representation of Reality' (1987), Pp, 345-8; 401; 403; 405-7." In *Modern Literary Theory,* edited by Philip Rice and Patricia Waugh, 265-72. London: Arnold, 2001.

Willans, Geoffrey, and Ronald Searle. *The Compleet Molesworth.* London: Parrish, 1961.

Wilson, A. N. *The Victorians.* London: Arrow, 2003.

Wittgenstein, Ludwig. *Philosophical Investigations.* Translated by G. E. M. Anscombe. Oxford: Blackwell, 1972.

Wolff, Robert Lee. *The Golden Key: A Study of the Fiction of George MacDonald.* New Haven: Yale University Press, 1961.

Wolfreys, Julian, Ruth Robbins, and Kenneth Womack. *Key Concepts in Literary Theory.* 2nd ed. Edinburgh: Edinburgh University Press, 2006.

Womack, Kenneth. "Ethical Criticism." In *Introducing Criticism of the 21st Century,* edited by J. Wolfreys, 106-25. Edinburgh: Edinburgh University Press, 2002.

Woodsworth, J. S. "Motto of Sturgeon Creek Camp, Winnipeg." Online: www.legends.ca/orphanages.

Wright, Iain. "Hermeneutical Ethics." *The Critical Review: Renegotiating Ethics: Essays towards a New Ethical Criticism* 33 (1993) 78-87.

Zanger, Jules. "Goblins, Morlocks, and Weasels: Classic Fantasy and the Industrial Revolution." *Children's Literature in Education* 8 (1977) 154-62.

Zipes, Jack. *Fairy Tales and the Art of Subversion: The Classical Genre for Children and the Process of Civilization.* New York: Routledge, 1991.

———. *When Dreams Came True: Classical Fairy Tales and Their Tradition.* London: Routledge, 1999.

Zornado, John. *Inventing the Child: Culture, Ideology and the Rise of Childhood.* New York: Garland, 2000.

Index

active hero, 140–49, 169
Adela Cathcart (MacDonald), 195
adventure, convention of, 68
adventure hero, 149–51, 169, 173
adventure school, 40
adventure stories, 179
Adventures of a Younger Son (Trelawney), 179
Africa
　impressions of, 110
　MacDonald's writings on, 46–47
　representing psychological landscape, 172
age of transition, 15
Aldrich, Thomas Bailey, 103
Alec Forbes of Howglen (MacDonald), 40, 48
Alice's Adventures in Wonderland (Carroll), 115
Alighieri, Dante, 120
alterity, responses to, 4
Althusser, Louis, 3, 141, 194
Alton Locke (Kingsley), 49
Andersen, Hans Christian, 1, 66, 85
Anderson, Elizabeth Garrett, 47
anti-imperialism, 24–25, 26
Ariès, Phillipe, 94–95
Arnold, Guy, 2, 27, 31, 34–39, 130, 142, 181, 193
Arnold, Matthew, 160
Arnold, Thomas, 11, 18, 141, 172
Arnoldian boy, 18, 19, 34, 128, 140, 141, 152

art, paradox of, 175, 209–10
Arthur, James, 111, 113
Arthurian legends, 126
Ashcroft, Bill, 108, 110, 118
At the Back of the North Wind (MacDonald), 2, 3, 8, 9, 40, 41, 48, 49, 53, 54, 77–89, 94, 97, 99, 104, 107, 113, 118–20, 123, 135, 146, 149, 150, 154, 193–94
authority, 108–9
authors, value of, 5
Avery, Gillian, 110

bad boy, as literary construction, 103–4
Baker, Samuel White, 28, 29, 140, 142, 206
Bakhtin, Mikhail, 149, 173
Bal, Mieke, 76, 90
Barr, James, 34
Barthes, Roland, 80, 189
Barzini, Luigi, 141, 143
Battin, Melba, 116
Beale, Dorothea, 20
Beattie, James, 25, 33
Bentham, Jeremy, 13, 16
Benthamite philosophy, 16, 17
Berry, Laura, 117
Biedermeier, 98, 99
Birch, Reginald, 106
black pedagogy, 100
Blake, William, 96, 97, 203

Blanch, Stuart, 71
Blixen, Karen, 208
Blyton, Enid, 105
Boas, George, 95, 119
Boehme, Jacob, 97
Booth, William, 17, 30
borderland, 99
boxing, 157–58
Boy's Guide to the Historical Adventures of G. A. Henty, The (Schmitt), 3–4
boys
  Arnoldian, 18, 19, 34, 128, 141, 140, 152
  education of, 100
  as heroes, 18
  needing civilization, 102–9
  as savages, 102–9
Bradstock, Andrew, 47
Brander, Michael, 28, 140, 142, 206
Bright Face of Danger, The (Fisher), 2
British Empire
  justification for, 177
  presumed beneficial, 191–92
British Socialist Party, 30
Broadlands Conference, 51
Broken Swords, The (MacDonald), 153–54, 155
Brontë, Charlotte, 100
Brooke, James, 135
Broome, F. Hal, 15
Brown, A. B. E., 36, 57
Burnett, Frances Hodgson, 106, 147
Burns, Norman T., 126
Buss, Frances Mary, 20
Butler, Josephine, 101
Butts, Dennis, 2, 33, 63, 67
Byatt, A. S., 138
Byron, Anne Isabella Milbanke, 45–46
Byron, George Gordon, ix
By Sheer Pluck (Henty), 7, 15, 21, 28, 32, 36, 41, 58, 101, 109, 136, 140, 141, 149, 163, 168, 173, 181–82, 196
Camomile Lawn, The (Wesley), 106–7
Campbell, Joseph, 72–73
Captain Bayley's Heir (Henty), 7, 34, 36, 53, 54, 63, 64–67, 168
Carasoyn, The (MacDonald), 99
care, female ethic of, 48
Carlyle, Thomas
  on character development, 127–28
  foreseeing the mechanical age, 16
  on heroism, 99, 130, 133–34, 145, 151, 155, 205
  influence of, 49–50
  influences on, 42, 97, 114
  on instability in society, 12, 14, 26–27, 199
  as spokesman for the age of contradiction, 22
  vision of the hero, 50
Carpenter, Humphrey, 2, 33
Carroll, Lewis, 115
Carron, Juliet, 122
Cat of Bubastes, The (Henty), 38
Cavallaro, Dani, 141
character development, 114, 117, 127–28, 133–34, 143
character education, 110–11, 113, 133
Charge of the Light Brigade (Tennyson), 155
Chartist Movement, 15–16, 43, 117
Chesterton, G. K., 70, 71, 75, 122, 202
child, the. *See* children
childhood
  as adult construction, 94
  colonization of, 91–92
  innocence and, 95–99
childlikeness
  goal of, 132
  retaining, 120–21

childness, 95–96
children
  abuse of, 92
  bordering spiritual and physical worlds, 98–99
  closeness of, to nature, 92, 93, 98, 104
  colonized depicted as, 179–80, 200
  compared with the colonized, 25, 91, 118
  constructs of, 10, 91, 94
  divinity of, 120, 121, 123
  education of, 95, 110, 132
  as embodied individuals, 94
  exploitation of, 118
  faith in, 119
  within the family, 93–94, 95, 98
  feminization in representation of, 105
  growth of, controlling, 108
  ideal of, 110
  idealization of, 106
  innocence of, 106–7
  linked with heroes, 91–92
  literature for, 1. *See also* children's literature
  orphaned, 92
  as other, 100, 107
  preexisting before birth, 97
  primitivism of, 105
  protection for, 118
  as saviors, 120–24
  sent overseas, 92–93
  spirituality of, linked with courage, 136
  taking responsibility for moral decisions, 113
  teaching adults, 119
  as victims needing support, 117–20
  Victorian ideal of, 78
  visual representation of, 96, 105, 107
Children of the Empire (Wagner), 92
children's literature
  bad boy in, 103–4
  distinction in, 1–2
  fairy tale restructured in, 115
  heroes in, ix, xv
  ideology in, 68, 69
  language in, 68
  maturation as element in, 61
  moving toward fiction and fantasy, 114
  used for moral preparation, 105–6
Child's Inheritance, The (G. MacDonald), 115
Christianity
  controversies within, 29
  muscular. *See* muscular Christianity
Christian Science, 29
Christian socialism, 11, 17, 20, 30, 165, 175
Cicero, 95
civilization
  freedom from, 179
  superiority of, 178–79
classical hero, 169
Clifford, Hugh Charles, 29
clothes
  characters and, 161–62
  childhood innocence and, 106–7
Cobbett, William, 199
Cobden, Richard, 41
coddling, 95
Cohan, Steven, 75, 88
Cohoon, Lorinda, 103
coincidences, 149
Coleridge, Samuel Taylor, 96, 97, 133
colonialism, 24–25, 91
colonized
  childlike heroes and, 121
  as children, 179–80, 200
  MacDonald empathizing with, 177–78
  perceptions of, 110

colonized (*cont.*)
    presumed inferior to colonizers, 110–11
    protection for, 118
    viewed as in earlier state of development, 179
community, hope for, 69
compassion, 16, 63–65, 68, 87
Comte, Augustus, 127, 148
Condemned as a Nihilist (Henty), 8, 38–39, 111, 117, 129, 134, 141, 142, 150, 173, 182, 185, 192
Coningsby (Disraeli), 125, 171, 184n49
Conrad, Joseph, 81, 82
Contagious Diseases Acts (1864), 20
Cooper, Anthony Ashley (Lord Shaftesbury), 17, 93
courage, 8, 136–38, 146, 153–55, 163, 164
Cowper-Temple, Georgina, 51
Cowper-Temple, William, 51
Crimean War, 35
cross-dressing, 161–62, 174
Cross Purposes (MacDonald), 13, 41, 112–13, 142, 151, 168
Cult of Childhood, The (Boas), 95
Cuthbert Hartingdon (Henty), 36

Darton, F. J. Harvey, 2
Darwin, Charles, 14, 24
Das Leben Jesu (The Life of Jesus; Strauss), 17
Das Wesen des Christenthums (The Essence of Christianity; Feuerbach), 17
David Elginbrod (MacDonald), 30, 121
Davin, Bernard, 131
Day Boy and the Night Girl, The (MacDonald), 164
de Burgh, Hugo, 56

Deconstructing the Hero (Hourihan), 140
degeneration, 70, 121, 195, 197–203
Degeneration (Nordau), 198
Delany, Samuel R., 203
Dentith, Simon, 18, 23, 24
de Saint Pierre, Bernadin, 92, 123
Descartes, René, 119
Destruction of Jerusalem (For the Temple) (Henty), 38
de Vigny, Alfred, 96
Dickens, Charles, 17, 49, 73
difference, 178–79
displacement, 54
Disraeli, Benjamin, 18, 26, 37, 68, 125, 126, 171, 198, 204
diversity, acceptance of, 179
Don Juan (Lord Byron), ix
doubt, 14, 15, 51
Dramatic Illustrations from the Second Half of The Pilgrim's Progress by John Bunyan (MacDonald family), 49
Dreyfus affair, 30
dryads, 82
Duin, Julia, 34
Dumas, Alexander, 96
Dunae, Patrick, 130

education
    availability of, 113–14
    for the colonized, 118
    for control and socialization, 203
    enjoyment and, 131
    gender and, 99, 100
    inculcating moral character through, 99, 105–6
    influence of, on children, 110
    maturation and, 114
    for the urban poor, 197
Education Act (1870), 19, 22, 23
Edward, Charles, 40
Edwardes, Michael, 192
Edwards, Lee, 165

Elias, Norbert, 170
Eliot, George, 17, 160
Emig, Rainer, 22, 203
Emile (Rousseau), 92
empire. *See also* British Empire
    educating for, 29
    integral to British national life, 28
    justification for, 21, 176
Empire (Ferguson), 193
Empire and the British Character (Tidrick), 27–28
empire fiction, 27
emulation
    benefits of, 128–30
    encouragement of, 151
England. *See also* Victorian era
    acceptance in, of doctrine of empire, 26
    colonial operations of, 16, 22
    debates in, on science education, 18–19
    economic slowing in, 26
    legitimizing expansion, 24
    poverty in, 17
    public school system in, 11, 18, 19, 28–29, 141, 143, 172
    racial attitudes in, 23–24
    re-creation of, 172
    superiority of, 24, 179–82
    wars fought during Victorian era, 23
Erasmus, 127
Erikson, Erik, 143
escape, 126
ethical criticism, 4, 197
eugenics movement, 26
evangelical movement, 179
everyman, becoming hero, 206. *See also* heroes, as everyman
evil, innateness of, 99–100
exotic, control of, 210
exotic spaces, 25, 28, 193
    in the mind, 90
    physical, 90
experience, role of, in character education, 133–34
exploration, 28
Eze, Emmanuel Chukwudi, 32–33, 180

Facing Death (Henty), 13, 35, 142
factory child, 118
failure, 148, 151
Fairy Tale in Education, The (Greville MacDonald), 132–33
fairy tale hero, 135, 167–69
fairy tales
    characters in, 63–64
    christening motif in, 83
    compassion in, 63, 87
    literary, 3
    motifs of, 63, 64
    narrative of, 63, 68, 76
    pattern in, 66
    perception of, 3
    romances and, 88
    values of, 67
    as vehicle for social critique, 3
Fairy Tales and the Art of Subversion (Zipes), 2
faith, 29, 119, 123
Fantastic Imagination, The (MacDonald), 115
fantasy
    realism and, 1–2, 52, 53, 68
    residing between physical and spiritual, 89
fantasy literature, canon of, 46
father, as dominant authority, 107, 108
femininity, normative perception of, 156
Ferguson, John, 58
Ferguson, Niall, 193
Feuerbach, Ludwig Andreas, 17
Fichte, Johann Gottlieb, 145

fiction
  history and, 57, 58
  realistic, 55
Finucane, Elizabeth, 35
Fisher, Margery, 2
Flanagan, Victoria, 162
flawed hero, 151–55, 169
Ford, Harvey S., 136
Fordyce, David, 113
forests, in romances, 80, 82
For Name and Fame (Henty), 8, 112, 187
For the Temple (Henty), 7, 70, 93–94, 184, 185, 186–87, 192
Fox, George, 97
Fox, Geoffrey, 27
France
  colonial ideas in, 24
  superiority of, 24, 178–79
Freire, Paolo, 113–14
Frye, Northrop, 52–53, 54, 61, 62, 71, 72, 80, 112, 132, 172, 174–75, 177
Furst, Lilian, 67

games, importance of, 19
Garfield, Leon, 59, 210
Gaskell, Mrs. (Elizabeth), 45, 49
Gawain, 126
gendered heroes, 155–67, 169
Genette, Gerard, 59, 133
genre criticism, 52
genres, erasing boundaries between, 70–71
George MacDonald and Three German Thinkers (Hayward), 42
Gergen, Kenneth, 170
German Romanticism, 11, 42, 97
Germany, colonial expansion of, 24–25
Giant's Heart, The (MacDonald), 100–101
Gilligan, Carol, 48

girls
  behavioral standards for, different from boys, 104
  moral superiority of, 99, 100
Gittins, Diana, 94
goblins, 197, 200–203
God, childness of, 132
going native, 173, 195
Golden, Joanna, 76, 133
Golden Key, The (MacDonald), 2, 82, 85, 88, 99, 120, 123–24, 151, 166–67, 168
Good Things for the Young of All Ages, 8
Good Words for the Young, 8, 48
Gordon, Charles George, 126
Grand Human Being, 98–99
Gray Wolf, The (MacDonald), 43
Great Exhibition (1851), 16
great man, 50, 55, 99, 137, 145
Greek mythology, 82, 86
Green, Martin, 130
Green, Thomas Hill, 30
Greenaway, Kate, 105
Greenblatt, Stephen, 17, 202
Gregory, Marshall, 129, 199
Gualtieri, Claudia, 172
Guild Court (MacDonald), 49
Gunn, Giles, 202
Gunther, Adrian, 79, 80–81, 84, 87
Gutta Percha Willie (MacDonald), 41, 132

Haggard, Rider, 23
Hall, Donald, 20–21
Harpham, Geoffrey Galt, 134, 177, 197
Harrison, Frederic, 13
Haughton, Rosemary, 67
Hayward, Deirdre, 42, 97
Heart of Darkness (Conrad), 81, 82
Hegel, G. W. F., 24, 25, 33, 182
Heidi (Spyri), 106

Index

Hein, Rolland, 39–40, 42, 43, 73, 145, 202
Held Fast for England (G. Arnold), 31, 181
Henty, Frederick, 32, 35
Henty, George Alfred (G. A.), 23, 32, 204
   advocating good in all creeds philosophy, 39
   anti-academic stance of, 111
   assuming reader identification with characters, 130
   avoiding personal adulation, 131
   biographical information on, 31
   boxing and, 141, 157–58
   brother pattern, in writing of, 35, 37
   changing voice in work of, 58–59
   characters in, voicing political opinions, 27
   on children's place in the family, 93–94
   conventions used by, 68
   on courage, 154–55
   criticising English policy, 31
   critique of, 2, 68, 171
   developing child-hero construct, 91
   disguise in stories of, 61
   distilling political doctrines for young readers, 192
   early life of, 32, 33–34
   emphasizing character education, 110
   encouraging reader recognition and hero emulation, 172
   English boy heroes in writings of, 38
   ethnic portrayals by, 24, 181–84, 192–93
   fairy tale heroes in, 167–68
   first published novel of, 36
   fusing physical and spiritual, 126–27
   genres of, 1, 2, 171
   health problems of, 37
   heroes in, characteristics of, 3–4, 14–15, 19, 21, 36, 39, 41, 54, 65, 69, 103–4, 112, 126–27, 129–31, 134, 138–43, 147, 149–50
   historical sources for, 56–57
   Hyndman and, 30
   identity changes for heroes in, 173–74
   ideology of, on the British Empire, 67
   influence of, 5, 23
   influences on, 11, 32–34
   as insider in Victorian society, 32
   interested in natural history, 15, 32–33
   locations for stories of, 24
   lost-child motif in, 174–75
   mechanism in later adventure stories of, 27
   merging real and imagined, 89, 90, 206
   motivation for, 3–4, 38, 129, 186
   "native" characters in, 109
   as newspaper correspondent, 7
   political foresight of, 190
   popularity of, 67
   primary world of, 67
   propagating imperial myth, 185
   publications of, 6–8, 20
   racial views of, 22, 33, 180–81
   realistic fiction of, 2, 55, 58, 150–51
   reprinting of, 209
   on self-help, 13
   settings for stories of, 56, 62–63, 96
   similarities among heroes of, 138
   social critique by, 69, 178
   Stanley and, 28
   stepping out of historical time, 186–87

Henty, George Alfred (*cont.*)
  subversiveness of, 5, 38, 172–73, 185–86, 189–90
  supernatural elements in writings of, 59–62
  travels of, 36
  using speech structure to convey otherness, 182
  values in work of, 9–10
  on war, 190–91
  as war correspondent, 34–37, 56, 58
  women characters in, 101
  women heroes in writings of, 156–57, 161–63, 173–74
  writing on the position of the occupied, 185, 188–89, 192–93
Herder, Johann Gottfried, 25
heroes. *See also individual types of heroes*; Victorian hero
  active, 135, 140–49, 169
  adventure, 135, 149–51, 169, 173
  alternative, 143
  black, 6, 7
  character development and, 116–17
  characteristics of, 64, 76, 85, 169
  in children's literature, ix, xv
  classical, 135–40, 169
  contemporary, 209
  convention of, 68
  in defeat, 155
  English construct of, 10
  as everyman, 72, 127, 128, 142, 144, 151, 205
  fairy tale, 167–69
  female, 6, 8, 9, 36
  flawed, 6, 135, 151–55, 146, 169
  gendered, 135, 155–67, 169
  humanist concept of, 126
  ideal character of, 6, 9–10, 55
  image of, 1, 92
  importance of, for cultural history, 125
  influence of, on 19th-century England, 128
  as leaders, 128
  loss experienced by, 7
  morality of, 13, 109, 134
  narrative progression of, 77
  need for, 12
  19th-century construct of, influences on, 135
  occupying space of fantasy, 127
  as other and everyman, 205–6
  as outsiders, 135
  perception of the other, 176
  protecting the weak, 14–15
  relation to other men, 78
  sense of self, growing, 175
  spiritual awareness of, 126
  subjectivity of, 170–71
  superiority of, 134
  in unexpected roles, 142
  values of, 126
  as victims, 135
  youthfulness of, 143
Hero as Poet, The (Carlyle), 145
Hero as Prophet (Carlyle), 151
hero-victim, 76
hero-worship, 125
Hidden Life, A (MacDonald), 40
High Church Ritualist movement, 165
Higonnet, Anne, 96, 105, 107, 119
Hill, Octavia, 49
historical fiction, 59
history, fiction and, 57, 58
Hogan, Ann, 47
Hollindale, Peter, 209
homecoming, 63
Homer, 137
hooks, bell, 180
Hope of the Gospel, The (MacDonald), 96, 120
Houghton, John, 12, 14–15

Houghton, Walter, 125
Hourihan, Margery, 109, 130, 140, 142, 143, 158, 164–65, 166, 171, 180
Howard, Thomas, 202
Howe, Suzanne, 24, 57
Hughes, Thomas, 20, 34
Hugo, Victor, 96, 97
Hume, David, 24, 33
Huttenback, Robert, 130, 155
Hyndman, Henry Myers, 30

ideal
　physical vs. spiritual, 69
　progress toward, 68
identity
　escape from, 174
　recovery of, 174
ideology
　in children's literature, 68, 69
　publishing industry and, 209
imagination, 97, 132–33
imperialism
　cultural, 203
　importance of, to the English, 193
　justifiying, 179–80
India (Keay), 191
In a Different Voice (Gilligan), 48
individualism, 19, 128, 170
industrial society, growth of, 13
In the Reign of Terror (Henty), 34
inspiration, 126
interpellation, 3, 109, 194, 203
Invalid's Winter in Algeria, An (MacDonald), 46–47, 192, 194
Ireland, famine in, 16, 43

Jack Archer (Henty), 35
Jacobite Exile, A (Henty), 8, 142, 183, 185
James, Laurence, 31, 36
Jameson, Frederic, 72, 74, 86

Jane Eyre (Brontë), 100, 104
Jeffrey, Kirstin, 167
Jesuits, influence of, 110
Johannesen Printing and Publishing, 4
Jong, Erica, 151
Jordan, Gerald, 23
Jordan, Pamela, 15

Kant, Immanuel, 24, 33
Keay, John, 191
Kegler, Adelheid, 98
Kincaid, James, 118
King, Ann, 37
King, Don, 122
King of the Golden River (Ruskin), 85
Kingsley, Charles, 17, 20, 21, 32, 49, 135, 140, 144
Knight, George, 32

laissez-faire economics, 13
language
　in children's literature, 68
　mastery of, in Henty's stories, 35–36
La Touche, Rose, 36
Latter-Day Pamphlets (Carlyle), 199
Law, William, 97
Leclerc, Georges-Louis (Comte de Buffon), 177, 178
Leighton, Robert, 131
Levinas, Emmanuel, 4, 178
Levine, George, 5, 90, 127–28, 160
Lewes, George, 96
Lewis, C. S., 123, 132
Lewis, Naomi, 132
Light Princess, The (MacDonald), 48, 83, 84
Lilith (MacDonald), 42, 46, 51
literacy, 23, 111
literary-didactic split, 130
literary fairy tale, 3

Little Daylight (MacDonald), 48, 78–89, 99
Little Lord Fauntleroy (Burnett), 106
Little Savage, The (Marryat), 102
Lochhead, Marion, 99
Locke, John, 110, 111, 117
London Labour and the London Poor (Mayhew), 17
Lorenzo, David, 180
Low Church movement, 165
Lurie, Alison, 102
Lüthi, Max, 167

MacDonald, Charles, 44
MacDonald, George, 50, 96, 204
  accepting of imperialist activity, 154
  addressing societal degeneration, 27
  aligned with Christian socialism, 165
  alternative spiritualities in works of, 29–30
  androgyny in characters of, 104
  avoiding personal adulation, 131
  blending realism and fantasy, 150–51
  as boxer, 140
  on childhood as state of being, 122
  on character formation, 133–34
  character maturation in, 114
  Chesterton on, 71
  on children's place in the family, 93, 94
  contributing to Broadlands Conference, 51
  conventions used by, 68
  on courage, 154–55
  creating mindscapes, 81
  criticism of, 2
  critiquing materialism, 94
  death of, 51
  defending depiction of ideal characters, 67, 148
  depicting journey toward maturity, 131
  developing child-hero construct, 91
  didacticism in, 4, 114–15
  early years of, 40–43
  as editor, 8
  on education, 115, 132
  egalitarianism of, 196
  empathizing with the colonized, 177–78, 194–95
  exploring unknown psychological territory, 28
  on the fairy tale, 115
  fairy tale heroes of, 168–69
  as fairy tale writer, 2–3
  female child characters in, 9
  female heroes of, 164, 165, 167
  feminine qualities in children's writing of, 107
  first novel published, 48
  forced to leave pastorate, 18
  friends with feminist leaders, 101–2
  fusing physical and spiritual, 70–71, 89–90, 126–27
  gender roles in, 163–64
  genres of, 1, 2
  heroes in, characteristics of, 21, 69, 85, 126–27, 134, 139–40, 142, 104, 206, 207
  imperialistic representation and, 193–97
  importance of Scottish roots to, 39–40
  incorporating science into his stories, 15
  influence of, 5
  influences on, 11–12, 42, 97, 98–99, 145
  intent of, in writing, 3–4, 5, 48, 49, 74, 195–96

Index 235

MacDonald, George (*cont.*)
  library imagery in, 42
  male heroes of, 164–65
  on the masculine nature, 104
  as minister, 43–44
  mirrors in writing of, 50
  Modernism and, 81
  move to Manchester, 44–45
  on nobility and behavior, 112–13
  other world of, 172
  as outsider, 12, 39–40, 43–44, 46, 175, 177–78, 194–95
  physical/spiritual borderlands as motif in, 99
  on poetry, reading of, 144–45
  politics of attack in work of, 69
  poverty in works of, 41
  prophetic role of, 175–76
  protagonists of, 20
  publications of, 6, 8–10
  queerness in fiction of, 49
  on realism and character, 55
  reprints of, 210
  selfhood in works of, 173
  settings for stories of, 96
  significance of, to fantasy literature, 46
  as social critic, 14, 49–50, 89–90, 178, 199–200
  spirituality of, 41, 42, 43, 175
  spirituality in writing of, 9, 132, 144, 166, 173
  sponsored by Lady Byron, 45–46
  stereotypical language of, 196
  studying chemistry, 19
  subversiveness of, 4–5
  theology of, 83–84, 120
  women characters in, 77–78, 82, 101
  women's education and, 20, 45, 47–48
  on women's issues, 22
  on Wordsworth, 97–98, 115
MacDonald, George (father), 40
MacDonald, Grace, 50
MacDonald, Greville, 4, 16, 39–40, 41, 42, 43, 45, 145
  on goodness of girls, 99, 100
  on parents' intimacy with feminist leaders, 101–2
MacDonald, Lilia, 50
MacDonald, Louisa (Powell), 43–44, 49, 50, 101–2
MacDonald, Mary, 44
MacDonald, Ronald, 131, 140–41
MacIntyre, Alistair, 135–36
magazines, for boys, 27
Maier, Sarah, 114, 119–20
Manlove, Colin, 70, 81
Manville Fenn, George, 31, 32, 34, 37
Maori and Settler (Henty), 7
March to Magdala, The (Henty), 36
marginalized, need for, 203–4
Marshall, Cynthia, 166–67
Marx, Karl, 30
masculinity, 21, 140
maturation, 86, 99, 114, 175, 189
  as element in children's literature, 61
  process of, 131–33, 207
Maurice, F. D., 17, 18, 20, 45, 47, 140, 144, 165
Mayhew, Henry, 17
McCallum, Robyn, 76
McGann, Jerome, 192, 208–9
McGillis, Roderick, 97, 78, 116, 122, 133, 209
McKay, Helen, 43
medievalism, interest in, 126
Miles Christianus, 126
Mill, John Stuart, 14, 15, 114, 127–28
mindscapes, 81
mission civilisatrice, 24
mode
  differences between types of, 68
  fictional, 52–53, 62, 78, 80

Mode (*cont.*)
   generic, 82
   mimetic, 53
   mingling of, 61
   parable, 46
   romantic, 72
Modernism, 81
Montaigne, Michel de, 104
Montrose, Louis, 4
Moore, Caroline, 43
More, Hannah, 105
Morisonian heresy, 42
Mormonism, 29
Morphology of the Folktale, The (Propp), 63
movement, analogy of, 62
muscular Christianity, 11, 20–21, 140, 144, 198
Muscular Christianity (Hall), 20–21
muscular spirituality, 143–44
mutuality, 164

narrative, mood and voice in, 59
narratorial position, 133
natural selection, 14
Nesbit, Edith, 105
New Calendar of Great Men (Comte), 127, 148
Newbolt, Henry, 19
Nicholson, John, 152
Niemeyer, Carl, 142
Nikolajeva, Maria, 55–56, 61, 65, 70, 71, 86, 130, 161
nobility, behavior and, 112–13
noble savage, 104, 179
nonconformist movement, 165
Nordau, Max, 198
North and South (Gaskell), 45
Novalis (Friedrich von Hardenberg), 42, 96, 122–23
nuclear family, 94–95
Nussbaum, Martha, 197

On Heroes and Hero Worship (Carlyle), 22, 99, 128
On the Irrawady (Henty), 188
Onorato, Rina, 171, 175
Orange and Green (Henty), 33
Origen of Alexandria, 97
Origin of Species (Darwin), 14, 24
Österlund, Mia, 162
other
   awareness of, 175
   control of, 210
   identified with other races, 180
   preoccupation with, 178
   relationship with, 197
   representation of, 208
   turning into the English, 171
   us as, 176, 202–4
   us turning into, 197–202
otherness, 47, 63
   colonization and, 177
   conveyed through speech structure, 182
   defined, 176
   difference and, 178–79
   stereotypes and, 197
   view of, in Victorian era, 176–77
Out on the Pampas (Henty), 6–7, 58
Owen, Robert, 113

Pakenham, Thomas, 28
parents, superfluity of, 65
Parry, Milman, 191–92
Past and Present (Carlyle), 12
Paul, Lissa, 48
Paul Faber: Surgeon (MacDonald), 49, 120–21, 167
Pelagius, 95
Pennington, John, 143–44
personal example, cult of, 30
Pestalozzi, Johann, 119
Petzold, Dieter, 114
Phantastes: a Faerie Romance for Men and Women (MacDonald), 45, 46, 51, 73, 83, 99, 136, 206–7
Photogen and Nycteris (MacDonald), 86

Pinsent, Pat, 76, 209
Plague Ship, The (Henty), 162
pluck, 21
Plutarch, 137
Porter, Bernard, 25, 28
postcolonial criticism, 6
Potter, William, 2
poverty, 74, 75, 77, 117
Powell, Alexander, 43
power, directive, 60, 64
Pratchett, Terry, 57
Pre-Raphaelites, 126
Prickett, Stephen, 178
Pridmore, John, 115–16, 195
Princess books, 151, 168, 197
Princess and Curdie, The
 (MacDonald), 2, 8–9, 20,
 27, 48, 49–50, 66–67, 69–70,
 82, 94, 104, 121–22, 133,
 139, 142, 146, 148, 165–66,
 175–76, 198–201
Princess and the Goblin, The
 (MacDonald), 2, 8–9, 20, 27,
 48, 82, 85, 99, 104, 121, 146,
 174, 176, 200
Pritchard, Mari, 2
Propp, Vladimir, 63, 66, 75, 77
protagonists, identification with,
 130
protection, 118
Pruen, Hugh, 138
public school system, 141, 172
 ethos of, 11
 character development in, 143
 reform in, 18, 19, 28–29

quest tales, 54

race
 concept of, development of, 108
 dominant views of, 25
 issues of, linked with the urban
  poor, 25

 linked in home and foreign
  policy, 26
 stereotyping and, 24
Raeburn, Henry, 92
Raeper, William, 19, 39–41, 42, 43,
 44, 46, 47–48, 100, 144, 145
Ranald Bannerman's Boyhood
 (MacDonald), 8, 40, 48, 144,
 145–49, 150
Ransome, Arthur, 105
Reagan, Christopher, 126
realism
 distinct from fantasy, 1–2
 fantasy and, 52, 53, 68
 fictional, 55
 Henty's work critiqued as, 68
 idealism and, 67
 preference for, 3
realistic fiction, 55–56
rectifying principle, 76
redemption, 121–22
Reform Bill (1867), 22
Reis, Richard H., 114, 133
relativism, 15
religion
 controversy about, 14
 doubt regarding, 11, 14
*Renaissance of Wonder in Children's
 Literature, The* (Lochhead),
 99
reprints, market for, 209–10
revolution anxiety, 117
Reynolds, Joshua, 92
Richter, Ludwig, 98
Robb, David, 48, 49
Robert Falconer (MacDonald), 30,
 49, 50, 94, 146, 197, 201–2
Rohrich, Lutz, 76
*Role of the Child as a Route to
 Spiritual Reality, The*
 (Carron), 122
romances
 fairy tales and, 88
 forests in, 80, 82

romances (*cont.*)
  salvational logic in, 72
  themes in, 174
  transformation as element of, 74
Romantic movement, 96–98, 105, 116
Rose, Nikolas, 172
Rough Shaking, A (MacDonald), 3, 9, 40, 41, 53, 54–55, 62, 71–77, 104, 107, 113, 120, 135, 149, 150, 175, 194, 207
Rousseau, Jean-Jacques, 92, 104
Roving Commission, A (Henty), 150
Rujub the Juggler (Henty), 8, 60, 104, 109, 146, 151–53, 154–55, 185, 188–89, 192
Ruskin, John, 22, 24, 85, 114, 193
Russell, D. A., 137, 139
Russell, William Howard, 26, 35
Ryken, Leland, 71

Said, Edward, 24, 26, 179, 203
Saintsbury, Elizabeth, 145
Salvation Army, 30
savages, boys as, 102–9
Schmitt, Doug, 3–4
Scholes, Robert, 52
schooling, structured, 94–95
Schreber, Daniel Gottlob Moritz, 100
science
  education about, 18–19
  theology and, 15
scientific enquiry, 11
scientific investigation, 97
scientific racism, 24, 26
Scotland, controversies in (1840s), 41
Scott, Alexander, 18, 45
Seaboard Parish, The (MacDonald), 47
Seamon, Roger, 57
Search for a Secret, A (Henty), 36

Searle, Ronald, 106
Secret Garden, The (Burnett), 147
self, personal identity and, 171
self-categorization theory, 171
Self-Help (Smiles), 13
self-help philosophy, 16–17, 21, 128
self-improvement, gospel of, 11
self-schema theory, 171
Selous, Frederick Courtenay, 28
Selwyn, George Augustus, 135
service, as social concern, 165
Shaberman, Raphael, 40
Sherwood (Mrs.), 105
Shires, Linda, 75, 88
Shooting Niagara (Carlyle), 22, 26–27
Sidgwick, Anna, 101
Sidney, Philip, 128
Sinclair, George, 42
Sir Gibbie (MacDonald), 51, 55, 69, 77, 104, 113, 120, 148, 168–69, 196
Sleeping Beauty, The, 79, 83
Smiles, Samuel, 13, 16–17, 128, 133, 146
Smith, Jessie Wilcox, 105
Snow, C. P., 181
Social Democratic Federation, 30
social gospel, 29
socialization, of the urban poor, 197
social mobility, 13
social reform, 30
society
  criticism of, 5
  position in, 147
Soldier's Daughter, A (Henty), 8, 36, 138, 141, 156–60, 174, 182, 187, 189–90
souls, preexistence of, 97
South Africa, British policy toward, 31
speculum naturae, 95, 110
spiritual awareness, 97

Index

spiritualities
   alternative, 29–30, 51
   renewed look at, 26
Spivak, Gayatri, 177, 193
Spyri, Johann, 106
Stanley, Henry Morton, 28, 110
state, role of, 117
Stead, William Thomas, 26
Stephens, John, 1–2, 9, 68, 76, 176
Steward, James, 92
St. George for England (Henty), 139, 198
Stokes, Eric, 38, 181, 192–93
story, power of, 129
storytelling, changes in, 79–80
Strauss, David Friedreich, 17
Sturdy and Strong (Henty), 8, 129, 142, 173
subconscious, exploration of, 81
subversion, 4–5, 168
suffering, theology of, 83–84
superiority, 179–80, 182
Sutherland, Robert D., 69
Swedenborg, Emmanuel, 98–99, 145
Sybil (Disraeli), 198

tabula rasa, 95, 110
Tatar, Maria, 168
Tennyson, Alfred, 155
Tennyson, G. B., 42
texts, context of, 4
Theological Essays (Maurice), 18, 45
theology, science and, 15
Theosophy, 29
therapeutic thinking, 62n39
Thomas Wingfold, Curate (MacDonald), 49, 51
Through the Sikh War (Henty), 58, 136
Tidrick, Kathryn, 27–28, 57, 152
Tieck, Ludwig, 96
Tiger of Mysore, The (Henty), 8, 36, 41, 53–54, 58, 59–63, 122, 138, 143, 155–56, 174, 185, 190–91
time
   cyclical nature of, 122
   uncertainty of, 62
Tinderbox, The (Andersen), 66, 85
Todorov, Tzvetan, 67, 69, 77, 89
tolerance, 22
Tom Brown's Schooldays (Hughes), 19, 34
transfiguration, 72
Trelawney, E. J., 179
Triggs, Kathy, 145
Trollope, Anthony, 29
Troup, Robert, 42
True Confessions of Charlotte Doyle, The (Avi), 161
True to the Old Flag (Henty), 8, 57
truth, 15
Turner, John, 171
Twain, Mark, 103

uncertainty, 12, 14, 15, 49, 77, 97, 125
unknown regions, fascination with, 96–97
urban poor, as children, 200
utilitarianism, 13

values, 5
Vance, Norman, 160
Vicar's Daughter, The (MacDonald), 30, 46, 49
Victorian era
   change during, 12–15, 18
   children in, 10, 18, 78
   faith during, 29
   hope during, 18
   literature in, 5
   otherness as perceived in, 176–77
   politics during, 15–16, 17
   religions movements during, 29
   religious controversy in, 14

Victorian era (*cont.*)
    retreating into fantasy, 55
    women's role in, 161
Victorian hero, 126–28, 129, 135, 139–41, 144, 149, 151, 170, 208, 210
violence, glorification of, 140
Vitai Lampada (Newbolt), 19
von Ofterdingen, Heinrich, 122–23
von Schmid, Christoph, 98

Wagner, Gillian, 92–93
Walhout, Clarence, 5
Walpole, Hugh, 1, 3, 9, 130, 171
Walvin, James, 24, 26, 118–19
warrior hero, 126
Water-Babies, The (Kingsley), 32
Way We Live Now, The (Trollope), 29
wealth, related to decline, 138–39
Webb, Jean, 96–97, 204
Welch, Claude, 29
Wesley, Mary, 106–7
Westminster School, 33–34, 64
Westward Ho! (Kingsley), 135
What's Mine's Mine (MacDonald), 94, 195
White, Hayden, 57, 209
Wilberforce, Samuel, 17
Wilfrid Cumbermede (MacDonald), 197
Wilson, A. N., 12, 16, 17, 23, 28, 55
Wise Woman, The (MacDonald), 2, 8–9, 82, 85, 111–12, 114, 116–17, 120, 122, 133
With the Allies to Pekin (Henty), 27, 141, 184, 189
With Buller in Natal (Henty), 31
Within and Without (MacDonald), 44, 45–46

With Kitchener in the Soudan (Henty), 36, 39, 58, 109, 138, 168, 173, 191
Wolff, Robert Lee, 198–99, 202
Womack, Kenneth, 178
women
    associated with the moon, 86
    cross-dressing, 161–62
    education of, 20, 45, 47, 116
    impression of, in Victorian era, 47–48
    perceptions of, 110
    sacrificing identity, 160–61
    striking of, by men, 101
Women of Faith in Victorian Culture (Hogan and Bradstock), 47
women's movement, 20
Wordsworth, William, 96, 97–98
Wordsworth's Poetry (MacDonald), 115–16
worth, test of, 64
Wright, Iain, 189

Yeast (Kingsley), 49
Young Buglers, The (Henty), 7, 24, 35, 102, 104, 107–8, 131, 142, 149, 182, 196
Young Carthaginian, The (Henty), 38, 137–39, 170, 174, 186, 198
Young Colonists, The (Henty), 31, 58
Young Franc-Tireurs, The (Henty), 8, 36–37, 149, 156, 181
youth, linked with the British Empire, 171

Zanger, Jules, 197, 200
Zipes, Jack, 2, 69, 74
Zornado, Joseph, 91, 99–100, 108–9

www.ingramcontent.com/pod-product-compliance
Lightning Source LLC
Chambersburg PA
CBHW050849230426
43667CB00012B/2215